Advance Praise for

Resisting Neoliberal Schooling: Dismantling the Rubricization and Corporatization of Higher Education

The corporatization of higher education is undermining teaching and learning while eroding the public good and public interest across universities and colleges. Corporatization is an insidious process that leads to the dismantling of public institutions over time. Bringing together a number of amazing scholars and activists, this volume contests the neoliberal restructuring of universities and colleges. Anyone who cares about education and public institutions anywhere in the world should want to read this collection and share it with their students as well.
—Dr. Kevin Walby, Associate Professor, Criminal Justice, University of Winnipeg

As higher education continues to concentrate on standardization, efficiency, and profit, *Resisting Neoliberal Schooling* is a must-needed text that recenters justice, collaboration, and liberation as central to the act of teaching.
—Zane McNeill, editor of *Vegan Entanglements: Dismantling Racial and Carceral Capitalism*

The myth that formal institutionalized education produces open-minded and critical thinkers who possess "academic freedom" to pursue what they think is important is part of the lie that structures neoliberal societies. This book presents some seeds for realizing, resisting, and overcoming this reality to instead foster equitable and critical-consciousness raising educational systems grounded in individuals' and communities' own interests, needs and experiences.
—Nathan Poirier, Co-Director, Students for Critical Animal Studies

Anthony Nocella and colleagues provide a hard-hitting critique of the pernicious influence of neoliberalism, cultural chauvinism, and other forms of bigotry on our educational system. They also offer something even more important — possible paths for promoting its healing and transformation.
—Dr. A. Peter Castro, Professor of Anthropology, Maxwell School of Citizenship and Public Affairs, Syracuse University

This anthology presents a much-needed critique of the increasing rhetoric of return on investment (ROI) in public higher education. Drawing on critical pedagogy, the authors shed light on the assessment industry and offer multiple strategies on how to exit the homogenizing game of "academic excellence" performance goals.
—Dr. Mechthild Nagel, Professor, Philosophy, State University of New York, College at Cortland

Stokely Carmichael (Kwame Ture) famously identified the "white intellectual ghetto of the West" as the beating heart of America's investment in racial capitalism and its networks of oppression. As he explained in "Black Power," we teach, learn, labor, and live in a landscape of constant crisis, one produced materially and ideologically by our schools and universities. *Resisting Neoliberal Schooling* offers a way to understand that crisis as both ongoing and manufactured–designed to recreate, explain, and even commodify inequities rather than address or upend them. Destroying this neoliberal extractive system of education as it exists today represents an important step towards total liberation and equality.
—Dr. William Horne, Villanova University

Resisting Neoliberal Schooling: Dismantling the Rubricization and Corporatization of Higher Education is a critical examination of the mechanisms within the institution of higher education that reinforce systemic inequalities. This is a book, in the vein of the classic "Pedagogy of the Oppressed," that compels instructors and students alike to challenge the dominant paradigm and social arrangements in higher education that obstructs the diversity and inclusion many institutions are claiming to strive towards in today's world.
—Dr. Chandra Ward, Assistant Professor, Sociology, University of Tennessee

Resisting Neoliberal Schooling brings together an exceptional group of contributors, all united in their determination to bring new understanding and visibility toward the devastating impacts of neoliberalism across academia. Moreover, they offer hope as what can be done now to challenge, reclaim, and rebuild academia and education anew. On these fronts - and others beside - the book is a tremendous success, and an essential read.

—Dr. Richard J. White, Reader, Human Geography, Sheffield Hallam University, UK

This book could not come at a more urgent time. At a moment when we are facing multiple existential crises, it has never been more critical for the universities to be freed from the ravages of neoliberalism and restored to their potential role in providing humanity with skills, knowledge and ideas needed to meet the challenges of our times. From calling out the exclusivity, elitism, labor exploitation and commodification of higher education under neoliberalism, to examining how the corporations have taken over and used academic fields as forces of indoctrination into neoliberal ideology, to exploring liberatory and even anarchistic ways of freeing the universities from neoliberalism's death grip, *Resisting Neoliberal Schooling: Dismantling the Rubricization and Corporatization of Higher Education* is exactly the sort of education the corporate ruling class is buying out the school system in order to prevent you from getting!

—Laura Schleifer, Co-Director, Institute for Critical Animal Studies

This is a powerful critical read for all those concerned with democracy, freedom, and justice. Read this book and truly understand how education is the foundation of any healthy society. Defend education from standardization and corporations now!

—Tony Quintana, Co-Editor, Transformative Justice Journal

Resisting Neoliberal Schooling is a provocative and interesting read. Just about everything you need to know with respect to the ideological and economic assault on public education.

—Dr. Mark Seis, Professor Emeritus, Sociology, Fort Lewis College

With *Resisting Neoliberal Schooling*, Anthony J. Nocella II takes readers on a voyage to the roots of the contemporary educational system's discontents, its chronic and repeated frustrations, and its manufactured failings. We see anew the ways in which power adapts and adjusts, but never means its withdrawals, never intends to embrace structural and meaningful change. Power offers cosmetic change—check a box called "diversity," give a superficial nod toward "inclusion," mention "equity" at every opportunity—while resisting justice with all its might. Nocella helps us cut through the barbed wire of "rubrics" and "data," the smothering cotton wool of standardization, and illuminates a path toward an education based on wakefulness and liberation.

—Bill Ayers, author, *Fugitive Days: A Memoir*

Intentionally written to provoke critical engagement, and not for purely academic or theoretical goals, *Resisting Neoliberal Schooling: Dismantling the Rubricization and Corporatization of Higher Education*, manages to contextualize a wide variety of obstacles to inclusive and abolitionist pedagogy. Including personal narratives, contemporary research, and historical framing, the book encourages teacher-scholars to be more engaged in community justice through the classroom.

—Dr. Taine Duncan, Chair, Department of Philosophy and Religion, University of Central Arkansas

Resisting Neoliberal Schooling is an outstanding and powerful book edited by a brilliant, interdisciplinary scholar and wonderful person. This book is to fight for the effort to save higher education from corporatization.

—Lucas Alan Dietsche, Wisdom Behind the Walls

This work is riveting, and explores oppressive practices perpetuated by institutions involved in higher education in a critical and easy-to-follow manner. I recommend this material to anyone who aims to challenge dominant group supremacy in academia.

—Brock M. Smith, Co-founder, FourLifers Incorporated

Here is a collection of essays which promise to challenge many of our cherished beliefs about our education systems including our trust that they are open, diverse, critical, independent and serve no masters.

—Les Mitchell, University of Fort Hare Hunterstoun Research Fellow

Timing is everything, this book could not come out at a better time. We are facing so many issues that this book touches on. Read it, share it.

—Alisha Page, Director, Save the Kids, Graham, Washington

Resisting Neoliberal Schooling

Anthony J. Nocella II and Lea Lani Kinikini
Series Editors

Vol. 1

Resisting Neoliberal Schooling

Dismantling the Rubricization and Corporatization of Higher Education

Edited by Anthony J. Nocella II

PETER LANG
New York · Berlin · Bruxelles · Chennai · Lausanne · Oxford

Library of Congress Cataloging-in-Publication Control Number: 2023019679

Bibliographic information published by the Deutsche Nationalbibliothek.
The German National Library lists this publication in the German
National Bibliography; detailed bibliographic data is available
on the Internet at http://dnb.d-nb.de.

Cover design by Peter Lang Group AG

ISSN 2835-9275 (print)
ISSN 2835-9283 (online)
ISBN 9781636672625 (paperback)
ISBN 9781636672618 (hardback)
ISBN 9781636672595 (ebook)
ISBN 9781636672601 (epub)
DOI 10.3726/b20681

© 2024 Peter Lang Group AG, Lausanne
Published by Peter Lang Publishing Inc., New York, USA
info@peterlang.com - www.peterlang.com

All rights reserved.
All parts of this publication are protected by copyright.
Any utilization outside the strict limits of the copyright law, without the permission of
the publisher, is forbidden and liable to prosecution.
This applies in particular to reproductions, translations, microfilming, and storage and
processing in electronic retrieval systems.

This publication has been peer reviewed.

Dedication

This book is dedicated to those that seek another way of learning and educating that wants to do away with rubrics, assessments, standardized tests and quizzes, and high stakes punitive tests and schooling models. Long live liberated radically minded dropouts that want more than conforming into norms.

Contents

Acknowledgments	ix
Foreword CLIFTON SANDERS	xi
Preface RODERIC LAND	xv

Introduction
 Abolition Educators Dismantling Neoliberal Colonizer Standardized
 Schooling From Assessments to Rubricization
     ASHLEY COX, LAURALEA EDWARDS, ANTHONY J. NOCELLA II, DAVID
     ROBLES, AND EMILY THOMPSON
	1

1 *Dismantling Rubericization, Evaluation, and Standardization in*
   Neoliberal Conformity: Building Community Colleges as Anti-Racist
   Public Intellectual Places of Knowledges
     ANTHONY J. NOCELLA II
	15

2 *Combatting Stigma: Opposing Neoliberal Oppression through*
   Intersectional, Transformative Activism
     ELISA STONE
	33

3 *From Diversity to Justice: Expanding the Chief Diversity Officer "Roles"*
   of Equity and Inclusion into Justice and Community
     LEA LANI KINIKINI
	49

4 *Resisting Neoliberalism Through Anarchist Studies and Critical Animal*
   Studies Conferences
     ELIZABETH VASILEVA AND WILL BOISSEAU
	63

5 Faculty and Student Activism as Sites of Resistance to Neoliberalism in Higher Education — 81
ADALBERTO AGUIRRE, JR. AND RUBÉN MARTINEZ

6 Neoliberalism, Neopopulism and the Assault on Higher Education — 95
RICHARD VAN HEERTUM

7 Life Lessons Learned (L³) Inside a Neoliberal Capitalist Educational System — 111
VICTOR M. MENDOZA

8 Triple Helix: The Intertwining Strands of Biology, Ideology and Policy in the Neoliberal Revolution — 125
LAURA I. SCHLEIFER

9 Bad Education: President Obama and the Neoliberalization of American Education — 141
RILEY CLARE VALENTINE

10 Neoliberalism, Democratization, and the Re-Visioning of Education — 155
STEVE GENNARO AND DOUGLAS KELLNER

11 Has The Last Bastion Fallen? — 165
FRANK A. FEAR

12 Tied to the Loom: Alienation in the Neoliberal Academy, Anarcha-Feminism, and a Politics of Resistance and Care — 187
CAROLINE K. KALTEFLEITER

13 Take Down the Wall: Higher Education at SLCC as Liberation for Incarcerated Students — 201
DAVID BOKOVOY

Epilogue
Suggestions to University/College Trustees: An Interview with Anthony Joseph Nocella — 213
ANTHONY J. NOCELLA II

Afterword
Don't Look Anywhere! Learning Without Stock Markets — 219
PAUL R. CARR

Contributors' Biographies — 227

Index — 235

Acknowledgments

This book was possible because of all the contributors Clifton Sanders, Roderic Land, Ashley Cox, Lauralea Edwards, David Robles, and Emily Thompson, Elisa Stone, Lea Lani Kinikini, Elizabeth Vasileva, Will Boisseau, Adalberto Aguirre, Jr., Rubén Martinez, Richard Van Heertum, Victor M. Mendoza, Laura Schleifer, Riley Clare Valentine, Steve Gennaro, Doug Kellner, Frank A. Fear, Caroline K. Kaltefleiter, David Bokovoy, Anthony Joseph Nocella, and Paul R. Carr. All the wonderful beautiful people from around the world that wrote powerful, supportive reviews of this book Tony Quintana, Dr. Kevin Walby, Zane McNeill, Nathan Poirier, Dr. A. Peter Castro, Dr. Mechthild Nagel, Dr. William Horne, Dr. *Chandra Ward*, Dr. Richard J. White, Laura Schleifer, Dr. Mark Seis, Dr. Bill Ayers, Dr. Taine Duncan, Lucas Alan Dietsche, Matthew R. Sparks, Brock M. Smith, and Les Mitchell. I would like to thank all the organizations I have involved with too Save the Kids, Academy for Peace Education, Institute for Critical Animal Studies, Critical Animal Studies Society, Critical Animal Studies Academy, Peace Studies Journal, Green Theory and Praxis Journal, Wisdom Behind the Walls, Poetry Behind the Walls, Outdoor Empowerment, Justice, Equity, Diversity, and Inclusion for Social Transformation, SLCC's Department of Criminal Justice, SLCC's EDICT, Lowrider Studies Journal, Transformative Justice Journal, Journal for Critical Animal Studies, #NoYouthinPrison, Alternatives to Violence Project, Salt Lake Prisoner Letter Writing, Ecoability Collective, Total Liberation Campaigns, Utah Cycling Newspaper, Arissa Media Group, and SLCC's JEDI Senate Committee, SLCC's Faculty Senate, SLCC's FDAR Senate Committee. I would also like to thank my family mom, dad, sisters, my friends (Ben, Amber George, Richard White, Emily Thompson, Alisha Page, Reece Graham, Monika, Selinda, Dejesus, David Michael, Lucas, Erik J., Stormie, Cecile, Brett, Russ, Stephanie, Ryan, Peter, Laura, Lauren,

Chris, Amy, Kaela, Rich, Dan, Brock, Leslie, Cris, Kevin, Juone, Gina, Rita, Idolina, Brenda, Caleb, James, Nick, Ana, Liz, Kristin, Nancy Barrickman, Julia, Antonette, David Robles, Adam Dastrup, Kati Lewis, Ashley Cox, Hangar 15 Bicycle Millcreek (Ian, Tommy, Mike Hanseen, Lewis, Mike P., Chuck, Rob, Chris, Mark, and Joey), and my cats Emma and Lucy. I would like to thank an amazing beautiful person in my life Christine Camille. My family has been my support and rock through my whole life; I could not have done anything without them. I would finally, like to thank Dani and Jackie and everyone at Peter Lang Publishing who supports me on all my publications throughout the years. Dani is an amazing brilliant scholar and kind person. I thank her so much.

Foreword

CLIFTON SANDERS

For colleges and universities worldwide, particularly for public institutions in the West, the philosophy and praxis of neoliberalism dominates. National organizations, local and state legislatures and major business interests determine (with impunity) funding, incentives, resource allocation, curriculum design and program prioritization. Increasingly, and in this current moment of Critical Race Theory demonization, powerful economic elite interests are manipulating a virulent strand of populism and anti-scholarship in order to disembowel democratic norms and academic freedom, and further suppress marginalized voices and historical perspectives under the pretext of 'divisiveness'. Higher education—as scholarly knowledge, as knowledge for personal and public good, as empowerment gained from development of critical thinking and encounter with new ideas and ways of knowing—is heavily commodified and debased by a neoliberal/capitalist mindset which idolizes job training, 'hard-skill' mastery (that frequently categorizes humanistic knowledge as 'soft skills'), individuals as units of economic utility, and which tenaciously holds onto a myopic, materialistic illusion of success or failure in life as quantified by 'business analytics'.

Many scholars have written extensively on the toxic impacts of neoliberalism on higher education. I contend that this new contribution, *Resisting Neoliberal Schooling: Dismantling the Rubricization and Corporatization of Higher Education*, is far more than another welcome contribution to the current body of work. The wide-ranging collection of essays presented here together constitute a novel and innovative exercise in resistance. The opening overview by Anthony Nocella II et al. sets the stage for work presented by scholars, educators and activists representing the full spectrum of the higher education experience. Several essays come from my own colleagues at Salt Lake Community College in Salt Lake City, Utah.

I believe that it is very important for community colleges to be represented in this eclectic monograph. I have been a community college professional for nearly thirty years, starting as a member of the faculty and, for more than 20 years, serving as an academic administrator. In my judgement, community colleges are universally the least understood entity in higher education, even by educators and administrators. More telling, community colleges are the most vulnerable sites of rubricization and corporatization in higher education simply because they are thoroughly public entities without consistent, large-scale access to other kinds of support. Fund-raising and grant procurement are, when compared to long traditions of philanthropy to colleges and universities, a very recent part of community college culture. Community college educators and leaders need adequate resources to provide students with rich education and training to lead meaningful and productive lives. Nevertheless, community colleges are defenseless against the kinds of neoliberal false equivalencies and gaslighting that have consistently resulted in defunded higher education and co-opted institutional priorities.

There is enormous variation among approximately 1200 community colleges in the US. Community colleges are tasked with providing 'affordable' education, primarily via: (1) workforce training and professional education for immediate job seekers and workers in local industries, and (2) the first two years of course credits which can be transferred to complete a college/university baccalaureate major. Community college faculty are a professionally diverse community of educators who possess credentials spanning workforce occupational specialties, academic scholarship and lived experience. Together they serve the neediest students with the promise of education that liberates and transforms entire communities. What is often overlooked (to me at least) is a valuable kind of knowledge production that arises from community college teaching and faculty-centric scholarship. All too often, what passes as community college 'scholarship' comes from neoliberal think tanks and university scholars who, despite their alleged dedication to student success, critique community colleges primarily as defective institutions that must be micromanaged with less than adequate funding to improve student 'completion.' These critiques are often justified via a framework of statistical analyses of selectively constructed, often federated, data sets. Information curated in this way inevitably sacrifices nuance and valuable insight, and homogenizes variable inputs into a flattened output narrative, which then shamelessly fuels simple-minded political and other aggression in the name of reform.

In glaring contrast, the essays in this monograph by my colleagues, including Anthony Nocella II, Emily Thompson, Lauralea Edwards, David Robles, AC Cox, Lea Lani Kinikini, Elisa Stone and David Bokovoy provide rich firsthand knowledge and insight about neoliberal repression and resistance in the community college context. This is especially valuable because these humble stories describe programs, encounters and experiences that show how overlooked community college beginnings can flower into global significance and impact. I submit that this is far more common than one might think, and it is also an invitation by traditional scholarship to be taken back to 'school.' Despite dauntingly convoluted and idiosyncratic histories, often a result of bare-knuckled political will, and evolutions from various kinds of prior institutions, community colleges persist in hope because of the intrinsic worth and dignity of our students and communities.

If there is any silver-lining in the plight of community colleges under neoliberalism, it is truly the opportunity for faculty and administrators to be public intellectuals, seamlessly blending teaching and training with scholarship, activism and service. Many SLCC students are the first in their family to attempt higher education, and many come from marginalized communities. Yes, students need training for jobs and careers, but they also seek and find opportunities to grow and critically engage their present and future. That my colleagues resist the neoliberal constructions of their functions and assigned roles is no less than a labor of love toward students, and modeling the call to activism and public intellectual engagement.

The other essays in *Resisting Neoliberal Schooling* are equally superb, rich with careful historical analyses, passionate narratives of awakening and defiance, and models for organization, resistance, recovery and revisioning education for liberation and social transformation. Of course, this monograph will be of great value to kindred spirits, but there is much here to challenge scholars and readers of every ideological persuasion. As a utopian skeptic, I would not necessarily call myself an anarchist, but I will be re-reading these essays and I welcome them as my intellectual sparring partners and provocateurs to new ways of thinking, seeing and engaging my professional and other worlds with the valuable lessons and the deep, heartfelt insights herein.

Preface

Roderic Land

As we rest in a global society mired in conflict, inequities and ideological dogma, I am always curious about the role education—or lack thereof—has played in the creation of this condition. A condition that is void of love, compassion and any sense of humanity. A condition that values the cacophony of selfish individualism over the harmony of selfless collective work and responsibility. A condition that sees difference as a license to harm physically, mentally, and/or spiritually opposed to celebrating and embracing the value these differences bring to bear. While education is not the only factor to consider, it is indeed my belief that it has played a role as we have witnessed the push towards a curriculum and assessment that seeks to satisfy standards influenced by businesses and corporations.

Living in a time where members of local, state, and federal government is making a push to diminish academic freedom and the relevance of Humanities and Social Sciences by banning the teaching of "divisive" topics, critical race theory, and a more comprehensive American history is highly problematic. As a student of history, I think about the function of education during the early 20th century when America had a massive flow of immigrants coming to her shores. It was intended to tell a particular narrative to assimilate and build an allegiance to a country that many "New Americans" would call home. It was intended to tell a story about the promise of America; it told a story about the strength of America; and yes, it told the story about the greatness of America. However, what this narrative did not tell, was the dark side of America.

The content of this curriculum was often void of a major part of what shaped this country, slavery. Slavery was/is the foundation, the engine, the heartbeat of America's economic, political, and social structure. While this is not the focus of this book, it does provide context as to why we have witnessed such a strong governmental resistance to telling this part of the narrative, both historically and present day. This is a stain in the social fabric of these United States of America. An America in which many BIPOC (Black, Indigenous, People of Color) and people of the global majority cringe at the slogan, "Make America Great Again".

These virulent attacks on critical thought and liberatory forms of curriculum and pedagogy is in alignment with an earlier period in American history. As Giroux (2021) so aptly points out, these attacks are akin to the McCarthy and Red Scare period of the 1950s when there was a heightened sense of fear over the threat of communism which resulted in laws that banned the teaching of any subject or topic deemed unpatriotic.

The far Right-wing of the republican party has weaponized education and employed the power of persuasion to discredit and dismantle any approach to critically examine the historical legacy of racial injustice and structured inequality. Additionally, right-wing politicians have introduced laws to limit funding for higher education institutions that teach critical race theory. For example, a coalition of House Republicans introduced legislation that are designed to halt the teaching of critical race theory (CRT) in colleges and universities. A bill entitled the "Stop CRT Act," seeks to cut off all federal funding to schools that incorporate CRT into their curriculum. On Monday, March 21, 2022, republican controlled Tennessee state legislature passed a bill that prohibits higher education from teaching what they identified as "divisive concepts" related to racism, sexism, and social class. This bill also prohibits any monetary incentive for teaching this subject matter.

These attacks on and the censoring of higher education seriously compromises the ability to teach a more wholistic history and puts in the crosshairs of extremist, faculty and students who seek to better understand and address issues of social justice, racial inequality and other forms of oppression and social ills.

Ironically, proponents of neoliberalism place a strong emphasis on government restraint over government intervention. In addition to, personal wealth over the welfare of the community and public good, and individualism over collectivism. At a time when millions of college students lack access to basic needs, such as food and shelter, neoliberal policies exacerbate these insecurities. Not to mention the compounding effect of generations of discrimination underserved populations have endured.

In meeting this challenge, we must recognize that under the auspices of neoliberalism, the role of education in creating an informed and conscious citizenry has been extremely compromised by mis-information campaigns, privatization of education and the shift from higher education serving a public good to being market driven that obstructs many people from gaining access. Under these tenets, institutions of higher education are reduced to only preparing students to enter the workforce and will cease to be bastions of critical thought. This does not have to be a zero-sum game. There is space for both to exist where one does not have to be sacrificed and completely absorbed by the other.

However, higher education must continue to put forth the effort to achieve its promise. It must continue to fight for academic freedom, to be a space where ideas can be debated and not censored; a space where one can feel safe to respectfully express themselves and develop the critical thinking and social skills to engage a changing world; a space to interrogate and create solutions to the myriad of social ills that plague our society. Whether big or small, we all have a part to play. In reading this text, I hope you are well on your way to playing yours. Resist and re-imagine.

Introduction
Abolition Educators Dismantling Neoliberal Colonizer Standardized Schooling From Assessments to Rubricization

ASHLEY COX, LAURALEA EDWARDS, ANTHONY J. NOCELLA II, DAVID ROBLES, AND EMILY THOMPSON

Dismantling the Gap

Academia, i.e., formal education, is in an era shaped by neoliberalism, which defends its academic repression (Readings, 1997; Nocella, Best, & McLaren, 2010; Nocella & Gabbard, 2013; Chatterjee & Maira, 2014), behind corporate-factory schooling concepts such as—standardization, effectiveness, assessment, best-practices, efficiency, equality, fairness, and evidence-based practices (Giroux, 2014; Brownlee, 2015; Brownlee, Hurl, & Walby, 2018). These concepts are in place to end the fabricated socially constructed academic myth of closing the equity gap. Those who use the term "equity gap," are not critically thinking about the significant systemic issues that have built this socially constructed gap that reinforces a divisive superior versus inferior binary between middle class white students and the rest of the learner population. The terms "achievement gap," "equity gap," or "opportunity gap" stabilizes binaries for the sole purpose of shaming one group if they do not assimilate into the standards set by a dominant group that still clutches rigidly to their assumption that their notions of binaries, standards, and measures provide equal value and meaning to all learners. The critical problems with the socially constructed gap analogy are that they do not address three issues: (1) how the measurement of the socially constructed gap is grounded in supremacy; (2) how the results are imperialistic in that the superior group defines success such that the inferior group is forced to assimilate; and finally (3) those that are establishing and use the socially constructed gaps are erasing, silencing, and willfully ignoring the endless types of knowledge and learners. It must be noted that imperialism is conquering land and telling the original stewards of the land to assimilate into the dominator/oppressor culture, while colonialism is the conquering of land and exploiting people and land resources for profit. Neoliberal education is imperialistic by promoting assimilation. Promoting assimilation in any research or educational approach is antithetical to diversity and inclusion as it erases diversity of Black and white, as well as the diversity of Black and Indigenous cultures, behaviors, beliefs, and knowledges, such as critical race theory. Inclusion means these cultures, behaviors, beliefs, and knowledges are welcomed, acknowledged, and respected regardless of race or nationality. Neoliberalism is colonialist in that it co-opts equality for commodification by using terms like "equity gap" to justify its one-size-fits-all standardized curriculums that silence oppressed voices through actions such as boycotting critical race theory and banning terms that provide a map for anti-oppressive educational transformation (Williams, 2016).

A genuinely transformative learning experience is fostered when educators recognize every identity in human society has a theory, culture, epistemology, methodology, pedagogy, and many even have a field of study (e.g., lowrider studies, a new field, which is going global). Until all those identities and cultures are welcomed and honored in the learning space, education will continue to be an oppressive space for those who refuse to assimilate to maintain their personal and cultural integrity.

We cannot adequately speak about justice, equity, inclusion, or liberation when we fail to recognize diversity. Diversity, grounded in multi-culturalism, is the first step in social change. Not adapting education to include diverse perspectives maintains colonial dominance and excludes learners not from the colonizing culture. Multi-culturalism recognizes that there are multiple cultures within a room, yet multiculturalism exoticizes, commodifies, appropriates, and simplifies cultures into one large postmodern experience. The next step in social change is to create inclusion, where diversities are respected, acknowledged, and appreciated in spaces. Inclusion is essential before discussing what each identity needs to thrive within their framework of success. Without inclusion, educators will merely continue to exchange existing assimilationist practices for new assimilationist practices. Finally, after each group has what they need, liberation is achieved as a self-reflective actualizing cognitive, spiritual, emotional, and physical (i.e., holistic) act. When the oppressed are liberated and society changes altogether, we have social transformation.

Neoliberalism and neoconservatism are similar in that they work through capitalism, but for different results. Neoliberalism wants to promote capitalism through crisis and misfortune, such as poverty, suicide, depression, COVID-19, forest fires, floods, and incarceration. Meanwhile neoconservatism is collaborating and taking over governments to promote a country's values and interests. One is based on global economic growth, while the other is based on government political global growth. Neoconservatism, an individualist free market ideology wants global economic capitalism with conservative ethical values, which include being against communism, socialism, and other leftist movements. Neoliberalism wants global economic capitalism, with false facade of having inclusive and equity ethical values, such as promoting fair-trade coffee and chocolate and conflict-free diamonds. Neoliberalism would be to colonialism as neoconservatism would be to imperialism.

The Current Context of Education

The neoliberal agenda operates now as it did in the 1980s: through the political structures of regional accreditation and state requirements. Higher education institutions are accredited through regional bodies that dictate the standards institutions of higher education must meet. The Northwest Commission of Colleges and Universities (NWCCU) defines student success as students graduating from an institution and becoming gainfully employed (Northwest Commission of Colleges and Universities 2020 Standards, n.d.). They also require institutions to maintain a method of assessment that supports student success. The focus of accreditation on graduation and gainful employment reinforces the neoliberal agenda of preparing students to be human capital instead of improving their sense of self and the world in which they live.

Moreover, when these accreditation standards are put in the context of states like Utah, the home state of this chapter's authors, the neoliberal education agenda becomes reified in the worst kinds of ways. In 2017, Utah, whose motto is "industry," created the Utah Data Research Center (UDRC). This center is charged with maintaining longitudinal data on education, healthcare, and workforce as well as conducting studies for the legislature (Utah Data Research Services, n.d.). In 2019, they produced a report titled

"The Return on Investment (ROI) of Career and Technical Education." In this report, return on investment was defined as the time it took for the state to recover in taxes the amount of money it had invested in higher education. That is, based on the income tax tied to wages of graduates, how long did it take the state to earn the $66 million it had allocated to the technical colleges (Return on Investment of UTech, 2019). This reductive definition of ROI restricts the purpose of education to one of human capital rooted in colonialist and imperialistic definitions. When a state legislature defines education solely as producing a skilled workforce, the tools utilized by institutions to meet accreditation standards become equally reductive. Accrediting standards that require breaking down assessment and metrics by demographics utilize the same neoliberal and problematic perspectives as the equity gap analysis. As such, they become a tool of supremacy.

Assessments have historically been used to control students to maintain hegemony over knowledge, knowledge production, and normalcy. Assessments can be inclusive when they allow students to reflect on learning from their various cultural epistemologies. One size fits all assessment that prioritizes white epistemological worldviews is equivalent to assessing a marathon runner on the skills required to excel at basketball. Rather than using neoliberal business terms such as assessment and evaluations, activities can be reframed using ecological terminology such as reflection and growth. The word reflection invites people to apply their own way of knowing to a situation. Using words such as growth, sets an expectation that the purpose of the reflection is to identify opportunities for change. A key element in this reframing is naming the way of knowing so the cultural norms can be made explicit. When assessment is done from an objectivist corporate framework, the cultural expectations remain implicit, and thus create a sense of othering for students who do not come from a white heteronormative background.

The Tool of Supremacists

Those who use equity gap analysis engage certain assessments (e.g., standardized tests), rubrics, and metrics to justify their arguments, which are rooted in a pre-determined assumption that one-size education fits all. The presumption that all students should look and perform the same negates the need for any true research. If all students are expected to be the same, any deviation is caused by a deficiency in the individual. This conclusion is predetermined because it is grounded in supremacy.

Standardized tests are a tool that attempts to mask oppression with fairness claims. Standardized tests emerged in the U.S. in 1838 as a method to assess learning. The modern form of standardized tests that are scanned and graded by a computer emerged in the 1960s. One of the most popular critiques of standardized testing came in 1979 by the band Pink Floyd with the song "Another Brick in the Wall." As critiques built from critical thinkers, standardized rational modernists doubled down by introducing standardized tests into law, which was forced by public education in the U.S. and defended by corporate nonprofits and think tanks. Critical thinkers also argued that the tests were discriminating and privileging white wealth, able-minded, able-bodied, and heterosexual students.

Rubrics are another common tool used to assess student outcomes based on objectives defined by white supremacy culture. While claiming that rubrics create equality and ensure every learner is assessed the same way, they force students to assimilate to one-right-way established by the person with the most power in the classroom, the teacher. While Paul Diederich at Educational Testing Service was the father of the rubric in 1961, Charles Cooper at the University at Buffalo and Richard Lloyd-Jones at the University of Iowa, in 1977 published and gave structure to the term that so many are forced to use today, as a way to defend the university or colleges valued of equality and diversity. This emphasis on rubrics and performance assessments reinforced a focus on assessing student learning rather than assessing students for learning. As long as the emphasis is on learning assessment, students will be expected to meet outcomes defined by educators in the specific ways defined in a rubric.

A liberatory, decolonizing approach to learning would be to partner with students throughout the learning process and recognize that the priorities of learning the concepts and how that learning will be demonstrated may vary for each student. The hegemony of higher education has been changing from its inception as a form of religious control towards a corporate and militaristic form of control (Feldman, 1999; Giroux, 2007).

Rubrics, a tool to assess, is a problem within education for three fundamental reasons. First, rubrics develop structure, limiting creativity and freedom of ideas, knowledges, methods, theories, and experiences. Second, rubrics do not allow diversity of approaches and requires to a specific conclusion. Third, rubrics are constructed within a supremacist argument for fairness, equality, and equity. That argument claims there is little room for subjectivity, bias, favoritism, or prejudice, but in fact, the rubric defines a singular type of method and knowledge which rejects the diversity of each student. This assimilation imperialistic colonialistic assessment methodology is oppressive and identifies Knowledge, with a capital K, as a fact and Truth, rather than a one of many perspectives, i.e., knowledges.

The true battle for social justice is not in micro-aggressions, institutional practices, or social behaviors, which lend themselves to injustice. The true battle for social justice is systems grounded in a single theoretical framework (Adams & Bell, 2016; Ayers, Quinn, & Stovall 2009). Colonialism and imperialism, with the support of capitalism, promote training rather than education, which for-profit universities are adopting as they are striving to hijack higher education globally (Fanon, 1961). These for-profits adopting a training approach, which lacks critical thinking, creativity, and collaboration is about profit and exploitation, not democracy and citizenship. This training approach uses a theoretical framework of standardization to deploy academic repression on decolonizing critical theorists (Chatterjee & Maira, 2014). To create a system that educates rather than trains, we must recognize the assimilationist expectations of standardized testing and rubrics and stop using them (Fanon, 1952). The rubric is the post-assessment for the teacher to determine the student's grade and the instructions for the student to conduct the assignment. The outcome is predetermined for the student, thus any deviation using critical thinking or creativity will decrease their grade. Therefore, the student is being trained, not educated. Training is a set of actions for a specific outcome emerging from the corporate-factory industry and Taylorism school. Education has become a finely oiled factory to produce students into cogs in industries, companies, and corporations based on the efficiency model of education. The efficiency model of education comes out of standardization and promotes rubrication. This model is based on pathway academic advising, where students are told what courses to take, what assignments to complete, what format to adopt, and what style to perform. Training is not about changing, but conformity, effectiveness, and efficiency. Training is not about questioning, or equity.

I (Anthony J. Nocella II) argue for the complete oppsite of the efficency model of education, which is hands-off pedagogy. Hands-off pedagogy intentionally giving minimum instructions, directions, structure, framing, standardization, rubricization, and guidance for the purpose of allowing space and fostering of creativity, leadership, self-worth, freedom, problem-solving skills, risk-taking, adventure, liberation, peace, and cultivating metacognition. Therefore, there will be less directions, rubrics, standards, and instructions on what to do or what the learning objectives or outcomes are (to avoid promoting a deficit model of teaching). Traditional teachers commonly view this pedagogy as disorganized, not skilled, uneducated, and underprepared. Contrary to the traditional teachers' belief, expressive education and experiential education are hands-off pedagogy based, with the process and activity being the learning moment. Many hands-off pedagogues do not have syllabus or create the syllabus with the student and do not give direction, until direction is asked by the student(s). Further, the teacher/professor does not give resources, but rather waits for the student(s) to ask for resources or for the student(s) to search them out on their own through problem-solving skill development. Further, hands-off pedagogy promotes the liberal arts (the freedom of learning what you want) not pathways degree structure (where all courses are dictated to the student on what to take). This pedagogy is about getting lost in education and learning and not being rigid. Hands-off pedagogy, a very old and rigorous pedagogy, is intentionally not structured or outlined, but free-flowing, where the teacher is a facilitator and allows the student to discover the world and to become a scholar on their own.

Paulo Freire (2002), the founder of critical pedagogy, believed in two principles around education: that education should be for the student and that the student in collaboration with the teacher should dismantle that binary and create. The teacher facilitates an education and grading/assessment with all the students, which results in different grading/assessments for each student. The assumption that educational settings are fair and equitable is an illusion. Currently, the structure of education is set up as a banking model of education. Freire's explanation of this model provides understanding for the current oppressive educational structure that perpetuates common core standards, rubricization, and a system that deters diversity of thought and acceptance. The current education system is set to have students reaggregate what is presented to them. It leaves no room or acceptance for authentic, equitable practices. It is here that special education had something going for it, in that it creates an Individual Education Plan (IEP) for each student in a special education class. IEPs should not be only for students in special education but for all students; this is the only just and inclusive approach for a diverse student body (Nocella, Parmar, & Stovall, 2014). Using the IEP concepts and Freirian perspective, rubrics and other assessments could be re-envisioned to be a framework to measure the amount of diverse thought and critical thinking of each individual student. Critical pedagogy challenges syllabus, assessments, standardization, order, structure and colonialism, which in America is all defended by the Doctrine of Discovery, American exceptionalism, and Manifest Destiny (Fanon, 1961).

Liberation

Decolonizing, social justice, and abolitionist education; unschooling; anarchist, critical, transformative, disability, hip hop, feminist, punk, critical race and queer pedagogies are just a few of the educational approaches to dismantle neoliberalism, imperialism, colonialism, capitalism, neo-conservativism, supremacy, domination, oppression, and assimilation within academia and schools (Nocella & Juergensmeyer, 2017). These pedagogies are being academically repressed, but should be protected under academic freedom, which is the essential protective policy that leads to a healthy educational curriculum and a healthy democracy (Nelson, 2011; Schrecker, 2010). The essential foundation of academic freedom is based on the interdisciplinary and multidisciplinary liberal arts approach (from Latin liberalis "free" and ars "method").

These pedagogical approaches are founded by grassroot activist groups that continue to fight for liberation from the dominant sociocultural and sociopolitical spheres (Del Gandio & Nocella, 2014). To liberate education, one must first understand the systems and ideologies that lead education to be masked as neoliberal in the first place. White supremacy infests these spaces through the school-to-prison pipelines it facilitates. For example, Black youth are disciplined through the justice system at higher rates than their white counterparts for in-school misconduct (Alexander, 2011). The curriculum taught in schools continues to enforce and promote colonization and imperialism through outdated forms of standardization and neoliberal pedagogies such as rubricization. Rubricization, grounded in standardization, is the ridged conditioning of students to develop pseudo-research projects based on predetermined outcomes, rather than starting with a hypothesis, which would discover the outcome. Students then lead lives motived by these imperialist and elitist foundations—That typically avoid incorporating any form of critical race theory. Exploitive capitalistic processes and policies restrict access to these spaces, making them increasingly less diverse. While white supremacist values, colonizer-based attitudes, and capitalist ideologies are at the center, this collection of anthologies uncovers the depths of where this issue truly lies and how liberation can come to fruition.

Some great resources to investigate for social justice and social change are AK Press, PM Press, Lantern Books, Northern Sun Catalogue, Syracuse Cultural Workers, Democracy Now!, Earth First!, The Nation, Rethinking Schools, Dignity in Schools, Save the Kids, Seven Stories Press, Haymarket Books, Pluto Press, Autonomedia, Counter Punch, Arissa Media Group, Mother Jones, Verso Press, Radical Philosophy, Beehive Design Collective, Justseeds, Alternatives to Violence Project, Training for Change, Highlander School, Ruckus Society, Black August, Black Liberation Collective, American Friends Service Committee, Rainforest Action Network, Friends Committee on National Legislation, ADAPT, Critical Resistance, Youth Justice Coalition, INCITE!, Anarchist Black Cross, Institute for Critical Animal Studies, Jericho

Movement, American Association of University Professors, Civil Liberties Defense Center, Center for Constitutional Rights, National Lawyers Guild, Books Through Bars, 4StruggleMag, Alliance for Self-Directed Education, Eclectic Learning Network, and Peace and Justice Studies Association. These are just a small representation of the groups people can get involved with to create intersectional social justice and liberation (Crenshaw, 1989).

Outline of Book

This anthology is a collection of scholar-activists (Del Gandio and Nocella, 2014) from around the world who are challenging standardization, rubricization, and neoliberalism. Each chapter is grounded in theory, personal experience, and resistance. Chapter 1, authored by Anthony Nocella, describes how neoliberal values are perpetuated within community colleges. He describes many of the myths associated with community colleges that, when coupled with neoliberal tenets, undermine the mission of these affordable educational institutions. He concludes with ways to liberate community colleges from the neoliberal bind.

Chapter 2, authored by Elisa Stone (she/her/hers), describes how neoliberal education creates exclusionary spaces and limits learning. Stone describes her own experience with education and self-identity, along with stories of other people marginalized by the neoliberal agenda in higher education. Through these narratives, Stone shows how these experiences are examples of revolution outside the neoliberal classroom.

Chapter 3, written by Dr. Lea Lani Kinikini, brings forth a critical and personal critique of the role of a chief diversity officer (CDO) at Salt Lake Community College and similar roles throughout the state of Utah. She connects her own identity and experiences towards realigning CDO roles in an effort to move from equity and inclusion towards justice and community. She concludes these arguments by emphasizing the importance of countercultures such as Lowrider Studies and provides ten points that align with liberation.

Chapter 4, Resisting Neoliberalism Through Anarchist Studies and Critical Animal Studies Conferences, is authored by Elizabeth Vasileva and Will Boisseau. The authors disrupt neoliberal approaches, facilitated by academic conferences, by bringing forth elements of the Anarchist Studies Network (ASN) and Critical Animal Studies (CAS). They approach this piece with reflective insight offering both solutions and a holistic guide towards organizing an anarchist event.

Chapter 5, authored by Adalberto Aguirre, Jr. and Rubén Martinez, addresses the embedment and impact of neoliberalism within colleges and universities. The authors present various ways to challenge and fight against neoliberal practices and New McCarthyism. They challenge this neoliberal model by surfacing the importance of allyship, social movements, and academic freedom.

Chapter 6, by Richard Van Heertum, provides an in-depth understanding of how neoliberalism and neo-populism are assaulting higher education. He argues the importance of combating neoliberalism and neo-populism by detailing the parallels. In addition, he urges professors to openly combat attacks on science, reason, truth, and education. Richard provides solutions to this assault by emphasizing the importance of educators dedicated to social justice efforts in the classroom and the public sphere.

Chapter 7, written by Victor Mendoza, presents a personalized account of how his education and life have been influenced by the neoliberal education he was raised with in West Texas. Mendoza seamlessly weaves narrative and theory together to demonstrate how the white neoliberal agenda forces students to ignore their history and identity. In Mendoza's case, his school district attempted to retain its language diversity only to have that diversity stripped of its potency by the neoliberal ideologies.

In Chapter 8, Laura Schleifer describes the introduction of neoliberalism into education, showing that the removal of public funding allowed neoliberal think tanks and corporations to sweep in and fund faculty positions that promote neoliberal agendas (Washburn, 2006). Schleifer also describes how these positions in biology, psychology, and policy are infusing the American culture with neoliberal ideologies. In the end, this infusion of ideology co-opts the notion of academic freedom in the service of corporations and capitalism (Berube & Ruth, 2015).

Chapter 9, authored by Riley Clare Valentine, walks through the evolution of education from a social activity that cultivates our sense of self to the neoliberal notion of education as an investment. Valentine takes issue with neoliberalism's commodification of education as a market-only value. She also notes the challenges to our morality when education is restricted to economic value.

Chapter 10, *Neoliberalism, Democratization, and the Re-Visioning of Education,* written by Steven Gennaro and Douglas Kellner, presents a novel approach to navigating the ever-changing technological, global, and neoliberal experiences of the present day. The authors posit that expanded critical pedagogies in cultural literacy, social literacy, and eco-literacy are pivotal to the future of the education system. They offer that developing multiple critical literacy skills enables students and citizens to use emergent technologies to enhance their lives and create a better culture and society.

Chapter 11, *Has the Last Bastion Fallen?*, written by Frank A. Fear, focuses on the double-impact of neoliberalism and capitalism on higher education. The future of higher education is in the balance as the commodification of the education system infects the traditional vocational platform. The text serves as a call-to-arms for those in academia desiring to uphold higher education principles and society.

Chapter 12 is *Tied to the Loom: Alienation in the Neoliberal Academy, Anarcha-Feminism, and a Politics of Resistance and Care*, by Caroline K. Kaltefleiter. The author compares the plight of academics with that of textile workers, willing to give of themselves for financial security. The text presents anarcha-feminist theory and Post-Situationist anarchist thought to overcome the neoliberal degradation of the academy. Additionally, the author provides insight into the use of collective self-care as a means of freeing academics from the grips of the neoliberal machine.

Chapter 13, written by Dr. David Bokovoy, presents a first-hand look at the Prison Education Program through Salt Lake Community College. The essay describes the importance and necessity of the program, using first-hand accounts from incarcerated students enrolled in the program. The students share how the program has changed their outlook on their lives, their environments, and the importance of education in helping them navigate their environments and reintegrate into normal society.

Higher education promotes equity but operates within the confines of neoliberal principles. This text will expose educational spaces in the US to help empower a critical consciousness that can help lead towards action and liberation.

References

Adams, M., & L. E. (2016). *Teaching for diversity and social justice*. New York, NY: Routledge.

Alexander, M. (2011). *The new Jim Crow: Mass incarceration in the age of colorblindness*.

Ayers, B., Quinn, T. M., & Stovall, D. (2009). *Handbook of social justice in education*. New York, NY: Routledge.

Berube, M., & Ruth, J. (2015). *The humanities, higher education and academic freedom: Three necessary arguments*. New York, NY: Palgrave.

Brownlee, J. (2015). *Academia, Inc: How corporatization is transforming Canadian universities*. Fernwood Publishing.

Brownlee, J., Hurl, C., & Walby, K. (Eds.). (2018). *Corporatizing Canada: Making business out of public service*. Between the Lines.

Chatterjee, P., & Maira, S. (2014). *The imperial university: Academic repression and scholarly dissent*. Minneapolis, MN: University of Minnesota Press.

Crenshaw, K. (1989). "Demarginalizing the intersection of race and sex: A black feminist critique of antidiscrimination doctrine, feminist theory and antiracist policies." *University of Chicago Legal Forum*, no. 1. 139–167.

Del Gandio, J., & Nocella II, A. J. (2014). *Educating for action: Strategies to ignite social justice*. British Columbia, CA: New Society Publishers.

Fanon, F. (1952). *Black skin, white masks*. Grove Press.

Fanon, F. (1961). *The wretched of the Earth*. Grove Press.

Feldman, J. (1999). *Universities in the business of repression: The academic military industrial complex in Central America*. South End Press.

Friere, P. (2002). *Pedagogy of the oppressed*. New York, NY: Bloomsbury Academic.

Giroux, H. (2014). *Neo-liberalism's war on higher education*. Chicago, IL: Haymarket Books.

Giroux, H. (2007). *The university in chains: Confronting the military-industrial-academic complex*. New York, NY: Routledge.

Nelson, C. (2011). *No university is an island: Saving academic freedom*. New York, NY: New York University Press.

Nocella II, A. J, Best, S., & McLaren, P. (2010). *Academic repression: Reflections from the academic industrial complex*. Oakland, CA: AK Press.

Nocella II, A. J., & Gabbard, D. (2013). *Policing the campus: Academic repression, Surveillance, and the occupy movement*. New York, NY: Peter Lang Publishing.

Nocella II, A., Parmar, P., & Stovall, D. (2014). *From education to incarceration: Dismantling the school to prison pipeline*. New York, NY: Peter Lang.

Nocella II, A. J., & Juergensmeyer, E. (2017). *Fighting academic repression: Resistance, reclaiming, organizing and black lives matter in education*. New York, NY: Peter Lang Publishing.

Northwest Council on Colleges and University 2020 Standards. (n.d.). NWCCU. Retrieved September 21, 2020, from https://www.nwccu.org/accreditation/standards-policies/standards/

Readings, B. (1997). *The university in ruins*. Cambridge, MA: Harvard University Press.

Return on Investment of UTech. (2019). Retrieved November 27, 2021, from https://udrc.utah.gov/utechroi/index.html

Schrecker, E. (2010). *The lost soul of higher education: Corporatization, the assault on academic freedom, and the end of American university*. New York, NY: The New Press.

Utah Data Research Center. (n.d.). Retrieved November 27, 2021, from https://udrc.utah.gov/about.html

Washburn, J. (2006). *University inc.: The corporate corruption of higher education.* New York, NY: Basic Books

Williams, J. (2016). *Academic freedom in an age of conformity: Confronting the fear of knowledge.* New York, NY: Palgrave Macmillan.

1 Dismantling Rubericization, Evaluation, and Standardization in Neoliberal Conformity: Building Community Colleges as Anti-Racist Public Intellectual Places of Knowledges

ANTHONY J. NOCELLA II

Introduction

Teaching, service, and professional development are the three criteria of determining the neoliberal so-called worth/value of a professor. That is it. It is a simple three-part equation. A professor must have good teaching evaluations from students and an external evaluator, provide service to the institution such as be on a committee, and continue to develop professionally. Those are the community college basic criteria. At a four-year institution the three-part equation is slightly different, but should be addressed. The four-year institution determines the worth of a professor based on teaching, service and publishing. With many professors at community colleges dedicated to professional development and many professors at bachelor and graduate colleges and universities dedicated to publishing, there is a clear value being set for those that are at either institution. It is critical to understand and witness the difference of these criteria. Community college administration and governing bodies views the professors as not being fully prepared and accomplished, while the bachelor and graduate college and university administration and governing bodies view their professors as prepared and accomplished. This social constructed intellectual binary is reinforced also with the students and the students' assumed professional goals.

With a surplus of professors with doctorates not all of them can and/or want to teach at a four-year school, so to assume community colleges do not have professors with doctorates is today, a misconception. Further, more professors every year are wanting to leave the elitist institutions that promote competition amongst its faculty and with grant writing. The ten macro-faculty differences between community colleges and four-year institutions are:

1. Community college professors teach more courses per semester and do not have teaching assistants unlike many research universities
2. Community college professors publish less and do less research
3. Community colleges do more community and service projects
4. Community colleges often have more students with disabilities and first-generation students
5. Community colleges also are extremely more affordable and cater to the local level region more than the national or international level.
6. With the huge amount of teaching assistants and adjuncts, universities do not have a larger amount of overall faculty with doctorates.
7. There is a higher percentage of full-time faculty with doctorate degrees at universities compared to community colleges.
8. Community colleges have more professional and technical-based degrees, while universities often have more social science and advanced careers in sciences, law, and business.
9. Both institutions have nontraditional students.
10. Both institutions have students that do not go on for more degrees.

Higher education is changing with seven different macro-types of higher education: (1) community/junior colleges, (2) public research universities, (3) public colleges, (4) private colleges, (5) for-profit colleges/universities, (6) private research universities, and (7) technical colleges. It is not that one institution is better than another, rather that they cater to different wants and needs. Unfortunately, those in power have socially constructed elitism, which is annually ranked by different agencies such as U.S. News and World Report to determine what institutions have the most valuable, intelligent and successful individuals.

Neoliberalism

Too often neoliberalism is defined abstractly with jargon-filled explanations. Neoliberalism is a theory of doing good for self-interest that is commonly financial motivated. Corporations, nonprofits, agencies, individuals, and organizations can all be neoliberal (Giroux, 2014). The problem with neoliberalism is that it destroys morality, ethics, and humanity. It abolishes the idea of helping others for the purpose of caring for them and valuing peace and justice above external incentives, which if every act becomes neoliberal all relationships and friendships are had only for financial gain. Therefore, people will not want to uplift others if they cannot benefit from or exploit them. All relationships in a complete neoliberal society would be based on financial values, which is the direction in which we are headed if we do not educate, resist, revolt, rebel, and dismantle neoliberalism and capitalism (Marcuse, 1972; Nocella & Gabbard, 2013; Nocella & Juergensmeyer, 2017).

Neoliberalism is an old term that was used by critical theorists most often in the 1980s in a critique of global capitalism and imperialism by England and the United States (Best, Kahn, Nocella, & McLaren, 2011). Naomi Klein (2018) writes,

> In 1988, Canada and the U.S. signed their free trade agreement, a prototype for NAFTA and countless deals that would follow. The Berlin wall was about to fall, an event that would be successfully seized upon by right-wing ideologues in the U.S. as proof of "the end of history" and taken as license to export the Reagan-Thatcher recipe of privatization, deregulation, and austerity to every corner of the globe.

The North American Free Trade Agreement, World Trade Organization, International Monetary Fund, all appeared to support workers, consumers, and the environment, but in actuality these transnational Corporate-funded NGOs move jobs to other countries, provide a less healthy and quality product and destroy many ecosystems with the building of factories.

The difference between capitalism, an economic system and neoliberalism, a social theory, is that capitalism wants profit by any means and at any cost, while neoliberalism only wants to profit by appearing to help others. Capitalism has been exposed as the exploitive theory it is by the world, so to disguise itself, its has marketed it malevolence as acts of charity—oil companies donating to environmental groups, banks donating to homeless shelters, police giving out toys to Black youth, and public schools giving food to their students (Shannon, Nocella II, & Asimakopoulos, 2012). Neoliberalism is a performative theory, in that, one wants to appear good, in-order to financially profit. Therefore, neoliberalism defines being good as a means to an end and that end is making money. The more a company or individual appears doing good in a neoliberal society, the more they will gain financially, hence why so many corporations are supporting LGBTTQQIA+ inclusion and Black Lives Matter. Many corporations understand that these movements can build potential customers, which in turn, can garner more revenue for the company. It is here the utilitarian philosophy of valuing majority rule is extremely oppressive, subjective, and dangerous. Neoliberal social justice advocates identify People of Color as global majority, rather than fighting for a new ethic that demands more justice, equity, inclusion, diversity, freedom, dignity, and inevitable rights. It does not matter if there a particular population is the majority or minority statistically speaking, this is subjective logic, as who or what the majority and minority are identify can always be manipulated to favor whatever argument is being made. It is here that why utilitarianism is flawed.

All wars in modern history have all been fought for one reason—power and control over profitable resources such as land, water, oil, humans, minerals, and plants. The real neoliberal wars are not with soldiers, but with traders on Wall Street. Noam Chomsky (1998) writes,

> The 'principal architects' of the neoliberal 'Washington consensus' are the masters of the private economy, mainly huge corporations that control much of the international economy and have the means to dominate policy formation as well as the structuring of thought and opinion. The United States has a special role in the system for obvious reasons. To borrow the words of diplomatic historian Gerald Haines, who is also senior historian of the CIA, 'Following World War II the United States assumed, out of self-interest, responsibility for the welfare of the world capitalist system.' (p. 20)

The greatest neoliberal college and university slogan is, "we are here to serve the students," while the real neoliberal mission is, to create jobs for administrators and developing students to be cogs in the industrial-capitalistic-machine, while neglecting students' learning. As schools are to make workers and to be a business in the neoliberal schooling model, not - citizens, critical thinkers, foster democracy, or serve the community. If colleges and universities were here for the students and not for a job, we would in-act the following. First, we would make sure to not have standardized teaching and evaluating, as every student learns differently, and every student has a different mind. Second, every student learns better in smaller groups, so schools and colleges should provide smaller classrooms. Third, schools and colleges would be free instead of requiring most students take out financial aid and loans to receive higher education. Fourth, schools would be dedicated to education and learning as a process. Consequently, schools and colleges would abolition grades, which is one of the major factors why students do not attend or stay in these institutions. Fifth, have open enrollment policy for all students, which would be accompanied by personal counseling and individual education program (IEP) for each student, not just those with disabilities. Finally, schools should not be influenced by industry or by building pathways and degrees, but rather challenge industry to be more like schools and promote inclusion, equity, justice, democracy, and peace. These are the great values of the most respected philosophers and education theorist who warned us against exploitation, war, capitalism, oppression, and violence. Schools need to be liberatory and allow students to explore and to become lost—not found—in education (Freire, 1997). Students are too directed, bureaucratic, structured, standardized, and rubric-oriented. Schools are different than education and teachers are different than educators. Rubricization and standardization foster categorization and classification, which are tools of normalcy, a theory of fostering socially constructed sameness and to eliminate diversity and replace equity for equality. Normalcy occurs by voluntary conformity or violent assimilation. Rubrics are not being used in schools, colleges, and universities as guides of what to learn, but as tools to assess and evaluate what is deemed important knowledge and skills, which is a normalizing and monolithic. Schools are not places of learning with rubrics in place. Rather schools, acting like prisons, are penal sites of hegemonic violence, with rubrics, acting like probation and parole, are used as punitive tools of punishment (Nocella, Seis, & Shantz, 2018, 2020).. Joseph E. Flynn, Jr., Michelle Tenam-Zehach, and Leslie David Burns (2015) write in the Introduction: Why A Book on Rubrics? Problematizing the Unquestioned, in the book, *Rubric Nation: Critical Inquiries on the Impact of Rubrics in Education* (Tenam-Zemach & Flynn, Jr., 2015), writes:

> As Bourdieu and Passerson (1990) point out, 'Every power to exert symbolic violence, i.e., every power which manages to impose meanings and to impose them as legitimate by concealing power relations which are the basis of its force, adds its own specifically symbolic force to those power relations' (p. 4). If rubrics offer roadmaps to achieving particular outcomes related to particular standards, for example, who is determining the outcomes that will matter most (or at all), for whom, how, and to what effects? (p. xvii)

Rubrics, like artificial intelligence, standardization, tests, quizzes, and schools are valued-based in that these tools and institutions are grounded in a particular knowledge which favors certain philosophies and not others, therefore privileging certain cultures, while marginalizing others. We cannot argue for inclusion, diversity, justice, and equity, while favoring a monolithic educational model, that only allows certain types of knowledge. Epistemologically speaking we know that knowledge is rooted in culture. There are many cultures, cultures are always changing, and cultures evolve and end. Rubricization and standardization are theories to defend what knowledge is taught in schools, colleges, universities and limit teachers and professors from teaching anything contrary to that dominant and monolithic valued knowledge. This process is protected by normalcy, forced assimilation, and violence toward the student.

> Taylorism and Fordism were systematically applied far beyond their originally intended contexts of factory production to include the standardization of social systems (Clark, 1990), rubrics must be considered as at least potential instruments for use in the de-professionalization of teaching and teacher education, both of which require workers who must be afforded significant levels of autonomy and flexibility in order to be successful. (Flynn, Jr., Tenam-Zehach, & Burns, 2015, p. xxii)

Taylorism and Fordism is being supported today by corporatization of education. In higher education we are producing workers, not citizens. Companies are replacing society and the workplace is replacing democracy. Rubrics are not about thinking, let alone critical thinking, but rather a procedure. Rubrics are for training, where education, is to be complex, messy, and not to have an answer, but an exploration of being lost and liberated at the same time.

Pink Floyd called out schools as being factories of information, today those factories are corporations and industries which emerged two very standardized model of education or a hybrid of the two—corporate education or factory education, which both together in one of the three modalities establishes the academic industrial complex. Students come into schools, colleges, and universities in a standardized process, but while in the institutions are conditioned through rubrics, referred to as rubricization. If standardization is a 1.0 of the normalizing of educating into a factory model, then rubricization is 2.0. People defend and depend on rubrics as they depend on modules via Blackboard, Canvas, D2L, etc. These course hubs allow the professor to engage less with the students compared to a face-to-face course. Online courses, which have proven to be efficient in providing information to students, has yet to prove that the students will be critical thinkers with the ability to defend and engage in a democratic society. With professors conditioned to do less in the classes because they are so efficient they only need a grader, the only question that needs to be asked is if these shells are sufficiently efficient to disseminate information. It also must be discussed that with these online shells and with artificial intelligence (AI) universities, colleges, and schools might view full-time professors as they currently view adjuncts: as mere tools to be exploited and not as a living beings meant to share wisdom, knowledge, and to educate. AI is useful for schools, colleges, and universities to be a more efficient corporate-factory diploma mill of disseminating information, grading student work, saving money by replacing professors, and universalizing discussions with and responses to students. AI is dangerous for many reasons, but the top five are (1) it will marginalize economic disadvantaged groups more, (2) it will be racially prejudice as AI is designed predominantly by white scholars, (3) it will replace professors, (4) it is very costly,

(5) being emotionless to the students, (6) lack creativity, (7) lack morals and values, (8) lack human experiences in the workforce, (8) able to be hacked, (9) monolithic generation of misinformation, and (10) humans begin to depend on it. AI will replace many jobs in schools and colleges such as librarians, staff, and professors who do not participate in complex engaged learning practices (high-impacted practices) such as community service, conference presentation, publishing, interviews, organizing events, research, intellectual critical dialogues, study abroad, and immersion learning. Professors need to be more creative, engaged and impactful to protect their jobs from AI. AI is not a useful tool for education, as society has been fine without it for centuries. What AI is doing is striving to make learning efficient categorical and conformist, but that is an oxymoron. Learning is meant to be a complex, messy, unique, and transformative process, not a result, for each individual. AI could help with simple research and information gathering, but if educators fall asleep at the wheel, we will see the elimination of discussions in all classes on ethics and humanity from the liberal arts to the sciences.

Schools and teachers are tools in the academic industrial complex, a neoliberal front for democracy. John Dewey (2018) is turning over in his grave now that education is becoming fully about corporate development rather than building a healthy democracy. Fighting for democracy is a political and educational act. Dewey (2008) believes that miseducative experience is one that is grounded in becoming less desiring and disengaged in learning and creative thinking. There are many books coming out on why students do not value education. This framing is completely wrong. Students are not less desiring of education, they are becoming more aware of how education is becoming schooling and mechanical and not about learning, but about training. Public discourse is being replaced with dogmatic tweets and TikTok videos that lack critical thinking and analytical evaluation of social problems. Higher education today about the consumer and producer relationship where education is just a product to be purchased. Former First Lady Melania Trump BBC reported (2018) wore a green long jacket that said on the back of it in white paint, "I really don't care, do you?" which speaks to the apathetic ideology. The normalizing of not caring is the foundation of the Trump Era, which also promoted an anti-intellectual loyalist dogmatic value culture, similar to that of Nazism. Too often those that critique Donald Trump say his number one priority is wealth. I would say that while that is not wrong completely, because of his authoritarian style leadership, his biggest negative impact is unquestionable loyalty. Colleges and universities are taking a dangerous and anti-democratic turn by adopting competency-based education, which is where a student can test out of a course if the student knows specific information that the course covers. What is completely lacking in competency-based education, which can be engaged in a field or topic is the critical epistemological dialectical discourse. Cultural understanding of others in discourse is lacking in these competency-based education and online programs. Competency-based education reinforces a testing model based on a socially constructed monolithic hegemonic knowledge. This therefore suppresses the fact that there are many epistemologies, knowledges, and cultures, which view fields and topics differently. What is replaced is a generation of dogmatic noncritical thinkers who do not have the ability to create democracy or critical citizenship, but rather a capitalist oligarchy. Voting is being replaced with purchasing and to be opposed to a political decision, we boycott with our purchasing power, rather than protest the issue. The voting booth is checkout line, and the voting booth officer is being replaced with a cashier. Henry Giroux writes,

> But more is needed than defending higher education as a vital sphere in which to develop and nourish the proper balance between democratic values and market fundamentalism, between identities founded on democratic principles and identities steeped in forms of competitive, self-interested individualism that celebrate their own material and ideological advantages. Given the current assault on critical educators in light of the tragic events of September 11th, it is politically crucial that educators at all levels of involvement in the academy be defended as public intellectuals who provide an indispensable service to the nation. Such an appeal cannot be made in the name of professionalism but in terms of the civic duty such intellectuals provide. Too many academics have retreated into narrow specialisms that serve largely to consolidate authority rather than critique its abuses. (Giroux, 2002, pp. 112–113)

Scholars, researchers, professors, public intellectuals, students, and staff must organize, build unions and fight against the corporate conservative anti-intellectual agenda that is striving to hijack schools, colleges, and universities.

We must join the effort in abolishing schools and strive to eliminate the agendas, syllabi, outcomes, and evidence-based learning grounded in capitalism and colonialism (Albert & Chomsky, 2014). One cannot truly grade or determine one's knowledge, wisdom, effort, or intelligence, as these are all transformative experiences. We strive to measure transformative education, which is abstract, holistic, and mystical as love. Rubrics, tests, quizzes, grades, assessment, evaluations, report cards, ranking, and rating are all opinions betrayed by academia as objective intellectual Truth, but is is subjective at best and a tool of oppression as worst, designed by colonialism, enforced by imperialism, and benefited by capitalism. The oppression equation can be applied here as supremacy + domination = privilege, with supremacy being colonialism, domination being imperialism, and privilege being capitalism.

The Deficit Model

Community Colleges

Society has constructed that professors and students that are part of community colleges are intellectually inferior and are followers rather than leaders. This social constructed elitism is not only reinforced in society by nonprofit, for-profit, and government sectors, but by universities as well. Another institution that is reinforcing this social construction is community colleges themselves. They have an internalized oppression and inferiority complex, which must be dismantled if community colleges want to liberate the community and its students. The idea at the beginning of this article was about how community college professors need engage in professional development, while university professors publish. Community colleges too often invite university professors for professional development, rather than looking for community college professors within their institution or similar institutions that can provide professional development. Community college professors often have nothing to develop, but rather advance like all professors. Community college professors also do publish and should publish. Publishing allows the professor to advance their discipline and to study it via research while developing scholarship, such as a publication and/or presentation.

Don't Fall for the Gaps

Achievement gap displays the deficits between, most notably, wealthy youth and economically disadvantaged youth and Youth of Color and white students. The achievement gap, success gap, academic gap, opportunity gap, urban education, and the deficit model are not only problematic, but violent justifications for propaganda rationalizing why wealthy, elite white colonial, imperialist settlers are the 3Ss—successful, smarter, and superior. There is no gap, but different modes of thinking and acting, based on cultural differences. Therefore, no one can be culturally competent, because to be competent is to know and understand, but a white man can never know or understand what it means to be a Black woman in the U.S. Further, the concept of minority is problematic as the term is defined as less than, rooted all the way back to the 3/5 vote during slavery in the U.S. We need to understand that we cannot be culturally competent and strive to be Dangerous Minds (1995) a highly oppressive and white supremacist movement, where the only dangerous mind was the white teacher. This white supremacist teaching was challenged brilliantly in *Boyz n the Hood* (Singleton, 1991) where a young Black youth questioned the history of Thanksgiving and white settler colonialism by arguing how it was racist. In the beginning of the movie (Singleton, 1991) many of the students are not engaged and the teacher gives a traditional whitewashed history of thanksgiving. After the colonial lecture, the teacher tells her students,

> Teacher: And that's why we celebrate Thanksgiving, to commemorate the unity between the Indians, excuse me, the Native Americans, and the early English settlers who were called... Class?
> Class (in unison): Pilgrims.
> Teacher: That's right, the Pilgrims. Very good.
> Tre: The penguins!
> Teacher: Who said that? (1991)

The teacher and Tre then begin to have a disagreement in front of the whole class, with Tre using humor to dismantle the authority of the white teacher, by calling the pilgrims "penguins," consequently the students laughed. This laughter annoyed and disempowered the teacher. Tre the Black liberated self-confident student challenged white supremacist pedagogy being taught by the white teacher. His liberated being was fostered by his highly intellectual, powerful Black father, who regularly gave him and his friends lectures surrounding racism and classism. Tre noted to the teacher that all people are from Africa, for this reason the Teacher invites him to give a lesson standing up in front of the students at the front of the class:

> Tre (pointing to Africa on a map): What's the name of this place?
> Female Student: That's Africa. I know that.
> Tre: Right, that's Africa.
> Tre: Did you know that Africa is where the body of the first man was found? My daddy says that's where all people originated from. That means everybody's really from Africa. Everybody. All y'all. Everybody. (1991)

Tre taught that the Western educational system perpetuated racism and a false socially constructed narrative (Nocella & Socha, 2013). This scene in the movie stresses that public education in the U.S. is grounded in racism. It is important to note this because it stresses that education, while not segregated anymore, is being taught by mostly white teachers with a colonial white supremacist pedagogy. Schools are a powerful tool is implementing propaganda, such as the idea that women should not work in a company, but stay at home working to serve the needs of children and their husband or that Black people are not fit to be lawyers, which was told by a white teacher to

Malcolm X, while in school (X, 1998). School can be a place of liberation or a place of hell, which sad to say, is the case for many transgender youth, BIPOC youth, youth with disabilities, LGBTTQQIA+ youth, girls, and ESL youth. If it is a place of hell it normally pushes youth out and into the juvenile justice system, which manifests the school-to-prison pipeline (Nocella, Parmar, & Stovall, 2014).

Banning Social Justice Education

Most recently at the beginning of 2023 nationally many neoconservative politicians are striving to ban and dismantle equity, diversity, and inclusion (EDI), justice, equity, diversity, and inclusion (JEDI), and diversity, equity, inclusion, and justice (DEIJ) initiatives in kindergarten to college. These neoconservative politicians, such as Ron DeSantis is working on bills. such as, "Stop Woke Act" and anti-LGBTTQQIA+ youth and advocates bills, that challenge racism, sexism, ableism, classism, and all forms of oppression, which make neoconservatives feel uncomfortable and guilty. Neoconservatives are taking the playbook from neoliberals by blending corporations, lobby groups and schools together to push exclusive dogmatic-patriotic white supremacy agendas. This effort is strategized by introducing an extreme bill in kindergarten to twelfth grade to test the waters and to shock the public. This bill is meant to fail, while the second bill is meant to be noted as being revised and passed. Once the bill passes in kindergarten to twelfth grade, it is then introduced with the two-bill strategy in higher education. Further, this two-bill strategy is introduced in conservative states first then introduced in moderate states and finally introduced in liberal states.

Fighting Neoliberal Racism

To learn and teach about oppression, is key. Too often neoliberal teachers/professors/administrators/staff teach and learn about diversity and bullying, but not about how they, the system, society, and the institution and industry, are responsible and accountable for perpetuating oppression. Further, neoliberals often insert a simplistic surface level non-critical discussion, module, workshop, session, or lecture on equity and inclusion, which is even worse, because this poor check-box/module/session attempt to address oppression only tells those that are oppressed they are only worth a small segment of the larger course, workshop, conference, teach-in, lecture, training, and curriculum, which is taught by someone that is an apologist for the oppressor and an "All Lives Matter, can't we get over it, can't we all just get along" facilitator, which is just reinforcing the oppression and choking out oppression and the breathe of those oppressed even more. Teaching can be another form of violence and I argue within the school-to-prison-pipeline discussion, worse than police as teachers, and can condition marginalized students to learn a false history of their culture and hate themselves, i.e., internalized oppression (Nocella, Parmar, & Stovall, 2014). Case in point is the famous doll experiment with youth in schools, conducted in the 1940s by Mamie Clark and Kenneth Clark, African-American psychologists, which was fundamental in the will of Brown versus Board of Education, which was grounded on separate is not equal. The problem with ending segregated schools was that those in power, i.e., white America, were the teachers. The Black teachers were essentially eliminated from public schools. The Brown versus Board of Education case in 1954 gave rise to white teachers teaching that whites are superior and People of Color are inferior. This violent abusive behavior until the present, referred to by the establishment as teaching, was addressed so brilliantly in *Boyz N the Hood* (Singleton, 1991). This teaching is nothing more than 2.0 of colonialism. Colonialism started off visually and physically violent, with lynching, chaining, slavery, rape, muzzling, courting, dragging, and much more horrible acts. Today, colonialism is harder to identify as it puts its hand out as an ally, but it is a wolf in sheep's clothing. Malcolm X explained the dangerous of the white liberal:

> The American negro is nothing but a political football and the white liberals control this ball. Through tricks, tokenism, and false promises of integration and civil rights. (X, n.d.)

Those that are wanting to be allies and in solidarity, must not portray themselves as understanding or being culturally competent in what it means to be oppressed. I came up with the *Working to Be in Solidarity with Oppressed People* list (Nocella, 2019):

1. Be invited to the struggle not movement.
2. Listen.
3. Articulate one's commitment.
4. Explain one's skills.
5. Explain motivation and personal goals.
6. Be willing to follow and never lead.
7. Be willing to not get credit, but give credit to non-dominate voices.
8. Be willing to take accountability and own one's supremacy and domination.
9. Be willing to be challenged and be called out.
10. Be willing to learn new processes and cultural practices.

11. Be willing to take more risks.
12. Be willing to do more.
13. Be willing to not take money or other benefits
14. Challenge acts by white individuals and agencies that tokenize, patronize, and co-opt.
15. Be willing to leave and not blame others.

The above is only a list, the real work is in action. I have a common quote I tell people in activism: do something about it, or shut up. I am not saying that for everyone, but for activists. Activism is skilled position to escalate an issue until it is addressed by the opposition (De Gandio & Nocella II, 2014). Community members will complain, cry, yell, scream because of depression and anger, which we must allow space and place for as a form of therapy. Without allowed nonviolent expression, we will have chaotic violence.

Community Colleges as a Place of Community Scholars and Public Intellectuals

Community colleges, with their expertise and focus on community, first generation students, affordable education, regional and local social issues have a lot of opportunity for research and scholarship. My argument is that community colleges need to provide funding and resources to have a center dedicated community research and scholarship. Further, community colleges need to give attention to the scholarship and research of professors by rewarding, funding, publicizing, and giving them time. I am not saying the focus should not be less on teaching than research and scholarship, but rather if a community college professor is wanting to dedicate their time to research and scholarship, support and praise them for doing so. Community colleges need to dismantle anti-intellectualism in society, administratively, in the student-body, and in the faculty-body. Anti-intellectualism is rampant in community colleges because of the internalized oppression and inferiority complex. The center would implement this mission by using the 4Ps—produce, publicize, praise, and promote. Encourage faculty to *produce* scholarship by giving them financial and time release incentives, but not through threats, punishment, or requirements. Next, *publicize* the scholarship that the faculty have produced through social media, websites, media releases, and paper publications. Third, *praise* the faculty that produce through celebrations, awards, and other recognitions. Finally, *promote* faculty financially and with titles, and/or leadership roles.

Community colleges should be a bastion of activism, public intellectualism, and community organizing more so than any other institution in higher education (Giroux, 1988). The reason for why there is not activism on certain campuses is because many professors are not teaching or not allowed, due to academic repression, (Nocella, Best, & McLaren, 2010) to teach about critical issues, which inform the students of social injustices and oppression, which would excite the students to engage in organizing and activism. If one is not educated about an issue that individual cannot act on that issue, because they are not aware of it. Education comes prior to activism in all social movements.

People need to know what they do not know, including that social justice education and peace and conflict studies are internationally respected fields that have been developed formally since the beginning of the 1900s and for centuries prior to that if we are not speaking about academia, but decolonized education as well. To respect social justice education and peace and conflict studies, we must first recognize that if you are not in the field, admit it and learn from those in the field. Academics must stay in their wheelhouse and lane of expertise and learn from others. If academics and scholars strive to perform in a field they are not knowledgeable about, these will aid in the cooptation and destruction of the field.

Neoliberalism is benefiting financially through capitalist modes of behavior, which is portrayed as progressive acts that help others, while coopting three key terms—equity, inclusion, and justice. Do not always trust those that are working for equity, inclusion, and justice. What's key is to be critically aware of how these terms are used in combination with other terms such as closing the equity or academic achievement gap, which are colonial and white-centric agendas. Further, "diversity" and "urban" are often used by neoliberals to identify People of Color. These are code words of oppression. There are many more code words of oppression by neoliberals, but neoconservatives also have a list of code words and agendas. Neoconservatism is promoting tradition views from valuing hard work and school is important to picking yourself up from the bootstraps and an excuse is for losers for financial gains. Neoconservatism would like to think they are for schools and education, but in actuality they view students as cogs in a corporate welfare machine that drains the government of valuable resources.

Conclusion

Colleges, schools, and universities need to dismantle off- and on-campus neoliberalism and neoconservatism by (1) calling it out, (2) silencing it, (3) removing it, (4) destroy it, and (5) educating others on how to spot it in the future. Further, places of education need to end the use of tools of neoliberalism and neoconservatism, such as rubrics, standardized tests, assessments, evaluations, and trainings. Education should not be a factory, but a liberatory creative experience for social transformation. Foucault (1995) would agree that today schools are prisons, rather than places of joy, creativity, autonomy, and freedom, where discipline is not based on learning, but punishment, shame, fear, and control. Do not participate in collegiality or respectability politics, when it comes to oppression. There is no respectful way to tell someone they are racist, sexist, homophobic, transphobic, speciesist, ableist, statist, elitist, ageist, classist, or anthropocentric. State marginalized, not global majority; prejudice not bias; equity not equality; liberation not empowerment, academic repression not academic rigor; problematic and conflict not collegiality; discrimination not bullying; and diversity and privilege not success/racial/achievement/academic gap. We need to be for intersectional justice for total liberation, that is acted out through transformative justice and not restorative justice (Crenshaw, 1989; Nocella & George, 2019). Restorative justice is reformist, colonial, and oppressive. This world is not going to change if people do not start calling out issues directly, which will force difficult conversations and educating in a critical perspective. This does not mean canceling people, but engaging in accountability transformative dialogues. Cancel culture is not transformative justice, but rather another form of punitive justice. A critical, not from neoliberalism use, i.e., asking questions, but a critical from critical theory grounded in the Frankfurt School in Germany, who created critical theory, which is about analyzing social problems and working to end domination, authoritarianism, and oppression. True critical theorists must be for social justice and total liberation. This will include ending practices, departments, schools, evaluation tools, and changing everything we think we know about schools and colleges, which have turned into a mega-bureaucratic factory corporate schooling machine, spitting out diplomas in exchange for money.

References

Albert, M., & Chomsky, N. (2014). *Realizing hope: Life beyond capitalism*. Zed Books.
BBC. (2023, October 14). *Melania Trump says 'don't care' jacket was a message*. Retrieved from https://www.bbc.com/news/world-us-canada-45853364
Best, S., Kahn, R., Nocella II, A. J., & McLaren, P. (2011). *The global industrial complex: Systems of domination*. Lexington Books.
Bourdieu, P., & Passerson, J. (1990). *Reproduction in education, society and culture*. Sage.
Chomsky, N. (1989). *Profit over people*.

Crenshaw, K. (1989). *Demarginalizing the intersection of race and sex: A Black feminist critique of antidiscrimination doctrine*. University of Chicago Legal Forum, 1989: 139–168.

Del Gandio, J., & Nocella II, A. J. (2014). *Educating for action: Strategies to ignite social justice*. New Society Publishers.

Dewey, J. (2018). *Democracy and education*. Myers Education Press.

Dewey, J. (2008). *Experience and education*. Touchstone.

Foucault, M. (1995). *Discipline and punish: The birth of the prison*. Vintage Books.

Freire, P. (1997). *Pedagogy of the oppressed*. Continuum.

Flynn, Jr., J. E., Tenam-Zemach, M., & Burns, L. D. (2015). Introduction: Why a book on rubrics? problematizing the unquestioned. In M. Tenam-Zemach & J. E. Flynn, Jr., J. E., *Rubric Nation: Critical inquiries on the impact of rubrics in education*. (pp. xi–xxx). Information Age Publishing.

Giroux, H. (1988). *Teachers as intellectuals: Toward a critical pedagogy of learning*. Bergin and Garvey.

Giroux, H. (2002). The corporate war against higher education. *Workplace, 9*, 103–117.

Giroux, H. (2014). *Neoliberalism's war on higher education*. Haymarket Books.

Klein, N. (2018). *Capitalism killed our climate momentum, not "human nature."* Retrieved on May 21, 2020 from https://theintercept.com/2018/08/03/climate-change-new-york-times-magazine/

Marcuse, H. (1972). *Counterrevolution and revolt*. Beacon Press.

Nocella II, A. J. (2019). *Working to Be in Solidarity with Oppressed People*. Retrieved from http://www.criticalanimalstudies.org/2019/01/working-to-be-in-solidarity-with-oppressed-people/

Nocella II, A. J., Best, S., & McLaren, P. (2010). *Academic repression: Reflections from the academic industrial complex*. AK Press.

Nocella II, A., Parmar, P., & Stovall, D. (2014). *From education to incarceration: Dismantling the school to prison pipeline*. New York, NY: Peter Lang.

Nocella II, A. J., Seis, M., & Shantz, J. (2018). *Contemporary anarchist criminology: Against authoritarianism and punishment*. Peter Lang Publishing.

Nocella II, A. J., Seis, M., & Shantz, J. (2020). *Classic writings in anarchist criminology: A historical dismantling of punishment and domination*. AK Press.

Nocella II, A. J., & Gabbard, D. (2013). *Policing the campus: Academic repression, surveillance, and the occupy movement*. Peter Lang Publishing.

Nocella II, A. J., & George, A. E. (2019). *Intersectionality of critical animal studies: A historical collection*. Peter Lang Publishing.

Nocella II, A. J., & Juergensmeyer, E. (2017). *Fighting academic repression: Resistance, reclaiming, organizing and black lives matter in education*. Peter Lang Publishing.

Nocella II, A. J., & Socha, K. (2013). Old school, new school, no school: Hip hop's dismantling of school and the prison industrial complex. *International Journal of Critical Pedagogy, 4*(3), 40–54.

Shannon, D., Nocella II, A. J., & Asimakopoulos, J. (2012). *The accumulation of freedom: Writings on anarchist economics.* AK Press.

Singleton, J. (1991). *Boyz n the hood.* Columbia Pictures.

Tenam-Zemach, M., & Flynn, Jr., J. E. (2015). *Rubric nation: Critical inquiries on the impact of rubrics in education.* Information Age Publishing.

X, M. (1998). *The autobiography of Malcolm X.* Bantam Doubleday Dell Publishing Group.

2 Combatting Stigma: Opposing Neoliberal Oppression through Intersectional, Transformative Activism

Elisa Stone

she/her/hersIntroduction

It seems to me that the major problem with stigma is this: most folks choose to think the problem is not us. Higher education only reinforces our sense of othering in this regard, and even with deep, honest introspection, we may not see past ironically self-perpetuating shame and guilt. To understand why, we must realize we are enmeshed in a system fueled to reinforce the very oppression it purports to critique and subvert. With an awareness of neoliberalism's funneling resources and manipulating ideologies to favor existing systems of privilege and power, one quickly sees that

> rather than providing space for intellectual thought and worldly experience, the academy has become an adjunct to corporate profit. The average college campus is ground zero for licensing agreements; construction contracts; outsourcing of bookstores, venders, concessions and food, laundry, traveling and printing services; corporate sponsoring of buildings, events, speakers and campus programs; patenting of intellectual property rights; and corporate funding, ownership and direct influencing of research. Such corporatization transforms students into customers, teachers into workers, administrators into CEOs and campuses into market populations." (Gandio, 2010)

This chapter will be a personal and socio-cultural endeavor to forge transformative, partnership-based activism in a community college environment and beyond.

Embarking on a personal quest to combat stigma, I accepted a challenge from my colleague and took the Harvard implicit bias test: (Project Implicit, 2011). I scored neutral on everything for which I was tested, meaning that according to the test, I do not unconsciously favor or disfavor any particular group. This left me to my own consideration of where to go next. As the daughter of a college English professor, higher education always seemed to me to be a hallowed space where oppression could be tamed in a civilized, egalitarian environment. I romanticized college as a time and place in one's life where books, ideas, and studies as a buffer to adulthood would rectify authoritarian miscarriages of justice and indignities students endure in K-12. Now, as a college English professor myself, I'm forced to face the influence of neoliberalism in perpetuating capitalism's worst tendencies of corrupting earnest scholarship in favor of existing systems of wealth and power, whether those systems are visible or masked. In the Queer Studies classes I teach, I invoke Audre Lorde's words "The true focus of revolutionary change is never merely the oppressive situations which we seek to escape, but that piece of the oppressor which is planted deep within each of us" (1984). To that end, I seek to rectify when I make missteps regarding my privilege or opinions, diminishing my ability to be in solidarity with those experiencing stigma and oppression. What helps me is having friends, family members, and loved ones who are diverse and candid. Without the guidance of my own eclectic Greek chorus dispensing their collective wisdom to question concepts/tangibles like my "white privilege tears," I suppose I would have remained the naive but inquisitive version of younger me, raised in rural Idaho near the setting of the movie *Napoleon Dynamite* (Hess, 2004). From deep into the archives of childhood, I've wanted to help foster a just and equitable world. And in my envisioned world, people of conscience band together to combat stigma.

I was reared in the kind of town that could easily have murdered Matthew Shepard. I honestly believed I had never seen a gay person, despite having a gay brother, a "butch" lesbian bestie, and being bisexual myself, an identity I wasn't able to claim until well into adulthood. It's hard to explain the denials and erasures in oppressive communities unless you experience them. I admit avoiding the boy in high school choir who was "known" to be gay. I recall sitting in silence while my Mormon seminary teacher, during school hours, made endless "gay Ray" jokes and brought to class the wedding invitations of same sex couples his wife pilfered from the printing company where she worked so he could mock them. Silence is condoning; I was silent. Conversely, when I left Idaho to attend Utah State University, I immediately discovered the Gay/Straight Alliance and pretended to study near their meetings, telling myself I was curious to see a gay person. Before long the complete ordinariness of the attendees launched me out of incognito; soon I was a regular at meetings, and when my sister arrived at USU, she became a life-long ally and the President of the GSA. This is how cycles of stigma, both externally/communally generated and internalized, are disrupted, one person at a time, rebuilding the world through a new lens rather than staying glued to the dingy porthole of bigotry.

Gatherings and conversations in safe havens can catapult us to activism, pivotal to cultural transformation whether or not one agrees with activists' strategies. By the time I had my son and daughter, they were raised with two dear friends—a gay couple—as their cherished godparents, and didn't fully witness homophobia until I sojourned to Brigham Young University-Idaho to protest their LGBTQ+ discrimination policies with Soul Force Freedom Riders, despite the embarrassment to my parents, both employed there, and despite the danger as my former 4th grade teacher showed up with a loaded shotgun and threatened to shoot not only our little band of protestors as we stood in a line holding pictures of our families, but all of the TV, radio, and newspaper reporters as well. The Police Chief, my former neighbor who was rabidly homophobic in my youth but was inexplicably, touchingly kind to the protestors, shooed the would-be shooter away. She came back a second time, still out for blood. Such was my experience of a private religious college in small-town rural America.

But what of academia as a whole, where higher education purports to create utopias where freer-flowing discourse unfetters us from the constraints of stigma and oppression? Despite the ever-present hierarchies dividing academia into tiers where community colleges appear on the bottom rung, what of our unique positionality to be on the front lines of empowering social justice endeavors? (Beebe, 2015). We must be aware of, and actively resist neo liberalism's tendency to commodify: "Education either functions as an instrument which is used to facilitate integration of the younger generation into the logic of the present system and bring about conformity or it becomes the practice of freedom, the means by which men and women deal critically and creatively with reality and discover how to participate in the transformation of their world" (Friere, 2005, p. 34). How might a student respond to the possibility of such transformation? Student editor for the *Globe Newspaper SLCC* Heather Graham reminds us that

> The community college environment is the perfect place to help students understand basic concepts of intersectionality. Community colleges have a lot of diversity within their student body in terms of race, ethnicity, sexuality,

gender, ability, and socioeconomic differences, making it a good environment to apply the understanding of intersectionality. The ability to recognize, accept, and embrace different spaces that people come from and the variety of lived-experiences their individual identities face is a precious skill far beyond the boundaries of academia. Encouraging students to welcome these intersections, normalize them, and celebrate them can change the world. (personal communication, April 20, 2020)

Heather's words echo the rhetoric of bell hooks, one of my muses as a student in search of meaning: "Multiculturalism compels educators to recognize the narrow boundaries that have shaped the way knowledge is shared in the classroom. It forces us all to recognize our complicity in accepting and perpetuating biases of any kind. Students are eager to break through barriers to knowing" (hooks, 1994, p. 44). This in turn, echoes Lourde's admonishment to recognize the oppressor within, and the pragmatism of educators choosing to take that implicit bias test.

Undoubtedly, academia does grant us a haven; it may have taken us multiple proposals and years, but Salt Lake Community College finally opened the Gender & Sexuality Student Resource Center that had been a vision and dream of so many of us for so long. Safe spaces matter. I have the honor of co-creating community for students who tell me they are queer, not out to their parents, families, or communities of faith, and feeling they will never be accepted in the places they've always called home. I have the fulfillment of being an advisor to a Queer Student Club much like the one I once spied on; I help students plan events, advocate their needs, and enjoy the nonjudgmental, welcoming company of their chosen family even when their biological families have, quite literally, abandoned them. These are gifts I hold close to my heart. But are they enough?

There are many ways to misread our positionality. We are not saviors. We do not always get to prevail against the barriers our student face outside and within our protected spaces. We might move away from being detached academics or careerists in favor of the scholar-activist identity civic engagement endeavors have infused into college culture. But the pressure to impart victorious narratives about high-impact learning practices can obscure the realities of nonsuccess. In collaboration with a filmmaker colleague and graduate students, my anti-stigma work took me to South Africa, assisting with an anti-stigma campaign for the Desmond Tutu HIV Foundation. One of the people I befriended was a young man named Atti, 20 years old, a Xosa tribal member living in Gugulethu, Cape Town, who dreamed of being a doctor. Atti took my hand and proudly showed me his favorite ice-skating rink on our group outing; I remember my heart sinking as I stood with our band of

Black young people watching only the white South Africans skating, as the fallout of apartheid remains. I met Atti in October 2016. I was elated the Foundation asked me to return in April, when I would be invited to attend a Peace with Justice Award Ceremony in honor of Desmond Tutu, to hear him speak, and to have coffee with him. I hoped to bring some of the teenagers from the township with me to meet "The Arch," as they fondly refer to Archbishop Emeritus Tutu. Four months later, Atti passed away. Rather than facing the scrutiny of transitioning to the young adult clinic and having people judge him for having HIV, which, incidentally, he was born with, Atti had gone off his government-sponsored medication and died on February 9, 2016. Despite our well-intentioned filmmaking, PSAs, and workshops to combat stigma, we couldn't prevent Atti from becoming a statistic in a country with "the biggest and most high-profile HIV epidemic in the world, with an estimated 7.7 million people living with HIV in 2018" (AVERT, 2020). Closer to home, my LGBTQ+ advocacy, activism, and protests didn't prevent my own gay brother from twice attempting suicide during his time at Brigham Young University. Our aims at utopian ideals may fall far short of their marks. And yet we must press on, with the integrity to account for our foibles, however unflattering or off-mission they may be.

My measure of how I'm doing ethically is predominately based on the opinions of the least empowered beings in my world—including the way I treat animals. As Tutu has said,

> I have spent my life fighting discrimination and injustice, whether the victims are blacks, women, or gays and lesbians. No human being should be the target of prejudice or the object of vilification or be denied his or her basic rights. But there are other issues of justice—not only for human beings but also for the world's other sentient creatures. The matter of the abuse and cruelty we inflict on other animals has to fight for our attention in what sometimes seems an already overfull moral agenda. It is vital, however, that these instances of injustice not be overlooked." (Huffpost, 2013)

I point this out because I find that activism involving stigma and oppression is habitually siloed—one chooses a cause, such as combatting racism, or misogyny, or homophobia, and then lasers in without seeing the interconnectedness of all oppression, including that of non-human animals. It is common in Queer Studies to foreground intersectionality. I invite guest speakers visiting my classes to share their unique perspectives and identities in open conversations I could never inspire on my own. But I've noticed with social justice circles that we lack intersectional activism.

Books such as Will Tuttle's *The World Peace Diet* have helped me connect my varying identities around anti-stigma work so I can feel consistent in the way I choose to live within and outside of academia. I find it's just as easy to incur enemies for my 18+ years as a vegan as it is to gain friends among colleagues and non-profit community organizations who support my LGBTQ+ activism. I have started to understand the pushback is not merely personal, nor is the issue solely about animal rights. Moving forward from pioneering books like Carol J. Adams' *The Sexual Politics of Meat* (1994) demonstrating the intrinsic ties of carnism, patriarchy, misogyny and oppression, Tuttle explains how the first capitalists "were the herders who fought each other for land and capital and created the first kingdoms, complete with slavery, regular warfare, and power concentrated in the hands of a wealthy cattle-owning elite" (2016, p. 18). He argues that "by commodifying and enslaving large, powerful animals, the ancient progenitors of Western culture established a basic mythos and worldview that still lives today at the heart of our culture" (p. 19). He invokes Riane Eisler's *The Chalice and the Blade*, which draws from anthropologists and historians to argue for two types of societies: partnership (women and men generally equal and cooperatively working as the norm for tens of thousands of years) and dominator (patriarchal cultures dating back five to seven thousand years ago based on the herding of animals) (p. 19). Tuttle uses Eisler's work to contrast foraging and gardening communities vs. weaponry and warfare associated, respectively, with partnership vs. dominator cultures, surmising "violent conflict, competition, oppression of women, and class strife, according to Eisler, need not characterize human nature but are relatively recent products of social pressure and conditioning brought by the invading herding cultures whose dominator values we have inherited" (p. 20). Partnership-based societies are key to more equitable relations among all living beings.

This is why I refuse to believe that intersectionality and activism are limited to human issues or to mere ideologies; they are interwoven into the daily, intimate moments of our individual and collective lives. All around me in academia I see layers of denial—that white folks involved in anti-racist circles can't be oppressing People of Color—that sexual harassment isn't still a daily problem for gender and sexual minorities—that participation in the most horrific forms of violence by way of food and lifestyle doesn't matter, shouldn't be an issue. And yes, of course it makes sense that diet and privilege are connected. Does that mean, though, that we should decide oppressed communities should be excluded from a diet that protects them from diseases? (Campbell, 2016). Surely, as Aph Ko articulates in "Vegans of Color and Respectability Politics," "we need to stop expecting Eurocentric vegans to correct systemic racism. We need to let oppressed folks articulate their own movements using their own voices" (2017, p. 81). Until we stop denying the inter-faceted nature of stigmatism and oppression, evolving eludes us.

That is, until change is the only option. As I started writing this during the Covid19 outbreak, it seemed clearer than ever that greater unity is the only way out of our dystopic disfunction. As my student Sony Smith pointed out,

> Some external stigma that has been happening recently has to do with the Asian Americans. Since the COVID-19 outbreak there has been an increase in violence and hate speech towards this group of people. Violence towards this group was declining for years but, since the coronavirus is here it's rapidly increasing, and I think that's really scary. African Americans are still being treated unfairly but that's nothing new. It's really sad seeing how people can hate a huge group of people who haven't done anything wrong. The world is becoming a very dark place. This can cause some groups to not feel safe being at school, especially Asian Americans. I can see bullying increasing or even fights breaking out over this pandemic. (personal communication, April 23, 2020)

Only a month later, the horrific murder of George Floyd gut-wrenched us into full awareness of the unfathomably unjust continuation of systemic racism dating back to police force genesis as slave patrol (Kappeler, 2014). In addition to blatant racism and abuses of police power, this case brought into sharper focus the paralyzing legacy and divisiveness of neo liberalism:

> This moment has been a triumph for Black Lives Matter activists, but once the plumes of tear gas dissipate and compassion fatigue sets in, the real beneficiaries will likely be the neoliberal Democrats and the capitalist blocs they serve. Nearly all of the Democrat leadership who 'took a knee' against racist policing, have openly opposed Medicare for All, free higher education, and the expansion of other public goods, but their technical reforms to reduce excessive force incidents and prosecute police for misconduct are the perfect way of displaying commitment to racial justice, while perpetuating the very pro-market logics and class relations that stress policing and mass incarceration were invented to protect. (Johnson, 2020)

As activists rally to demand justice, the divided society engineered by power-based disparities causes well-intentioned people to remain weary, wary, and worse. Globally, locally, and internally, we must emerge from our silos and find new ways of connecting. But how?

Whenever I'm in doubt, which is often, I ask students like Sony. They are my teachers and collaborators in academia, and in life. I asked what they thought about stigma, oppression, and how to make academia a truly ideal communal space. I also asked some of my colleagues their thoughts on these questions: *What are some ways the external stigma of being an oppressed minority, the internalized stigma from socialization, or the irony of being a stigmatized person who nonetheless oppresses others' lives might be addressed, and even overcome, within the culture of a community college learning environment?*

    The first response I received from a colleague let me know I should reconsider my language as I posed these questions. The use of the word minority and its denotation of "less than" in numbers can also connote "less than" in worth. They offered some resources to help unpack this idea, and a metaphor that stood out most was from Wesley Morris, who writes of "how 'minority' becomes a designation of passenger status in a car somebody else is always driving" (2019). I thought of the time I was asked to oversee our SLCC Community Writing Center's Salt Lake Teens Write Program, designed to pair teens and mentors in a reciprocal, mutually beneficial learning experience. The program's literature when I came onboard said we were seeking "underserved" teens, and I cringed at how it sounded. I learned from our AmeriCorps Vista volunteers who visited classrooms to recruit teens for this opportunity, that people commonly misread the word "underserved" to mean "un-deserved," as in "not deserving." Eventually we prevailed on our Director to compromise with the phrase "underrepresented" teens instead, and our program managed to win awards as we grew. Still, we never got past the deficit-based connotations of "under" in our ethos.

    Language might not seem like a big deal, but it can contour a student's experience in academia. For example, the inclusion on college application forms for a gender other than "male/female" helps non-binary and transgender students know they are recognized. The same is true for calling students by their chosen names and pronouns consistently throughout their college experience. To a transgender student who has transitioned, they may consider their birth name to be their "dead name" and feel traumatized whenever they hear it. A traumatized person doesn't have the best chance of an equitable learning experience. Language is power, and if we're serious about equity and inclusion, we need to adapt inclusive language. Consider the story of Nick Arteaga, an SLCC alumni with whom I collaborate to help plan the annual genderevolution Conference sponsored by the Utah Pride Center. Nick is our Conference Chair. Nick's experiences deserve space, and this is what he would like us to know:

> As a pansexual, non-binary transmasculine person with passing male privilege, my understanding of external stigma of an oppressed minority has magnified. Growing up as a Latina, cisgender woman, assigned female at birth raised in a Mexican household with strong influence from an occult, religious background, I never had much choice of anything. I was a subordinate in many capacities as a woman of color. Whether it was by society's standards, church doctrine, or my family's eyes, there was not much more potential than to be submissive, procreate life and pay homage to the patriarchy and machismo that strongly enveloped

my thoughts, my actions and the way I saw myself and the world. Upon realizing I was transgender, and leaning more towards masculinity, I came to terms with the fact that I am not a woman. It was a relief to relinquish the weight of such responsibility. Yet, I conveniently absorbed and practiced all the misogyny and toxic masculinity I was exposed to growing up and celebrated my newfound privilege. It has allowed me to see the world from a different perspective and has truly shown me the great imbalances experienced as a minority on contrasting wavelengths. As a transgender person, I am constantly rejected by society for not being cisgender. As a 'male passing' individual, I have more privilege than I did as a woman. As a person of color, after transitioning, I am still brown, so I will never bask in the privilege of being white. However, I am still entitled to more opportunities than I ever was before and I benefit from all of that, in everyday life. I am taken much more seriously and am visible in spaces I never was before.

When I applied for college back in 2014, in the earlier stages of my transition, I had to apply as a female, and use my government name to enroll. I had to constantly remind my teachers, especially when bigger assignments came due that I was who I said I was and still one semester nearly did not receive credit on an entire course because I was using a different name in everyday life than the one given to me, legally. I had panic attacks and severe bouts of anxiety working on group projects and using school email to communicate as it was set up with my government name. I got tired of explaining why it was different and it derailed my focus from schoolwork to self-preservation; my own mental health and safety. I had to choose a bathroom on campus, separated into two archaic and binary options that don't necessarily apply to me and how I identify which made going into public all the more treacherous. There is so much fear on restrooms in public spaces, I would recommend gender neutral signage or no signs at all. Just restrooms. Whether it was being genderfluid, queer, a person of color, a first-generation college attendee in my family or second puberty, I did not fit in anywhere. I did not pass, but also was terrified of being outed, so I kept to myself and missed out on a lot of socialization and connection with my peers.

I think a lot of the adversity I faced could be minimized and mitigated by offering more amazing queer studies courses, gender studies, cultural and humanities classes as general, required courses or even free electives. If colleges were to reward credit hours for volunteer work and community service it would encourage folks to learn about all the distinct and rich culture of diversity that exists in the world, especially on campus. I think we should consider making college tuition free to accomplish equity in an educational setting. It's easy for wealthy, white, conservative families to send their own off to college and other educational institutions which continues to perpetuate systemic racism and classism and wealth disparity. Generally, the privileged can pay their way through school or be awarded scholarships, graduate and choose successful career paths as where oppressed minorities are only qualified for capitalistic slave labor work with below cost of living wages. What's the point of higher education if we do nothing to empower everyone but use it as an advantage to continually marginalize those who are already oppressed? What is the point of being an intellectual if we don't know how to take care of our own and uplift one another? Once we stop segregating and upholding outdated expectations of human identities, we can truly celebrate ourselves and each other. We lose nothing by being empathetic and equitable to those with less. We win when we work together and make higher education (among other commodities) accessible and accommodating to all. (personal communication, April 23, 2020)

On a similar trajectory, I became acquainted with Lillian Thando Naluyima (Thando) first as an SLCC student helping me educate 6th graders about the legacy of Dr. Martin Luther King, Jr. in our program called "Beloved Community," where the children create photo essays we showcase in our campus art gallery. Thando and I remained connected as they enrolled in my Queer Studies class, then went on to start their own non-profit organization in Uganda, an LGBTQIA+ leadership camp focusing on human rights, sexual and reproductive health, activism, affirmations, and creating a safe space (https://www.facebook.com/PinkTriangleUganda/). We continue to collaborate as Thando guest lectures in my classes and works for our SLCC Gender & Sexuality Student Resource Center. Thando's response deserves space:

> Privilege is pervasive; it can be as complicated as the intersectionality of different groups of people at a Community College or as simple as black people not feeling safe to wear facial masks during COVID-19 for fear of being stigmatized as "dangerous" or "threatening". As a middle-class queer black woman and international student, I am an example of someone that is at the crossroads of almost every intersectionality you can think of. I have more points where I receive stigma than most groups of people. I do not say this because I want sympathy but rather to start a conversation about what it is like. As humans it is crucial we better understand one another and the chains of oppression we put around one another's necks when we stigmatize each other.
>
> For starters, the external stigma of being an oppressed minority is visible every day when I go to classes and do not see professors or administrators that look like me. It is apparent in the patriarchal and hyper "western culture" view and lenses dominate in all my classes. All too often my classes are so "Americentric" it is as if they are the only country on the planet yet back home in Uganda we are more versed in the politics of all countries around the world. It is going to a science class knowing that people around you might already have a subconscious view and think you are "inferior" or just be waiting for you to make a mistake so they can compartmentalize you with all the other "minorities" in their mind in a negative box that does not get equal treatment and is ignored. In fact, the only time they want to pull the box out is maybe once a year during Black History Month or on Martin Luther King Jr. Day otherwise it is invalidated, oversimplified, and put away. Minorities, unlike the majority, have to carry the burden of being an ambassador, every day 24-7 in a world that does not trust, validate, or appreciate us as equals.

Waking up every day for a role you never signed up for is exhausting in a system that makes it significantly harder for you to navigate. People do not realize how the pressure to conform to a dominant culture can be stressful and truly negatively impact your health physically, socially, and emotionally (hence statistics on deaths of 2nd generation African-Americans). Racism is real and it kills people slowly generation by generation each time shaving off a few years and adding on the next. When I mean adapting to a culture I mean getting used to being treated a certain way, questioned unnecessarily, misunderstood, and rarely truly listened too. At this point I know where your mind is going you think I am exaggerating or complaining but the truth is I am not. I need you to listen, not just read the words on the page but listen with your heart. You know the history of this country. People used to take their families for picnics and watch lynchings in the 1930s. The inequities in education, healthcare, income, property ownership, incarceration, wealth, life expectancy are wide and blatantly obvious. I am asking you to wake up to your inner humanity and truly listen and put yourself in my shoes.

As a black queer Ugandan woman, living in the American culture I have learned a great deal. Your culture has taught me a lot about how the 'majority' views people like me. As an African your culture teaches you to automatically feel 'sympathy' or 'pity' but yet you want me to pay 2x the tuition as an international student, as a woman your culture teaches that we are '2nd best' 'not quite good enough' (to have equal pay, control over our bodies, or equal representation), as a black woman your culture teaches that we are 'misunderstood' 'bossy' 'hyper-sexual', and then when you add queer to the mix this brings in a whole different dynamic of 'erasure' 'invisible' 'predator'. Yes, all of these things are stigma and stereotypes. Not a single one of them can be used to describe me but yet I find myself internalizing the fact that I know that many of you are thinking these things. At which point I have to then try to buffer or always be on my 'A' game so that I can dispel the stigma. I am here to tell you I am just one person and this is too much work for one person. The irony of being a stigmatized person in this culture is that I am the one most conscious and aware and in addition to deflecting your stereotypes I also am the one that gets stuck with the burden too often of educating you. Of helping you see what you are doing to me and people like me.

There is so much we can learn from each other but when you choose to shut me out and stigmatize me you are only hurting yourself because I am you. We are all one and the same. You are missing out on conversations, cultures, food, insight, friendships, relationships, and human camaraderie you cannot fathom. The oppression you place on me does not end. This cycle of 'exclusion' rolls on and pulls in your children and mine until we wake up and realize we need one another socially, emotionally, physically, intellectually, and bottom line as fellow humans. Scientists have shown when you put diverse groups of people together to solve problems they think of solutions unheard of. WE need each other and until we realize that we will not heal wounds of the past or move forward together rather we will continue to sacrifice minority students to fight a losing battle against stigmatization. Especially, queer students of color as they face more stigmatization than almost any other group of people.

> I need the help of the college and all students. This a battle we must all fight and it starts with the college continuing its efforts to improve on truly advocating for its students. I respect and I am grateful for the steps that have been made to help minorities but I am here to tell you they are not nearly enough and we make up a large percentage of the student population and by providing equitable opportunities you make the entire college stronger. The future is diverse and by being truly anti-racist and actively inclusive the college can continue to be trailblazers for equity and justice in the world that too often permits minorities to exist but fails to push them to thrive and reach their true potential. The future cannot afford for us to fail or be stunted by the stigmatization any longer.
>
> The following actions could be taken to actively advocate for minority students like myself placed in a position where I have to constantly deal with stigma even when I don't want to. The first step is to acknowledge that there is a problem and that my voice is valid. Second, I am tired of bearing this burden alone so I am asking you to LISTEN. That means genuinely trying to understand where minority students are coming from and what we are dealing with. We are already bearing a significant portion of the stigma and it is too heavy to carry alone. Third, more queer and ethnic faculty and staff need to be hired. Fourth, the college needs to play an active role in fighting stigma (marketing), curriculum and having more conversations about oppression. Things will never get better if we don't try and talk things out. Fifth, the school needs to provide more scholarships to minority and international students. Sixth, the school needs to get more families involved either through service or ethnic food nights to make them feel welcome. Seventh, the school needs to provide more leadership training programs and opportunities to minority students. Eighth, the college should provide mentors and life coaches to all minority students with faculty that look or identify as they do. Ninth, the career services at the college especially need to be aware of privilege and the stigma minority students have to deal with. They should work to give them every possibility to get information about all the opportunities available. Finally, the college needs to play an active role in fighting stigma associated with mental health and provide free counseling services for all students. As minorities bearing a significant burden of stigma we would greatly benefit from having opportunities for self-care as we carry a lot on our shoulders. (personal communication, April 23, 2020).

Thando's rhetoric rings true to all I have observed and heard from marginalized students including those who are undocumented. It's clear that both Thando and Nick are invoking specific, concrete actions. We must get past the book club/literary salon approach to anti-racism, inclusivity, and equity and start taking meaningful, measurable, sustainable, collaborative action.

To come full circle, I'll offer the wisdom of my colleague Bernice Olivas, the fellow SLCC English Professor who challenged us to take that implicit bias test:

> The most critical way that stigma can be addressed is to cultivate a culture of transparency within a learning environment. This means keeping our focus on actions, reactions, and repercussions of actions. It's very difficult to do since we are all deeply invested in the ideology that a racist person is a bad person. To successfully overcome stigma we have to step away from that ideology and re-frame racism as a learned behavior that can be un-learned. Members of a learning community must be able to point out an action and name it as racist so that the community can work together to do damage control and to make sure it doesn't reoccur. The hard part is doing this without alienating the actor or the person acted upon. (personal communication, April 22, 2020)

Again, action and ideology must coincide for dialogue and transformation to occur withing the community college culture. We must be self-aware and open to dialogue to avoid the harmful speech, beliefs, and behavior that oppress others. Despite our reputation as a more student-focused (as opposed to research-focused) place of learning, we are nonetheless part of the academic industrial complex: "While most colleges are still nonprofit institutions, their primary function is to serve the neoliberal enterprise. This happens in at least three ways – by targeting student-consumers, channeling students into corporate careers and contributing to rather than reducing social stratification" (Gandio, 2010). The co-opting of education into an extension of capitalism that "provides tax breaks for the rich, reduces spending on social programs and welfare, expands corporate control and eradicates labor rights, environmental protections, drug and food regulations and even national law" (Gandio, 2010) jeopardizes our ability to cultivate true scholarship as modes of dialogue, inquiry and reflection are subsumed by corporate/government/academic agendas of wealth and power that increase the divide between the privileged and the oppressed, often first-generation students whom our mission is to serve.

Liaisons with community activists and non-profit organizations can help us divest ourselves from perpetuating and placating the systems of oppression we are so adept at critiquing. We must realize, though, that the non-profit industrial complex can be just as problematically colonizing and oppressing as other systems of power ruled by neoliberalist ideologies and practices (Violence, 2017). Books like *INCITE! The Revolution Will Not Be Funded: Beyond the Non-Profit Industrial Complex* grant us a window into strategies to transform, and even bypass the pitfalls of non-profits' tendencies to subvert political goals in favor of government and foundation mandates.

My own departure from the absurd confines of the community in which I was raised was nurtured by academia—sitting outside that first Gay/Straight Alliance meeting helped me take a pivotal step, in an inquisitive environment, to transcend judgments and embrace my authentic identities. When I speak about stigma, I invite my audience to review the myriad photos we all seem to have of our lives these days—if most everyone you spend time with is exactly like you, how will you learn to navigate the world in a meaningfully equitable way? I've discovered elation in catapulting so-called comfort zones, to listen, and learn, what we can say, and do, to create transcendent experiences for all. As an activist, I've faced deflating moments of indifference, hostility, alienation, retaliation, and threats of violence, none of which I would trade for the illusive comfort of doing nothing or waiting until everyone is onboard. Transformation will require us to risk departure from our business-as-usual, rhetoric-only approaches to social justice and meaningful change. Though education has its own underclass of exploited adjuncts and underpaid professionals, hooks' words ring true to the potential unique to education in general, and community colleges in particular: "The classroom remains the most radical space of possibility in the academy…Urging all of us to open our minds and hearts so that we can know beyond the boundaries of what is acceptable, so that we can think and rethink, so that we can create new visions" (1994, p. 12). Community colleges are dynamically situated to help ourselves, our students, and our communities cultivate a partnership-based society. Alliances among activists and allies are a catalyst for a partnership-based approach to education. Let our revolutionaries show us the way.

References

Adams, C. J. (1994). *The sexual politics of meat*. Continuum.

AVERT. (2020, April). *HIV and AIDS in South Africa*. Retrieved from Global Information and Education on HIV and AIDS: https://www.avert.org/professionals/hiv-around-world/sub-saharan-africa/south-africa

Beebe, A. E. (2015, April/May). Serving for social justice. *Community College Journal*, 58–66. Retrieved from http://www.sbcc.edu/presidentsoffice/files/articles/Social Justice.pdf

Campbell, T. C. (2016). *The China study*. BenBella Books.

Friere, P. (2005). *Pedagogy of the oppressed*. Continuum.

Gandio, J. D. (2010, August 12). *Neo-Liberalism and the Academic-Industrial Complex*. Retrieved from Truthout: https://truthout.org/articles/neoliberalism-and-the-academicindustrial-complex/

Hess, J. (Director). (2004). *Napoleon dynamite* [Motion Picture].

hooks, b. (1994). *Teaching to transgress: Education as the practice of freedom*. Routeledge.

Huffpost. (2013, December 27). *Desmond Tutu on animal welfare: We must fight injustice to animals*. Retrieved from Huffpost: https://www.huffpost.com/entry/desmond-tutu-animal-rights_n_4509188?guccounter=1

Johnson, C. (2020, June 9). *The triumph of Black Lives Matter and Neoliberal Redemption.* Retrieved from nonsite.org: https://nonsite.org/the-triumph-of-black-lives-matter-and-neoliberal-redemption/

Kappeler, V. E. (2014, January 7). *A brief history of slavery and the origins of American policing.* Retrieved from Eastern Kentucky University Police Studies Online: https://plsonline.eku.edu/insidelook/brief-history-slavery-and-origins-american-policing

Ko, A. (2017). Vegans of Color and Respectability Politics. In A. K. Ko, *Aphro-ism: Essays on Pup culture, Feminism, and Black Veganism from two sisters* (pp. 76–81). Lantern.

Lorde, A. (1984). *Sister outsider: Essays and speeches.* Crossing Press.

Morris, W. (2019, January 23). Is Being a 'Minority' really just a matter of numbers? *The New York Times Magazine.* Retrieved from https://www.nytimes.com/2019/01/23/magazine/is-being-a-minority-really-just-a-matter-of-numbers.html

Project Implicit. (2011). Retrieved from Project Implicit: https://implicit.harvard.edu/implicit/

Tuttle, W. (2016). *The world peace diet.* Lantern Books.

Violence, I. W. (2017). *The revolution will not be funded: Beyond the non-profit industrial complex.* Duke University Press.

3 From Diversity to Justice: Expanding the Chief Diversity Officer "Roles" of Equity and Inclusion into Justice and Community

Lea Lani Kinikini

Becoming a Chief Diversity Officer in Recognition That Disrupting and Transforming

I have always fought for equity, inclusion, and justice for those that are oppressed. My own people Tangata Moana (People of the Sea, or, as the settler United States labels, "Pacific Islanders") were violently incurred upon during the European "Age of Discovery" in the 16th to 18th centuries and then whose indigenous archipelagos spanning one-third of the planet were carved up and colonized politically by European, Euro-American and Japanese empires leading to global warfare in which my peoples were played like pawns. Today I still organize in the Global South, nationally on Turtle Island, and in my small Pacific Islander community in Salt Lake, Utah in the lands of the Utes, Paiutes, Goshutes, Shoshone and Dine.

I first was introduced to activism to combat systemic oppression when I used to steal books from the Salt Lake City Public Library and Barnes and Nobles bookstores in Salt Lake City. My friends were stealing booze and cigarettes, but I wanted copies of George Jackson's *Soledad Brother*, *The Autobiography of Malcolm X*, Eldridge Cleaver's *Soul on Ice* and Sanyika Shakur's *Monster Cody* all the Black power and liberation books I could find. These foundational texts laid cornerstones in my activism—I knew that the oppressive interlocking systems were criminalizing my friends and family. As a youth, my friends and family became increasingly subject to state discipline, through exclusion, alienation, school pushout, juvenile arrests and youth court, to adult detention, jail and longer prison sentences. In college I went on to read classics *The Souls of Black Folk*, *The Autobiography of an Ex-Colored Man* and *Invisible Man*, solidifying my realm of understanding Pacific Islander struggles on stolen Native land, inside of the deeply resonant chambers of Black Liberation and Resistance that saw solidarity with the global North-South oppression of the Third World. We stood on the shoulders of giants and were not the first to seek and find knowledge in pursuit of liberation.

I began to understand it was the School to Prison Pipeline where my activism started, and where now twenty years later, as a mid-career professional scholar working in equity, diversity, inclusion, and transformative justice, that my path to becoming a Chief Diversity Officer became clear. Today, I am pushing for adding justice to the portfolio, is one that begins with equity in acknowledging the land I stand, write, and fight for is that land of the Utes, Paiutes, Goshutes, Shoshone and Dine (Navajo). I say this as a member of a blood line well versed in recognizing that *kelekele ʻoku uʻu*—"the land bites"—and in this equity, can recognition of truth furnish a transformative justice that will change whiteness as it recognizes settler colonialism is the root of diversity inequities, and indeed the framework of diversity as a jurisdiction that awards some bodies an ethnonationalist race-privilege, over others, supporting the total myth of control that there exists a melting pot (there was but for phenotypically-near fox).

I wanted to become a professor so I can write and conduct research on my people, rather than a white neoliberal settler doing it for or on us. My journey in higher education was always destined to move fluidly between often-reified, but always crumbling jurisdictions.

After recognizing and valuing other identities in a population such as a college or university, there must be the action of equity, meaning supporting the oppressed from a negative state to a zero state.

After the oppressed groups in the given population in a college or university are provided equity they must be included also referred to as inclusion. Most institutions in higher education have moved to equity and inclusion, but not justice. Justice supports the oppressed groups from a zero state to a positive one. The oppressor, which benefits from oppression is in the positive state.

A court of equity, equity court or chancery court is a court that is authorized to apply principles of equity, as opposed to those of law, to cases brought before it.

People are depositioned inequitably by race-ordered, heteronormative ableist capitalist settler legal and governance systems which interlock to create the education systems, governed by politically-voted embedded hierarchies, including boards, chancelleries, minsters, and so and so forth. Interlocking systems that certify and invest equity in privilege and passing bodies, over and at the expense of "other" marked bodies, based on hierarchical valuation equations of utility and regularity: the more homogenous, the more efficient the beast can be. Hence the rapid tenacity of monitoring, metrics, data in the neoliberal project of higher education in the 21st century.

From Diversity to Justice: Oppressed Knowledges

Salt Lake Community College is the Salt Lake County's and the State of Utah's only comprehensive community college, combining the State's early-20th century and post-war liberal trade school with the leftist socialist community college of the 1960s. In the higher education hierarchy, comprehensive community colleges are positioned as the failed experiment of socialism and labor industrial capitalism. Trade schools like SLCC merged and bloated in bureaucracy and now has identity crises bottom of the heap but led by upper class neoliberals whose administrative competence dovetails uncomfortably with a discontent professoriate tradition, of doctors, masters, and bachelors to professional practitioners of the trades—essential building blocks of global modernization.

To some CC's are the school you go to if you can't or don't wish to afford a four year school, or a common perspective can't make it into a four year institution: the outcasts, who if arraigned appropriately can go through the higher education pipeline and achieve uniformity with the success scion of success, be it lawyer, doctor, engineer, or software genius if male or if female secretary, nurse, dental hygienist. Or simply a better cog in the working class: an electrician, a mason, a carpenter, a composite, mechanical engineer, electrical engineer, etc. Increasingly community colleges even in conservative, slow to acknowledge let alone admit system-wide problems with mass educational inequity, hyper incarceration and the "racial injustice" of all categories—policing, housing, health, education and access. We are waking up that their very market model forces them to look at how to relate, i.e. successfully recruit from communities that traditionally feel no propensity to go to college because of the dominance of White affluence in creating biased and discrimminatory exclusion systems.

During the contraction of higher education globally after the financial crises of 2008/9 and now, ten years later, the online learning social-distancing disruption of the Coronavirus Pandemic, it seems that community colleges are in a zone of crises restructuring. Community colleges in Utah are overshadowed by the State's four-year institutions some of which were founded as community colleges, and then became "dual-mission" to offer 4-year degrees. In such a volatile post-millennial context, the equity, diversity and inclusion priorities are challenged by the low ebbs and are less elevated by the high tides of economic promise lifting all boats: more and more all boats, and the people in them, are sinking in the tidal waves of neoliberal labor markets and rapid change making technical careers unstable to a certain degree and two year liberal arts or academic degrees a high risk endeavor.

In such a volatile and unstable context, we can note the rapid changes afoot when looking at the State of Utah's merger of the two Boards governing higher education which is underway during the Coronavirus Pandemic. First the Utah State Higher Education Board of Regents is the governing body for the Utah System of Higher Education (USHE). USHE partners include "Talent Ready Utah" (formerly Utah Futures), school and college savings plans, and student loans institutions; the financial wellness of the State dovetails nearly perfectly with the state motto: a single word: "INDUSTRY", with the omniscient symbol of the British colonial Beehive scion of industrial colonialism underlying the austerity of a Scandic-Anglo-Saxon "Pioneer" moral virtue of thrift and perseverance bound to the Protestant ethic theorized by Max Weber. For Mormon religious culture, it is peculiarly bound up with the missionizing morality of a civilizing whiteness and the white race saving fallen and inferior races of dark-skinned peoples believed to be the ancestors of Native Americans, whose narratives animate Mormon holy scripture.

The Utah Legislature grants the Board of Regents the power to control, manage, and supervise USHE; the Utah Legislature determines its funding priorities through the USHE. The Board's major responsibilities include the power-laden processes of selecting and evaluating institutional presidents, setting policy, reviewing programs and degrees, approving institutional missions, and submitting a unified higher education budget request to the Governor and State Legislature. We can also note the post-secondary educational board that governed trade education in Utah was the Utah Technical or UTECH whose mission was industry and capital demand -driven: "To meet industry needs for technically-skilled workers and promote economic development by providing market-driven technical education to secondary and adult students"[1].

The two boards, USHE and UTEC are currently in the midst of a merger. UTEC board is 100% White; USHE board and its staff appears tokenistic, with a few "diversity, equity, and inclusion" roles, at lower and mid-levels. Diversity, equity, and inclusion (the "holy trinity" of EDI/DEI) is premised in Utah not only by the taint of a racist dispositive built on the bedrock of Euro-American settler exceptionalism and a sense of order of things and white supremacy as a great chain of being hierarchy in which Utopian ideals (and for Mormons, exaltation or perfection in becoming gods) and the unpredictable technological horizon of Artificial Intelligence eclipsing the former essentiality of the human laborer. A narrative imperative of "butts in seats" revenue model that concedes to prioritizing equity, diversity and inclusion insofar as there is a speculative underlying value for pushing for DEI/EDI to hire high level administrative positions such as Chief Diversity Officers/Special Assistants to the President/Vice-Presidents or Vice-Provosts of Diversity and Inclusion, et cetera.

While the deep and abiding structure of institutional racism persists in a perennial kind of viral latency of half awake (or what contemporary praxis favoring or drawing from Freud calls "unconscious bias") and overt bias based on class and body privelege /identity politics (racism, gendered violence, disabled exclusion) (becoming/being) this chapter positions the duty of the CDO to cultivate spaces of decolonial and class resistance and ensuring special equity initiatives grow into projects and programs that work to dismantle the school to prison that infuses equity where equity has been stripped and opportunity foreclosed through process of overt marginalization (as in the lack of funding in lower income tax schools and ZIP codes or poor neighhorhoods/ghettos/redlining). A deficit model of diversity management, rather than a profit model that secures justice and equity first and foremost as in the interest of the majority. Speaking back against this, and against the factory and worforce model of education over the model of education for social liberation a la Paulo Friere and Gramsci at the headwaters, yet these transformative and critical education models are less of what drives community colleges, in favor of a deficit model that sees agents/subjects as a problem, rather than the ground or foundation as being the problem[2]. Out of sync with the realities of movements of people, ideas, and capital and this is causing the State's social dysmorphia around power control community and race, compounded by multiple inequities of COVID-19 and ongoing crises in a failed racial injustices of policing and safety of some over others, coupled with of course, the deep legacies of intergenerational wealth disparities on the axis of culture, class identity, race and body (gender, disability, ageist, etc).

Unsettling Order and Industry: The Beehive State and Pedagogy of Oppression

Settler colonials from Northern Europe and the British Isles and the U.S. imperial state is premised on the erasure and forfeiture of Native peoples and

Native land titles. The State of Utah is a settler state in the unceded lands of the Utes, Paiutes, Goshutes, Shoshone, and Navajo as in the Mormon Church's expansion west of the Mississippi. Inasmuch as the imperializing necropolitics levied against First Nations, former slave classes stolen as property from African nations, Southern-Eastern European, Middle East, Asian-Pacific and Native and indigenous peoples aided and abetted by, eugencism and Cartesian empircism underwriting science and law. The politics of nation-state formation using forced removal, militarism and land entitlement dispossession through Treaties, Acts, Proclamations, is animated by a settler racism, which is racial class servitude to European settler affluence underwritten by class oppression and marginalization.

Salt Lake County spreads out like an immaculately planed grid emanating from ground zero of the Mormon Temple. The lake for which Salt Lake derives its name is a remnant of an ancient sea, filled with an evaporating brine leveled from a desiccated underworld named by Native Utes Pi'a-pa "Great Water". They also called it Ti'tsa-pa or "Bad Water". The settler territorialization of Utah is equally great and bad. Three years after their shovels dug into divert the stream beds and rivers coursing from mountaintops of the Ti'tsa-pa sea, the European settlers officiated the titling of their claims to Native land with the legislative passage in U.S. Congress of the Organic Act declaring a "Territorial Government for Utah" under federal jurisdiction. Specific in this Organic Act was the explicit exclusion of "Indians" from this new settler government; the insertion of a script of forced abstention. A refusal to "face off" furnished settler claims and conscripted Native lands and bodies into an ongoing and permanent condition of refusal of justice. The Utah Organic Act was the most extensive land grab since the Louisiana Purchase in 1803.

"This is the land of promise, and the place for the city of Zion," declared Joseph Smith in 1832 as he met with some 300 of his followers in Independence, Missouri and received his first "revelation" on how their god desired their grid should be ordered, a vision that progressed as they moved west and settled in Ute lands. Three years after their shovels dug into divert the stream beds and rivers coursing from mountaintops of the Ti'tsa-pa sea, the Euro settlers officiated the titling of their claims to Native land with the legislative passage in the U.S. Congress of the Organic Act declaring a "Territorial Government for Utah" under federal jurisdiction. Specific in this Organic Act was the explicit exclusion of "Indians" from this new settler government; the insertion of a script of forced abstention. A refusal to "face off" furnished settler claims and conscripted Native lands and bodies into an ongoing and permanent condition of refusal of justice.

The notes on Joseph Smith's Plat of Zion drawing specified that all streets were to be 132 feet wide. These created square blocks of 10 acres measuring 660 feet on each side. A center tier of blocks containing the storehouse and temples was wider, with blocks that measured 660 by 990 feet. Each half-acre lot was 66 by 330 feet. The curious orientation of each plat contains one mile square; all the squares the plat contain ten acres each, being forty rods square.

Although the settler narrative celebrates overcoming persecution for "peculiar doctrines" like plural marriage and blood atonement, the settler history lines up with a national settler meta-narrative of white entitlement to Native land through the doctrine of Manifest Destiny built upon a bedrock of the papal Bulls of Donation.

"You will observe that the lots are laid off alternately in the squares;" Brother Joseph wrote, "in one square running from the south and north to the line through the center of the square; and in the next, the lots run from the east and west to the center line. The lots are laid off in these squares, north and south, all of them; because these squares are forty perches by sixty, being twenty perches longer than the others, their greatest length being east and west, and by running all these squares, north and south, it makes all the lots in the city of one size."

"This is the land of promise, and the place for the city of Zion," declared Joseph Smith, the Protestant Mormon prophet in 1832 as he met with some 300 of his followers in Independence, Missouri and received his first revelation on how their god desired their grid should be ordered a vision that progressed as they eventually moved west.

The Beehive State has an oppressive biased education, built by the Mormon protestant ethic and missionizing patronization and disdain for dark skinned folk. The education system designed to support "The Beehive State" industries. For every 100 white students that complete, only 77 students of color do. 1 in 4 students of color will start but not complete a program, degree or certificate.

I find myself saying, "we're The People's college" in order to emphasize our fiduciary duty to taxpayers. The Hobbesian social contract between the taxpaying people and the administrators of an institution is rarely stated from the position of the people (the disempowered) and remains fixed at the masternarrative of the upper class educating the underclass to help save and uplift them from poverty. I say this often to bureacratic divisions of employees feeling disempowered and frustrated with the neoliberal chessboard management structure. County taxpaying residents ought to understand they are equity investors in our college—its "your community college".

C.D.O.s: *strategic disruptor or docile pawn Going Beyond Diversity, Equity & Inclusion: tactical survival tips from a fresh-in first year C.D.O.*

Quod fere totus mundus exercet histrionem ("because almost the whole world are actors") -attributed to Petronius.

High-level positions in diversity, equity and inclusion are largely catalyzed as a concession (in a way, a moral panic) reacting to escalating County/City/State demographics in which the white normative settler studentbody is transforming to one of Others: Muslim, Immigrant, Queer, Trans, Disabled, and "other races": Latinx, Black, East Asian and Southeast Asian, Pacific Islander, Hawaiian, Native American plural student-bodies. The catalyst is neoliberal mainstreaming and a management for change framework to support neoliberal metrics such as "we want our students to see themselves reflected in the teaching faculty", tied up with students of color as deficits that require extra help to "catch up" to their white counterparts. Given the decline of college enrollments across the board, and in particular the "completion gap" between White versus Black/Others", coupled with the concomitant disproportionate overrepresentation of such in prisons and jails.

On February 18th the Chief Diversity Office of Salt Lake Community College invited the Exonerated Central Park Five to a take centerstage of the Grand Theater[3].

During the course of the evenings talk, three positions struck a chord of resonance in me:

"Occupy these spaces" (meaning education & courts of equity and justice)
"We're playing Chess not Checkers" (meaning strategic moves and maneuvers of occupation).

Pawns- The people and citizens /plebeians: students, part-time staff
Knights- The military/student affairs administrators / full-time staff.
Bishops- Religion/faculty and teachers / hierarchy of tenure-track and adjunct.
Rooks- The educational industrial complex/neoliberal castles under occupation by White Supremacy and settlerhood.
Queen- Feminism and white women's empowerment in service of white settlerhood.
King- The corporate head/ scion/ president/white supremacy capitalist patriarchy—neoliberal education in service of white ethnonationalism.

While a C.D.O. can run the gamete from change agent to pawn, a scholar, researcher and writer, and administrator new to the job. Its more than a diplomatic role: it's an emissary of change and change is always resisted. To flip the script—i.e., to reverse the squares of the executive order (checkerboards originally being an accounting board) is to reverse every fiber that institutes racism at the institution. Solid Ground defines Institutional Racism as "the systematic distribution of resources, power and opportunity in our society to the benefit of people who are white and the exclusion of people of color. The term "institutional racism" was first used in 1967 in the book "Black Power: The Politics of Liberation" written by Stokely Carmichael.

So who would want to be a Chief Diversity Officer (C.D.O.)? I think most like me fall into it by accident[4]. When I was a kid, a serial documentary "So You Want to be a Doctor" fascinated me. It was about the educational requirements to get into medical school, following the journeys of would-be doctors. The same title "So you want to be a doctor" also lends itself to further study around C.D.O.s because the entire job is a new phenomenon. Such "roles" were set up in the early 70s as White colleges and universities began to integrate Black and African students: a multicultural education administrator and later in the post-1987 corporate Chief Diversity Officer, working off a collaborator model with little functional power, and much symbolic power.

Some come with a law degree or an Equal Employment Office or human resource or education administration background. An administrative role in the management/overseer vs. proletariat/exploited Faculty laboring category. They have a dangerous hypervisibility. They are there often in teams of 1, to change systems, but models vary from collaborative to structural. Some like me have a PhD usually in humanities or social science, or some like somewhere in between. For me, I was applying for jobs in a saturated market in my field of teaching, and the administrative area of institutional change management happened to apparently find my curriculum vitae appealing.

While the suffering of the decline of the robust protections of the professoriate and their erosian in the era of Trump (Nocella, Et. Al) we find the client-customer (students) is a triangulation of "role-playing" as administrator monitoring "roles" proliferate strategically emboldening on the one hand, a neoliberal data-driven, market-based sterile approach towards career and workforce education and training business corporate superstructure and in-depth critical consciousness of social inequities as critiques of settler colonialism and capitalism on the other. Some of these are new Vice Presidents of areas of "analytics" reliant on statistical specialization and computer technology, alogarithms; to addressing the gross social indicators of racism and classism resulting in widening disparities between classes underlied by racism and interlocking systemic oppression.

When I came onto this job as Chief Diversity Officer, I had very little exposure to the "role" or awareness of the challenges that would come with it. Was the role of the Chief Diversity Officer to shift structures in a context of Utah orderliness, disruptive change perspective: scholar, practitioner, admimistrator—put on a pedastal? How realistic is it?

At the of the Chief Diversity Office's portfolio is Hip Hop and Lowrider Studies under developement as a transformative critical and radical field to address inclusion and decenter Euro-American culture. Rather than addressing a diverse student body in an outdated neoliberal and colonial method/approach that strips identity, class and culture, Hip Hop and Lowrider Studies is cutting-edge, ground-breaking, lead out rather than follow the national dominant trend on transforming systemic bias, recentering inclusion and equity on countercultures that are empowering, just and equitable. Lowrider Studies has recently joined the community-based diversity research projects under the umbrella of the Chief Diversity Office Portfolio as a new inclusion and equity project for community transformation to support equitable access to postsecondary adult education connecting communities of learners to college resources which are overwhelmingly supported by an increasingly diverse tax base.

Critical scholarship in community colleges—transformative justice and equity in service of diversity and inclusion where we are—bringing our countercultures in

The Martin Luther King Jr. planning committee had set up a D.J. on stage with a black draped table and a lowrider bicycle which glistened a bespoken subtlety in the highlights. One committee member questioned what a lowrider bike had to do with Martin Luther King Jr. As the chair of the committee I brought up the connection that Lowrider culture, born of the centuries of resistance of Chicano/a/x cultures in the Western Settler United States in the mid-20th century of American steel and class politics labor resistance of increasingly hostile settlerism in the form of a nexus of prison-police brutalities bespeaking a systemic rot of major proportions. I said although lowriding could be seen by some as peripheral rather than central to black history. I didn't want to decenter Black power movements and the month that White settlerhood appropriates as "Black History Month". The committee wished to center that solidarity with Black resistance is also *Chicanx* travelling culture resistance to White Supremacy. Lowrider culture evidenced on main drags, streets demarcating color-coded / ZIP coded "red lined" areas designated for "immigrants" and Black migration from the Deep South to the land of Oranges and Hollywood, whose legendary racism is immortalized on the silver and golden globes of Anglo-American industrial global empire—now in decline.

Lowriders resist white settler power and privelege as a decolonial remnant that before white pioneers and settlers were here, there are a continuity of Native and indigenous and Spanish catholic settlers from southern Europe colonials / "conquerors". I said that settler colonialism thrives on a divisive multi-spectrum color-coding that is deformed into colorism and splintered by the multiple realities of dark-skinned peoples being the global majority. Highways through interstate migration as an example of a resistant aesthetic politics that Mexican culture speaks back to *Anglo hyphen American* occupation and colonization after the *Treaty of Guadalupe* and the ongoing racism and xenophobia Anglo-American settlerhood evinces on Black, Brown and Other bodies collectively particularly as the "balance" of racial domination is facing its "tipping point". I shared that by 2040 all cities would be a new majority and that *Chicanx* cultures (from Mexico, a colony built on the conquistadors rubble of *Azteca* and *Mayan* civilizations. I shared it was a resistance to White Power.

I shared that in the heritage history months, created and sanctioned by the State not only helped raise awareness of the othering. I told them, this is a still a journey in progress, and the numbers don't lie: what Public Enemy said in 1987 as the Iron Curtain was being (un)drawn: this was about fear of a Black Planet—a planet that always already had existed, and whiteness and settlerhood (rights) was constructed around the "deservingness" of some to die, and some to live—the necropolitics of an imperialism of whitening, of whitewashing the Black Planet through a whitewashed lens.

In the middle of the stage was a vertical sign saying, Utah Reintegration Project. is seeding/planting equity roots within a Europeans-enslaving/ imprisoning-Africans, Chinese, Italian workers settler context that places ad-hoc and marginalized "minority" status on all newcomers after the "founder event" the aura of Pioneer Day, the spectral proliferation of church and state still linger in the orderly grid or "plat of Zion". In an era of Coronavirus the image of washing the taint off of the hands in twenty second intervals is reminiscint of the ways in which White settlerhood commits to washing the taint of imperial violence off of its own blood stained hands and simultaneously containing the germs of "others"– Like Lady Macbeth, the compulsion effects the kind of equal parts denial and abjuration that defines settlerhood.

Like Lowrider Studies, their purpose is to manifest new possibilities, identify and redeem foreclosed opportunities, and rectify inequities in the schooling system established by Anglo-American settlers in response, more or less, to the changing demographics, particularly in the situation of Salt Lake Community College. Lowrider Studies is an emergent transdisciplinary field of study and an ideal carrier for action research and community transformation. Originating from the Southwest lands of what contemporary Native and Indigenous Studies scholars re-claim title as Turtle Island (North America), lowriding is a Mexican-American / Chicano/a/x cultural art form. Drawn on as a community engagement approach Lowriding disrupts and decenters a single Anglo-Eurpean settler narrative by re-centering Chicano/a/x and Native genealogies to land. Lowrider culture honors deep time, modern transformation, and heralds connection to cultural roots and indigeneity pre-Guadalupe Treaty. Lowrider culture resists a multi-faceted and hyper-violent legacy of Anglo-Saxon Protestant settler imperialism. and is an area of emergent study which documents the fine arts and countercultural resistance that lowriding communities build through art, relationality and honoring deeply rooted/routed identities of resistance. Lowriding allows genealogies of family lineage to contest and resist settler state. lowriders curate extra-state identities that resist and undergird a decolonial industrial working class politics and insistently priveleges the 200-hundred years of Anglo-American violence on Native, Indigenous and Mexican/Chicano/a/x peoples with long tenure and equity claims to the American Southwest.

10 points for a Liberatory C.D.O.J.

1. **Power to All People**: Outreach to taxpayer bases who pay but don't use community colleges and universities.
2. **Resisting**: the donor and student reification patronage model designed to oppress marginalized students further
3. **Decolonial** education models decentering the European colonial schools as prime example of plurality of tansformative educational approaches that work for All
4. **Scholarship not Opinion**: Dexterity over specialization: portfolio model dexterous over specialization particularly if community colleges are merged with technical or trade programs, always center disruptive theory and insist on building university partnerships as priority
5. **Influencing**: Build Rapport with all levels of leaders. Establish and leverage strategically planned lateral coordination and cross-coordination—get others to do this work. Recognize your biases in who you tend to build with, and consciously expand to All
6. **Undertake** Strategic Total Assessment Review (STAR)
   Insist on vital "mini-C.D.O. roles at the senior leadership level to provide stability and continuity.

Resist on grounds of racism that any new position at senior leadership level that is not hierarchically superior be eliminated/reversed for affirmative action
7. Merge and cut redundancies of "roles"; Retire white supremacist roles
8. **Insist the Budget must be Covered**: foundational commitment: bootstrapping is oppression if its Systemic change
Survival:
Plan on major resistance, have short term stop gap systems but be very clear and get a long-term plan for restructuring
Set tone for Awareness & Self-embracing: identity & culture of change
9. **Judge not**: policing the academy vs. Changing the proceedures, practices, policies small steps at a time
10. **Thriving**:
    a. Scholar: bedrocks of change are critical theory
    b. Tenured: Safety for disruptions, career on-ramps and off-ramps, battle fatigue
    c. Well funded: Shoe strings get broken

Conclusion for a Chief Diversity, Equity, Inclusion and Justice Officer

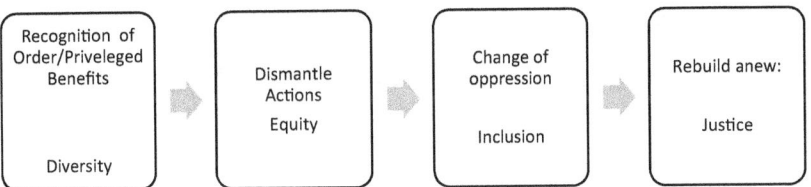

In conclusion, we need to move from simply recognizing apolitical, objectivist detached numbers of groups of people to justice for those people. Justice and education cannot and should not be detached from one another. Education, must (1) challenge order of things, (2) dismantle things, (3) change orders, and (4) rebuild new things. In this four-step process education will make people feel uncomfortable, especially those that are losing their power.

Notes

1 The Utah System of Technical Colleges consisted of eight Technical Colleges governed by a Board of Trustees who represent businesses, industry, trades and

apprenticeships from every region of the state. The work of the Trustees is overseen by Utah's Commissioner of Technical Education.

2 See "The 'Equity' picture is actually White Supremacy at work", Sippin the EquiTEA, Nov. 27, 2018. https://medium.com/@eec/this-equity-picture-is-actually-white-supremacy-at-work-59f4ea700509

3 – a remnant of the "New Deal" architecture projects –

4 I trained in a small interdisciplinary field called Critical Pacific Cultural Studies an empowered, pivoted, and postmodern/post-Cold War Pacific Islands Studies (area and geo-disciplinary counterparts to e.g. Asian Studies, Black Studies et cetera) that critiques imperialism, colonialism and neoliberalism and seeks redemption of alternative knowledges and epistemological philosophies that counter-narrate the dominant western civilization narratives.

4 Resisting Neoliberalism Through Anarchist Studies and Critical Animal Studies Conferences

ELIZABETH VASILEVA AND WILL BOISSEAU

Introduction

The impact of the pandemic on the world has left a lot of academics and researchers uncertain about the value of in-person academic conferences. On one hand, it is better for the environment, often cheaper and (in some ways) more accessible to attend virtual conferences, and on the other hand, the in-person communication, informal chats and atmosphere are essential elements a lot of us miss. At the Anarchist Studies Network (ASN), we have always been both critical and excited about getting comrades together and have always faced a few additional anarchist-specific questions when organizing events. In the following paper, we would like to reflect on some of the elements of ASN and Critical Animal Studies (CAS) organizing and offer our thoughts and solutions. We hope that this will serve both as a way of providing a bit of transparency of the organizational process, and perhaps can offer a bit of utility as a "guide" for people and groups who are thinking of organizing an event.

To begin with a little introduction, we are two anarchist academics. Elizabeth Vasileva is one of the co-convenors of the Anarchist Studies Network and has been involved in the organization of the Anarchist Studies Conference for the last six years, and has also been a paid conference organizer. Will Boisseau is a member of the Institute for Critical Animal Studies (ICAS) and has organized ICAS conferences in-person and online, as well as animal liberation panels at ASN conferences.

This paper draws on anarchist studies and critical animal studies and contributes to recent work in radical critical pedagogy, Social Justice Education and decolonizing pedagogy. Our aim is to disrupt and challenge neoliberal universities in which students and conference participants become consumers, the labor of academics and other workers is exploited and in which standardisation and selfishness is encouraged.

Academic conferences are not everyone's cup of tea. While some people see them as perks of the job and an opportunity to travel to nice and/or exotic locations on university expenses, others find scrutinising their own or other people's research combined with intense socialising difficult. This is exacerbated by the marketisation of education and academic research, where academics are expected to churn out new research all the time, perform the role of experts and review their peers work for free, as well as build careers at any cost. Academic conferences are extremely exclusionary, often charging hundreds just for attendance and offering overpriced accommodation, making them a very profitable part of universities' income. Even casually meeting fellow academics has been monetised through a framework of "networking", an activity that universities consider so vital that they organize workshops for doctorate researchers to be trained in (for instance, the funding body CHASE, Consortium for the Humanities and the Arts South-east England, offers workshops in academic networking as part of their annual conference). Combine this with the rampant sexism in academia, with young female academics often targeted by "celebrity academics" at conferences, it is no surprise that a lot of people have mixed feelings about them.

To organize an anarchist conference, the first thing to consider is what is valuable about conferences that needs to be salvaged from the hands of capitalism. The value, as we see it, is twofold. First of all, research and knowledge production don't happen in isolation. Most people need to read, write *and* talk to other people to be able to develop, crystalize and complete their research. This often happens in a myriad of organic ways, such as talking to friends, mentors, colleagues, etc. and it often happens in conferences, which is a space particularly designed for people to present their research to others. Leaving this space of knowledge production to the market forces of capitalism is reducing our ability as a movement to produce knowledge in anarchist ways. It also means that our research is more and more marketized and shaped by the state.

Secondly, because of the way academia is organized, most academics specialize in a narrow field of studies. Meeting people who are interested in the same topic can be hard and conferences are often the only place where that can happen. Conferences, particularly when there is space for more informal socialising, can be a beautiful place to make new friends from all over the world. It is important to acknowledge that anarchist academics are very few and far in between, often found in unexpected places, such as business departments, linguistics, sociology, music, among other more obvious ones like politics and history. Building a network for mutual support and cooperation was the purpose of starting the Anarchist Studies Network and its conference has become an important event for its members.

Having established this, we needed to ask ourselves how can we make an academic conference radical? What are the ways in which we would do it differently as anarchists? These are practical questions and we will try to outline our thinking and solutions to these problems. The first thing that needs to be decided before organizing a CAS or anarchist studies conference is who will do the organizing and how will that organization be structured. Usually, academic conferences would have a leader of sorts, either an established academic in the field, a paid organizer or another professional body making the decisions, with a small group of other academics, admin and PhD researchers to carry out the necessary tasks. Most of that labor is unpaid and considered a privilege, a valuable experience, and gives one the opportunity to attend the conference for free. Depending on the conference, the organizing structure is more or less rigidly hierarchical with little scope for people on the bottom to make decisions or implement changes they consider important. This can be a particularly disempowering experience for young academics who feel the boundaries of exclusion but are not in a position to challenge them.

One of the main considerations for ASN and ICAS is to internally organize in a way that gives everyone agency. Following the Spinozian framework beautifully outlined in *Joyful Militancy* (Bergman & Montgomery, 2017), we orient our anarchism towards enabling and supporting each other. In this sense, the purpose of the having an organizing group is to increase everyone's capacities to be and respond to the world, rather than stifle desire and creativity. This approach centres the creation of structures of mutual support and experimentation to show that *other worlds are possible*. Thus, anarchist scholar-activists may draw on tried and tested organizational approaches such as the key anarchist structure of affinity groups and consensus decision making. Although affinity groups are not so commonly used in academia, they provide a useful model for organizing in small groups in any context. The affinity group has become an established anarchist approach, through which activists can plan and undertake actions in small closely knit groups, typically between 5 and 12 members, through consensus decision making. The affinity group is regarded as better suited to carrying out direct actions in which it would not be possible or practical to organize with a large group of people. In affinity groups organization is non-hierarchical, voluntary, temporary, designed for a purpose and no larger than necessary. This small group structure lessens "the chances of internal hierarchies developing" and theoretically increases the likelihood of achieving consensus (Wilson & Kinna, 2012, p. 330). In theory, a conference organizing committee could operate much like an affinity group, working towards establishing trust, unifying thinking and holding tension in productive ways.

One established anarchist method of decision making within affinity groups is through consensus. Consensus is a method of decision making which is designed to produce "non-hierarchical and non-authoritarian" outcomes "because everyone agrees" to decisions (Wilson & Kinna, 2012, p. 335). Meetings are often facilitated "to ensure everyone's voice is heard" by using "tools and procedures" to help groups "reach decisions in a collective way" (p. 335). The use of consensus has not only "come to be seen as a fundamental principle of anarchism", but for many anarchists "consensus and anarchism are all but synonymous" (p. 335). A conference organizing committee might want to use consensus decision making as an ideal, but we are aware that such a structure is not always possible. Often in informal organizing work, the bulk of tasks fall on the shoulders of one (or a small number) of organizers. Rather than serving to share the load, the need to achieve consensus can actually cause an additional workload for the key organizer as they are constantly having to chase up comrades to confirm whether they agree to a decision. This is not a critique of comrades, or a critique of consensus decision-making, but an attempt to be as honest as possible about the problems of anarchist organizing.

In practice, we believe that most comrades are well-versed in consensus decision making and do not need to be educated in the value of it for anti-hierarchical organizing. The issue is not an ideological one, but a practical one, such as lack of time, resources and energy to dedicate to organizing the event. We are all so often involved in a range of other projects, and an ad-hoc established organizing committee might not produce the same commitment to the conference as its members might have to other projects. This often results in the need to have one person make urgent decisions on their own. In small organizing groups, where mutual trust has already been established, group members may find it quicker and easier to adopt a majority rule system (on the understanding that if the majority agreed with a decision then it is likely that consensus would be reached). In this situation, where one person is taking on the majority of work, it might be practical for the group to enable them to make planning decisions alone, perhaps with larger decisions being put to the entire group. Even the Animal Liberation Front that had a non-hierarchical affinity group structure and used cells that operated using consensus, recommended that:

[o]ne person should be chosen as the leader of the group. This doesn't mean that person has any special power or privileges, and it often won't come into play at all. But if during an action things go wrong, someone will need to make split-second decisions, and in this case there is no time for democracy. (ALF, N.D., p. 5)

It might similarly be wise for a conference organizing group to appoint a main organizer. It is important to recognize that people will have competing demands, academic workloads and other activist projects, and not everyone in a group will be able to take on as much work as everyone else. However, there is one key rule to being part of an organizing group—if you say you're going to do something, you have to do it. This rule has been key for activist groups whether organizing conferences, direct actions or leftist international football tournaments (Simpson & McMahon, 2012). A commitment to doing what you say you are going to also lessens the time and emotional labor that key organizers would otherwise spend on constantly checking the progress of projects. It also serves to strengthen the larger movement by building trust and long-lasting relationships.

Organizing committees might also want to think about what platforms they use for conference planning. Given that most of organizing is done online these days, security and practicality are of primary importance. For instance, the group may decide that WhatsApp is not a suitable platform given concerns about data collection and the questionable ethical practices of Facebook (O'Flaherty, 2001). There are a range of more secure apps and software to enable data-sharing, facilitate consensus decision-making and swift communications, such as Loomio, Discord, Signal, Telegram among others. Groups might want to use project management software like Trello or Zenkit. We have found that the most efficient way is to utilize a platform that people are already using on a daily basis, as people are less likely to regularly check an app with single-use value. However, we firmly recommend everyone use secure communication platforms at all times, not just for conference organizing.

Planning

In this section we will briefly consider some issues that might emerge during the planning phase of organizing an anarchist studies or CAS conference. As mentioned previously, we believe that organizing committees might want to bear in mind the overall aim of making a conference a radical space that challenges the neoliberal hegemony of the university.

Once the organizing committee is in place, the first issue is to find a suitable venue for the conference. For an academic anarchist studies or CAS conference it might be obvious to hold it at the university or academic institution of one (or more) of the key conference organizers. A CAS or anarchist studies conference may be trying to attract a range of "academic" speakers (meaning aligned to an institution) and speakers and participants not from an academic background. With this in mind, conference organizers may consider whether a public venue, rather than an institution, may be a more appropriate venue, as some people may be put off attending a conference at a university which they presume will be stuffy, pretentious and not relevant to everyday activism.

The most important consideration when choosing and finding a venue is to make sure it is fully accessible to all conference participants, particularly people with disabilities. This means at minimum wheelchair accessible, hearing loops, and a variety of visual signage to accommodate all needs. This is important for all conferences, but particularly so for a CAS conference because CAS has been influenced by the eco-ability movement. The eco-ability movement is now at the heart of CAS. Eco-ability is essential for understanding anti-domination theory that explores how capitalist destruction of the planet intersects with the oppression of animals and disability oppression (Nocella, George, & Lupinacci, 2019). If possible, the conference organizers could appoint a (dis)ability action group who would be able to review the conference rooms and accommodation to make sure that they are fully accessible. Conference organizers also need to consider people with hidden disabilities and organizers should champion neuro-diversity. This needs to be taken into account in every aspect of conference organizing, starting with the call for papers, to the accommodation and final debrief. Conference materials, for instance, need to be dyslexia-friendly and provided in large font. The venue must accommodate companion animals who may help people for a variety of reasons, including being therapy dogs to help people with anxiety. The conference programme should be organized with appropriate breaks in between talks. Ideally, the venue will have the option to set up a quiet room for participants and creche for children and young people and be generally a pleasant venue with comfortable seating, presentation facilities, well-lit, with the option to have gender-neutral toilets, etc. If the conference is held online, this presents a whole new range of accessibility issues. A main one is the time zone to hold the conference in in order to accommodate scholar-activists form around the world. The Punk Studies Network online conference was held over several days in different time zones to best facilitate a global scholar-activist base (Punk Scholars Network, 2020). Organizers might want to consider sending detailed step-by-step guide on how to use the conference software, which needs to be both written and video format, as well as setting up a practice session for people who need extra support. It is impossible to write an exhaustive list of all issues to take into account when ensuring accessibility, but in our opinion the most important thing is to make sure that support has been offered to participants on a regular basis to foster a community of acceptance and normalisation of different ways of being human.

Holding a radical conference at a university has the benefit of taking radical ideas and ways of organizing into the belly of the beast. This means that for a short period of time, anarchist praxis will come up against the neoliberal bureaucracy of the academic institution. There are organizing issues which might emerge, such as, the university administration may insist on using their contracted (non-vegan, extremely overpriced) catering suppliers, or they might insist that campus security is present. This can feel limiting and annoying, but we have often found that it is possible to figure out ways of going around it. For instance, at the 2018 ASN conference, we used non-university local vegan catering co-op, which set up in a local park next to the university building where the conference was being held. Since it was not on university ground, there was no objection to the catering service. However, sometimes this might not be possible and the organizing committee might want to double-check the conditions for committing to a space before making their final decision.

Finally, when picking a conference venue it is important to take the environmental impact into account. It is hardly appropriate to host a talk about green anarchism only for people to fly from all over the world to attend. This risks the conference giving off the same energy as G7 leaders flying short distances on internal flights to talk about creating a "green recovery" (BBC, 2021). There are inventive ways that conference organizers can reduce the carbon footprint of a conference. Of course, organizers can encourage the reduction of air travel where possible, such as by making sure that there are alternative transport links to the destination. We particularly encourage people to hitchhike and car-share when possible. CAS and anarchist studies conferences also have vegan catering which helps to address the contribution of the livestock sector to greenhouse gas emissions. The Intergovernmental Panel on Climate Change estimates that "agricultural emissions account for 10-12 per cent of the global total and that by 2030 agricultural emissions are projected to grow by 36-63 per cent" (D'Silva & Webster, 2010, p. 36).

Organizers could invite participants to present papers via online video platforms, or it may be decided that the most environmentally friendly option is to hold the entire conference online. As we previously mentioned, because of coronavirus there has been a huge rise of online conferences by necessity. On the other hand, anarchist scholar-activists are desperate to return to the camaraderie and free exchange of ideas that only a face-to-face conference can bring, which makes it unlikely that we will shift to online conferences on a permanent basis. However, it is possible that organizing committees will decide to alternate between one face-to-face conference and one online conference, or smaller online events with one big conference every two years.

Once a suitable venue has been found, organizers may begin to consider the overall conference theme. Themes are not a necessity, but they help to structure the general trajectory of the conference and often serve to express commitment to ideas. The themes might revolve around the key CAS principals of supporting direct action, promoting total liberation, building solidarity, alliances and total liberation, deconstructing binaries (Best, Nocella. Kahn, Gigliotti, & Kemmerer, 2007). CAS promotes critical dialogues between movements and disciplines and encourages a collaborative approach, and so a conference theme may appeal across movements and disciplines. Conference themes, for instance, can serve to bridge gaps between disciplines and emphasize commitment to supporting underrepresented groups.

The conference organizers should be aware of the barriers to academia that some communities face, for instance the fact that the animal rights movement is overwhelmingly white (Best, 2014, p. 85), and women and non-binary people are generally underrepresented in academia. To encourage the participation of scholar-activists who are also traditionally underrepresented within anarchist studies and CAS, the conference theme might reflect contemporary activist struggles such as Black Lives Matter, decolonisation, defending critical race theory. For instance, Anarchist Studies Network explained the reasoning for having a theme of "decolonization" at their 2018 conference:

> The purpose is twofold: to stimulate discussion of colonialism and racism as forms of oppression that anarchists oppose, but which continue to be felt in anarchist organising; and to welcome individuals, groups and communities who have not previously participated in ASN events. By recognising the legacy of non-western and anti-colonial thought and action in the anarchist tradition, we wish to strengthen the ties between contemporary anarchists and decolonial theory and practice in the struggle against oppression, and to use the recognition of racist and Eurocentric practices and mind-frames to open up the event to marginalised groups. (PSA, 2018)

The theme should also be relevant to contemporary activism, for instance the 2020 Anarchist Studies Network conference had a theme of "Anarchy in Crisis" which drew a range of participants focusing on how anarchists had stepped up to support communities and provide mutual aid during the coronavirus crisis (Anarchist Studies Network, 2020). However, conference organizers should be aware that there are always people who would rather present on another topic, so some flexibility and understanding is encouraged.

Organizers may discuss whether to invite a keynote speaker. The majority view in anarchist studies and CAS circles seems to be that inviting a keynote speaker promotes hierarchical thinking and should therefore be avoided in favor of a horizontal structure where all participants are equal. The alternative view is to invite a speaker from a traditionally marginalised group (in academia) or an early career academic, for instance a postgraduate student. This approach would give a scholar-activist who is just starting their career a leg-up which they might not get otherwise. CAS seeks to create a particularly welcoming and nurturing environment to new scholar-activists (Poirier, Bernatchez, & Nocella, forthcoming). If keynote speakers are invited then it is important to make sure that these are not all white men, and also to think about the geographical spread of where speakers are coming from. On a practical level, conference organizers will have to think about their budget as keynote speakers often request to have their travel, accommodation and honorarium paid.

CAS conference organizers will be especially keen to ensure that there is an appropriate gender balance because both the modern animal advocacy movement and CAS were strongly influenced by the early feminist concern for animals (Adams & Gruen, 2014, p. 30). Indeed, it was the emergence of ecofeminism that led to CAS scholars linking speciesism, sexism and patriarchy. In particular, the CAS themes of intersectionality and total liberation should be upheld in an ecofeminist analysis that believes that feminism entails an opposition to oppression and hierarchy in all forms. The vast majority of animal advocates are women, but as Marti Kheel (2006) explains, women "are disproportionately represented in the more mundane work entailed in running an organization" (p. 312). Women traditionally do the legwork of the movement often performing thankless backroom tasks, and taking part in direct action, without recognition as official leaders or theorists. To promote an appropriate gender balance organizers could again think of issues associated with the conference theme and keynote speakers. Academic conferences can be competitive and dominated by extrovert male voices, so CAS and anarchist conferences have to think about creating a positive, nurturing and supportive environment. Some examples of how this could be done is ensuring that there is a serious and consistent outreach to academic and activist places where there are more women and non-binary people, such as feminist groups, gender studies departments, feminist and gender-queer spaces, LGBTQ organizations, etc. For the ASN, this outreach has included gathering contact information and sending the call for papers to these groups repeatedly in the lead up to the deadline, which worked extremely well for the 2016 ASN with theme anarcha-feminism. Commitment to gender diversity shouldn't end there, as conference organizers need to ensure suitable childcare facilities to make the conference more accessible, as well as ensure that spaces for queer-only people and women-only are present. However, the biggest challenge in creating a more gender-equal space is actually reflecting on and changing internalised sexism, homophobia and/or transphobia among participants. This is a much slower process and it relies on work done outside these conferences as well, in particular to educate, reflect and actively work to dismantle patriarchy within ourselves and our communities. Unfortunately, no safer spaces policies or guidance from organizing committees can substitute for that work and we believe it should be understood as a collective responsibility within that space.

Another major issue to consider in terms of accessibility and inclusivity is how affordable the conference is. In most basic terms, the conference organizers will need to make sure they cover the expenses of the conference, whilst also offering low-waged and free tickets. CAS and anarchist studies conferences have always tried to make participation as cheap as possible, offering a sliding scale of tickets with some free, some low and some high-priced tickets (but always significantly lower than other academic conferences). In fact, the 2020 ASN conference incurred so little costs by being organized online that participants paid a token £1. This price was set to deter potential "trolls" or fascists which had been known to crash anarchist events online. The sliding scale of ticket prices is designed to ensure that higher-waged people subsidise lower waged participants, so that everyone can have access to the same food, drinks, venue, etc. Any additional money left after covering expenses goes to unfunded participants. This often takes the form of supporting participants to travel to the conference, purchase internet access or headphones, or pay for accommodation during the conference. At the ASN, we also aim to support anyone who comes to the conference, regardless whether they are presenting or attending. Although a small act, this is also a way of combating state and neoliberal thinking which places value on people only insofar as they are "productive" and generate value for the event itself by presenting a paper. We reject this and believe that everyone who attends our events is valuable and important.

Commitment to anti-racism and building solidarity with comrades from the Global South also brought the issue of how we support these comrades materially. For instance, before the fifth Anarchist Studies Network conference in Loughborough, themed around decolonialisation, a crowd funder was launched to support those who would not otherwise be able to afford to travel and stay in the UK. The reason for this was because:

> This year, we are inviting anarchists from all over the world to share their research and ideas about Decolonialisation. This has posed us with a new challenge. We would really like to give a chance for comrades from underrepresented (usually far-away) places to attend, make friends and present their work. This is invaluable for a conference about decolonising. However, the UK is often an expensive place for unwaged comrades from the global south to travel to, or spend time in. Even people who are waged often struggle with currency conversion rates. (Anarchist Studies Network Crowd funder, 2018)

The crowd funder was incredibly successful and gave us the opportunity to support a number of comrades from around the world to attend.

The conference in action

In this section we briefly discuss situations that might need to be considered during a radical CAS or anarchist studies conference. It is important to reiterate that we come from a place that sees universities as sites of struggle, and so the conference should be about supporting students and workers in struggle, creating an inclusive and supportive environment and supporting the wider movement through protests or prisoner support.

Market-orientated reforms seek to turn universities into seemingly neutral sites of knowledge exchange, in which students (or conference participants) pay a fee in return for a certain amount of knowledge, or at least a certificate that it is hoped will boost their future employment prospects. Radical conference organizers should remember that universities are living and breathing sites of struggle. Universities are sites of struggle for students and for diverse groups of workers including lecturers, support staff and facilities staff. Conference organizers might want to support students when they are in struggle. For instance, during the Covid-19 pandemic, students in the UK organized rent strikes that were designed to combat the marketisation of higher education. As Rent Strike explain:

> These campaigns aim to make on-campus accommodation more accessible for the economically disadvantaged, the marginalised and the physically disabled. However, without a full-blown movement for a free and democratic education these campaigns act at most as a bulwark to the full marketisation of universities. Universities running as businesses mean that students are seen as numbers, staff are put on more precarious contracts and pay, and money is diverted to expensive PR, advertising and management salaries—the aim of which is to make the university look good, rather than actually be good. (Rent Strike, N.D.)

Conference organizers should be aware and be supportive (or active participants) in these campaigns. For instance, scholar-activists could support student occupations by arranging teach ins. Conference organizers should always support workers in struggle and never cross a picket line. In fact, ASN conferences might want to deliberately opt to be held in an occupied location or site of struggle to show active support and build solidarity.

As a minimum level of solidarity to other species, and as a way of disrupting the animal-abusing norm of neoliberal institutions, CAS and anarchist studies conferences should adopt all vegan catering. The ASN conferences usually use Veggies catering, a radical local workers cooperative who have been "supporting campaigns for human and animal rights, environmental protection and social justice since 1984", and have found themselves victims of undercover police operations because of their campaign work (Veggies, N.D.). The adoption of vegan catering may prove contentions for anarchist conferences that are not exclusively focused on animal rights. Peter Neville (1990), writing in the anarchist quarterly *The Raven*, rejected vegetarianism because it could alienate potential working class recruits. Neville felt that "ramming vegetables down people's throats at the bookfair or anarchist meetings can induce a sense of culture shock" in which potential recruits would say that "anarchist ideas are fine" but reject "anarchist lifestyles" (p. 281). As recently as 2012 some anarchists still rejected the presumption that anarchist book fairs and conferences should use exclusively vegan catering (*Le Monde Libertaire*, 2012). However, there has been such a mainstreaming of veganism in recent years that it seems less likely that vegan catering would produce a "culture shock", and vegan anarchists should make the argument that human, animal and earth liberation are interrelated and one could not be achieved without the other (Best, 2014). In addition, this argument seems to erase many working class comrades who are indeed vegan and take animal liberation seriously, thus creating an artificial barrier between working class and other anarchists.

Neoliberal universities are soulless places in which private security and the police clamp down on any civil disobedience that disrupts the institution's pursuit of profit. It is important that conference organizers support Cops Off Campus initiatives. The North American Cops off Campus coalition explain that they aim to:

> challenge every school administration's commitment to – and use of – policing, which disproportionately violates Black, brown, Indigenous, queer, trans, disabled, and poor people and ultimately renders all members of educational campuses and their surrounding communities less safe. Further, it corrupts the mandate of spaces of education to educate rather than to violate and police. We

are committed to a free university in every sense, equally accessible to all. (Cops off Campus, N.D.)

This is important for anarchist studies scholar-activists who are also aware of the potentially serious repercussions for researchers, particularly given the imprisonment of Rik Scarce (2005) for refusing to testify to a federal grand jury about his interviews with animal rights activists. Conference organizers might be inviting speakers and groups from around the world who have faced police brutality or police spying and so in order to create a safe environment for all it is vital to support Cops Off Campus. This is especially important in relation to immigration enforcement and conference organizers need to be doubly vigilant when helping participants obtain visas and travel permits.

When it comes to online conferences, organizers might need to consider whether to record the conference. Recording the conference can be a useful way to increase accessibility or as outreach, but it is also important to consider the risks and limitations it poses. Recording an anarchist studies conference presents problems when people want to talk openly about revolutionary ideas. Given the fact that scholar-activists will be discussing movements which have faced police brutality and repression, and the fact that right wing groups and media trawl through leftist posts for nefarious reasons, we have previously decided not to record the event. In addition, not recording the conference allows everyone to stay in the moment and feel comfortable about speaking openly.

As a small gesture of solidarity and remembering anarchist and animal rights political prisoners who are serving long jail sentences, organizers might want to include activities such as prison letter writing workshops. Such small acts of solidarity can provide "a moment to breathe, to remember those fallen and those in cages, to remind ourselves of why we remain committed to the Beautiful Idea of anarchism" (June 11, N.D.). The Anarchist Black Cross Federation (ABCF, N.D.) offer support guides and resources which can be used for prisoner writing workshops. The ABCF stresses the need for supporters to

> be reliable, consistent and stable, some things you might keep in mind before offering a type of support, and then not being able to provide it in a short while... it is very important to be honest and upfront about what you can, and are prepared to do. If you can only offer some kind of support on a limited or inconsistent basis, tell them. If it is a type of support they can depend on regularly, tell them. (N.A.)

At a conference, it is likely that support will be limited, one option is setting up a table with birthday cards for animal rights and anarchist prisoners which can be signed by conference participants throughout the conference. There are numerous prisoner support resources available online (June 11th, Certain Days, Prisoner Solidarity, Anarchist Black Cross, Fight Toxic Prisons, Alliance for Global Justice, Prisoner Advocacy Network, the Ella Baker Center, the National Lawyers Guild, Prisoners Literature Project). Of course, the need for support has increased during the Covid-19 pandemic where "people in prisons, jails, and detention centers are at high risk of infection and have seriously abridged access to health care and hygiene within facilities." (Beyond Prisons, N.D. N.A.)

Finally, one crucial thing to remember is that no event or organizing committee is perfect and should be held to the highest anarchist ideals. This is often a learning process for all of us and, as such, needs to be a safe space to offer and receive feedback and criticism. In the spirit of mutual support and care, organizers might want to ensure there are channels to offer feedback, such as a general assembly at the end of the conference, and/or an online survey and/or anonymous suggestions box. In the same spirit, people offering feedback might want to consider what is the most productive way to do so, and what kind of feedback is appropriate. In particular, we are referring to the DIY ethos of ASN and CAS conferences, where, if you want something done, you do it yourself (given that you have the capacity to). It is thus useful to think whether the participant or group can solve the problem themselves before asking the organizing committee to get involved or offering feedback. This includes any issues, such as tech, room space, and issues around sexism and racism in the space. Ultimately, we want these spaces to enable people to be together in productive joyful ways and we want to give everyone the chance to contribute to producing the space in the way they want it to be. As an organizing committee, this often means going above and beyond your way to make people feel welcome and comfortable in the space through meeting, greeting and introducing people, being friendly, approachable, dismantling internal hierarchies in the form of "activist credentials" and knowing when to step in and when to step back. As Cindy Millstein rightly observes,

> Being good to each other, forging new social relations in the shell of the old, isn't going to end capitalism, smash the state, or nix all oppressions. It is nevertheless the prefigurative half of this herculean task. We also simultaneously need to constitute and experiment with new social organization. And both will only be as "good" as the dialectic between the goodness we struggle toward in our individual and institutional practices, growing, affirming, and reinforcing each other against all the hierarchical, oppressive horrors that batter us on all sides. (Millstein, 2014)

Conclusion

In this paper we have discussed some of the elements of ASN and CAS organizing and offered our thoughts and solutions to anarchist-specific problems that might arise when organizing conferences that challenge neoliberal institutions.

We have discussed the value of anarchist academic conferences and considered the importance of establishing conference organizing committees that create structures of mutual support and increase everyone's agency, such structures might mirror the anarchist affinity group model and be based on consensus decision making.

We considered issues which might arise during the conference planning stage, including finding a suitable venue that is fully accessible, choosing a conference theme, inviting keynote speakers and overcoming barriers to academia that some communities face. Neoliberal academic conferences are extremely exclusionary and the high cost of participation often means that it is impossible for unwaged or low-waged scholar-activists to attend, therefore finding solutions to issues around accessibility is key to organizing a radical conference.

When discussing the conference in action, we considered the importance of recognizing the neoliberal university as a site of struggle, and supporting initiatives such as student rent strikes or Cops Off Campus. We also discussed issues such as the catering and supporting political prisoners.

Of course, the discussions in this paper are not an exhaustive list of issues which might arise, for instance we did not mention the ASN open mic nights, which often produce some of the most memorable conference moments.

We know that other organizers will have different approaches, and we look forward to discussing the challenges that comrades have faced and the solutions they have found. ASN and CAS encourage a DIY (or Do It Together) approach, we look forward to learning from others and attending other radical conferences as the anarchist and animal liberation movements continue to grow and as together we continue to resist neoliberal institutions and build cultures and collectives based on solidarity and mutual aid.

References

Adams, C. J., & Gruen, L. (2014). *Ecofeminism: Feminist intersections with other animals & the earth*. Bloomsbury.

Alliance for Global Justice. (N.D.). Retrieved from https://afgj.org/

Anarchist Black Cross Federation. (N.D.). 'Support guide'. Retrieved from https://www.abcf.net/support-guide

Anarchist Studies Network. (2020). *Anarchist studies network conference 2020*. Retrieved from https://anarchiststudiesnetwork.org/asn-conferences/asn6-update/

Animal Liberation Front. (N.D.). *Animal liberation through direct action*. ALF.

BBC. (2021) 'G7 summit: How much carbon did Boris Johnson's flight generate?'. Retrieved from https://www.bbc.co.uk/news/57429106

Best, S. Nocella II, A. J. Kahn, R. Gigliotti, C., & Kemmerer, L. (2007). 'Introducing critical animal studies. *Animal Liberation Philosophy and Policy Journal*, 5(1), 4–5.

Bergman, C., & Montgomery, N. (2017). *Joyful militancy*. AK Press.

Best, S. (2014). *The politics of total liberation: Revolution for the 21st century*. Palgrave Macmillan.

Beyond Prisons. (2020). *Prisoner support guide for the coronavirus crisis*. Retrieved from https://www.beyond-prisons.com/prisoner-support-guide-for-the-coronavirus-crisis

Certain Days. (N.D.). Retrieved from https://www.certaindays.org/

Cops Off Campus. (N.D.). *About*. Retrieved from https://copsoffcampuscoalition.com/about/

D'Silva, J., & Webster, J. (2010). *The meat crisis: Developing more sustainable production and consumption*. Earthscan.

Ella Baker Center for Human Rights. (N.D.). Retrieved from https://ellabakercenter.org/

Fight Toxic Prisons. (N.D.). Retrieved from https://fighttoxicprisons.wordpress.com/

June 11th. (N.D.). *June 11, 2021*. Retrieved from https://june11.noblogs.org/

Kheel, M. (2006). 'Direct action and the heroic ideal: An ecofeminist critique'. In S. Best & A. J. Nocella II (Eds.), *Igniting a revolution: Voices in defence of the earth*. AK Press.

'Les animaux, ils sont gentils', *Le Monde Libertaire*, 18th October 2012, 18.

Millstein, C. (2014). *Organizing social spaces as if social relations matter*. Retrieved from https://theanarchistlibrary.org/library/cindy-milstein-organizing-social-spaces-as-if-social-relations-matter#toc2

O'Flaherty, K. (2021, January 24) 'Is it time to leave WhatsApp – And is signal the answer?', *Guardian*. Retrieved from https://www.theguardian.com/technology/2021/jan/24/is-it-time-to-leave-whatsapp-and-is-signal-the-answer

Poirier, N., Bernatchez, A., & Nocella II, A. J. (Forthcoming). *Emerging new voices in critical animal studies: Vegan studies for total liberation*. Peter Lang.

Political Studies Association. (2018). *Anarchist Studies Network conference 5*. Retrieved from https://www.psa.ac.uk/events/anarchist-studies-network-conference-5/asn5

National Lawyers Guild. (N.D.). Retrieved from https://www.nlg.org/

Neville, P. (1990). 'Anarchism and the sociology of food: A figurational approach'. *The Raven*, 11(3), 278–283.

Nocella II, A. J., George, A. E., & Lupinacci, J. (2019). *Animals, disability, and the end of capitalism: Voices from the eco-ability movement.* Peter Lang.

Prisoner Advocacy Network. (N.D.). Retrieved from https://www.prisoneradvocacynetwork.org/

Prisoner's Literature Project. (N.D.). Retrieved from https://www.prisonlit.org/

Prisoners Solidarity. (N.D.). Retrieved from https://www.prisonersolidarity.com

Punk Scholars Network. (N.D.). *Punk scholars annual conference 2020.* Retrieved from https://www.punkscholarsnetwork.com/blog/punk-scholars-annual-conference-2020/

Rent Strike. (N.D.). *Why we strike,* Retrieved from https://www.rent-strike.org/

Scarce, R. (2005). *Contempt of court: A scholar's battle for free speech from behind bars.* AltaMira.

Simpson, W., & Mcmahon, M. (2012). *Freedom through football: The story of the easton cowboys and cowgirls.* Tangent.

Veggies. (N.D.). *About.* Retrieved from https://www.veggies.org.uk/about/

Wilson, M., & Kinna, R. (2012). Key terms. In R. Kinna (Ed.), *The continuum companion to anarchism.* Continuum.

5 Faculty and Student Activism as Sites of Resistance to Neoliberalism in Higher Education

ADALBERTO AGUIRRE, JR. AND RUBÉN MARTINEZ

Introduction

When we hear statements such as, "resisting the police state," "resisting tuition increases in higher education," they bring to memory a popular statement issued by The Borg in *Star Trek: The New Generation* television series that "Resistance is futile!" One could interpret the statement that resistance is futile as suggesting that any attempt at change will fail or that the context for change has been altered to one that resists resistance. Our focus in this essay is on resistance to neoliberalism in higher education. Implicit in the discussion is the argument that neoliberalism has buffered itself in higher education such that its policies and practices are situated in the bureaucratic well-being of higher education. Higher education has arrived in its social and historical synergism to the point that neoliberalism is the vehicle for providing society with efficient and regimented corporate work roles. The perceived benefits of neoliberalism to higher education have altered the context for change to one that demands resistance by faculty and students alike.

The Emergence of the Neoliberal Model

With its roots in Adam Smith's ideas of free market capitalism in *The Wealth of Nations*, as modified by the German ordo-liberals and the Chicago School, neoliberalism served as the springboard for the economic doctrines of Margaret Thatcher and Ronald Reagan that resulted in the "emergence of a neoliberal model of global capitalism that serves to enrich powerful corporations at the expense of workers and ordinary citizens, while increasing social, political, and economic inequalities between nations" (Aguirre, Eick, & Reese, 2006, p. 1). Swept by the trade winds generated by globalization in the final quarter of the 20th century, neoliberalism embedded itself in the economies of poor countries so that business interests in rich countries could further exploit the availability of cheap labor and raw materials.

In this paper, we treat *neoliberalism* as a set of political principles and economic practices that promote an ideological mindset rooted in the beliefs that: (a) markets should be privatized and free in order to serve the public good; and (b) the state functions as a tool to promote the universalization of market principles and to defend individual or private monetary interests. We argue that the neoliberal emphasis on market *efficiency* and *accountability* has moved into public life and civic institutions, especially public education, in the United States. Under neoliberal principles, public education becomes a commodity, the school becomes a marketplace promoting "entrepreneurial subjects," and the political state uses its legislative powers to transform public education into an institution that meets individual or private monetary interests in an entrepreneurial society. Within the neoliberal view of public education students are socialized into agents for generating capital in a marketplace that invests education in joint ventures with the corporate/business elite sector that serve private interests.

The ideology of neoliberalism emphasizes, among other things, radical individualism, small government in the promotion of general welfare, privatization of government functions, and free labor—one "unhampered" by labor unions. In the neoliberal social order, individuals are free to pursue their interests without concern for the well-being of others or society. This is freedom without social responsibility and a form of unleashed greed grounded in the view that "I'm made my riches, it's your fault if you haven't made yours." Further, corporations are now considered persons with the same rights as people, although they are not equal before the law given their influence on policymaking through their multimillion dollar lobbying industry. This influence has resulted in pro-corporate policies that allow them to grow, concentrate capital, and extend their global reach at the expense of ordinary members of the population. Corporate influence has produced social inequality not seen in this country since the 1920s and has increased the rate of exploitation over the past five decades resulting in the stagnation in the wages of workers. Further, there is a punitive component to the imposition of neoliberal practices on institutions that characterizes neoliberalism as authoritarian. This feature of neoliberalism is embedded in performance based funding and the constant threat by legislators to cut funding to school

Neoliberalism in Higher Education

In 1962, 60 members of Students for a Democratic Society (1962) met at a UAW labor camp in Port Huron and drafted an agenda for their organization that called for a "new left" generation of college students that would pursue a truly democratic society in which more people could lead fulfilling lives. In what became *The Port Huron Statement*, the students criticized many of the institutions of American society, including higher education and the economy. They criticized the "university" for being governed by an administrative bureaucracy that eviscerated the creative spirit in students and transformed many of them into compliant servants of convention quietly accepting the "stock truths of the day" (1962, p. 4). The students called for educational reform grounded in the "independence and control that characterizes the teachers and students" (p. 31) and leads to "human beings with values and skills sufficient to live fully in the world" (p. 32). They saw the university as critically positioned in society to promote social change for the betterment of humanity. This required an alliance between students and faculty in promoting reform and wresting "control of the educational process from the administrative bureaucracy" (p. 49).

With regard to the economy, it is clear that the students perceived the emergent and liminal features of neoliberalism, although the term was not used to characterize the social order of that time. They called for the end to a "permanent war economy" controlled by rich and corporate elites "revelling in abundance" (p. 1). Such an economy should be replaced by one in which the "major resources and means of production…[are]…open to democratic participation and subject to democratic social regulation" (p. 31) and in which corporations are publicly responsible (p. 40). Finally, the students sought to protect free speech and the right to protest, which gave rise to the Free Speech Movement.

Two years later, in a 1964 address Mario Savio, leader of the Berkeley Free Speech Movement, stated "if this is a firm, and if the Board of Regents are the Board of Directors, and if President Kerr in fact is the manager, then I tell you something—the faculty are a bunch of employees and we're the raw material!" (Quoted in Seal, 2018: para. 1). Savio proposed that the corporatization of higher education would be resisted if students and faculty situated themselves as obstacles to its transformation into a corporate culture. While Savio identified change in the university as transitioning into a corporate culture, it was the confluence of other social forces that constructed a context for the entry of neoliberalism into higher education.

Several social forces facilitated the expansion of neoliberal practices in higher education (See Donoghue, 2008; Giroux, 2002; Steck, 2003). For example, between 1940 and the late 1970s higher education benefited from the infusion of funding from state, federal and private sources. The end of the Second World War almost doubled the number of students enrolled in college between 1940 and 1950 because of the large number of returning veterans using the G.I. Bill to pursue a college education (Williams, 2006). Universities continued to receive increasing support through the 1970s, but the political attacks on defunding the welfare state during the Reagan presidencies shifted the socio-political context in society to privatization. For universities, the emphasis on privatizing introduced neoliberal practices such as encouraging universities to profit from patenting research results as intellectual property and framing a university education as a commodity to be purchased at increasing prices, thereby transforming students into consumers. To decrease the cost of instruction, while increasing tuition, universities increased the use of contingent instructors, such as adjunct lecturers, to teach most of the courses offered by universities. In short, universities became an extension of a corporate model nested in a managerial culture that offered education as a profit enterprise instead of a societal good.

The neoliberal beliefs of the self-interested individual, a self-regulated free market, and free trade resulted in policies of deregulation, privatization, increased accountability, and fiscal austerity (Olsen & Peters, 2005; Venn, 2020). Increasing student enrollments, the courting of donors and their contributions, and growing public sentiment that "intellectual curiosity" should not be funded by taxpayers served as catalysts for infusing higher education with marketplace principles and practices (Giroux, 2010; Ingleby, 2015; Kandiko, 2010; Martinez, 2018; Olekenko, Molodychenko, & Sheherbakova, 2018). Neoliberalism created a context in higher education that linked learning with marketplace valuation, transforming students into commodities in an open market.

Neoliberal ideology in higher education altered the mission of higher education to contribute to society's well-being and personal growth; that is, the education of well-rounded persons and good citizens. The three pillars of higher education's integrity as a social and public institution–good teaching, research, and service–have been transformed by neoliberal principles into revenue generating enterprises. Reduced state funding and the infusion of marketplace principles and practices have resulted in the treatment of students as a revenue stream for raising tuition which, in turn, increases student dependence on loans benefiting private lenders, primarily those on Wall Street. Further, reduced state funding engendered pressure to increase the number of donors, especially those with deep pockets, which has served to expand the staff numbers in donor/development offices making them key stakeholders in the monetarization of higher education (Schulze-Cleven et al., 2017) and creating threats to academic freedom.

Neoliberal ideology transformed research grants into a tool for generating indirect cost benefits for bloated administrations and turned faculty into competitive predators in the pursuit of grant awards. In the neoliberal university, faculty who were successful in generating sizable amounts of research grant funding, call them "rain makers," also became commodities in the faculty market. The increased indirect cost benefits for higher education institutions from research grants promoted competition between institutions to determine placement on a hierarchical structure based on the generation of research awards and attendant monies (Gildersleeve, 2017). An institution's standing in higher education is no longer a reflection of its promotion of intellectual inquiry, but rather the institution's success in generating research monies and a portfolio of donorship and endowment.

Service is no longer treated as a public good, it became a means for the exploitation of students via student internships as free labor to industry. While students are recruited by businesses via internship opportunities where they perform work roles without compensation, students are required to pay for the class units. That is, in the neoliberal university students are encouraged to participate in internship programs that benefit business organizations; a benefit that comes with a cost to students but not businesses. Students are often advised that internship classes are not free because they will receive free work experience from the business community. Not surprisingly, higher education institutions utilize service to show state legislatures the value of higher education in their close ties with the business community. After all, legislatures are more likely to reward higher education with increased funding if there is a robust association with the business community. In the 21st century, the neoliberal university will face mounting social and political pressures to prepare students for future employment.

In summary, neoliberal ideology does more than just pursue business principles of efficiency and production on a large scale involving the merger of corporate cultures, education, and labor. Neoliberal ideology identifies bodies—students, staff, and faculty—as having a purpose in the production of profit for capital expansion via economies of scale tactics. In higher education, these tactics are identified as increased utilization of adjunct faculty in the classroom to eliminate the hiring of tenure-stream faculty; increasing class sizes to make instruction more profitable; and the promotion of impersonal online instructional delivery models to expand instruction beyond the physical classroom (Daniel, 2016). Virtual or online instruction is a cost-effective method in higher education that increases the scale of production by increasing the enrollment of students, accompanied by more tuition revenue beyond the structural limitations of the classroom. In short, higher education has become the victim of a hostile takeover by neoliberal principles that utilize higher education as a laboratory for economic practices and redesigning work roles for monetarizing the value of higher education.

Resisting Neoliberalism in Higher Education

Shahjahan (2021) suggests that one approach to resisting neoliberal higher education is by adopting postcolonial theories of resistance. These theories of resistance may provide strategies that enhance the understanding and willingness of faculty and administrators to resist neoliberal policies and practices. Shahjahan stresses *transformational resistance*, or the creation of new ways of being, knowing and doing to transform higher education. The notion of transformational resistance is a synthesis of Jeffress' (2008) critique of four modes of postcolonial resistance, namely cultural resistance, resistance-as-subversion, resistance-as-opposition, and resistance-as-transformation. Theories of postcolonial resistance, such as those found in the writings of Homi K. Bhabha and Franz Fanon, examine the concept of resistance as a means of attaining social and cultural transformation. However, the application of postcolonial theories in proposing strategies of resistance to neoliberalism in higher education can be expanded by focusing on the synergy between political power and economic structures in higher education.

Phipps (2017) has noted that universities are key neoliberal institutions which follow neoliberal principles nested in deregulation and privatization to promote the ideology that the social good is best served by the operation of market forces throughout society, one in which the state itself is controlled by the market in that it is organized along market principles. In the neoliberal university, research has become a commodity in a marketplace based on the valuation of knowledge production. The valuation of knowledge production results in the hierarchical placement of universities dependent on a system of competition for faculty and students. As such, faculty as service providers and students as consumers are commodities in the neoliberal university that strives to conjoin education as a process of self-betterment with economic productivity and with a market-based political state. As a result, with faculty and students as primary consumers and commodities, higher education is portrayed as promoting the social good by providing an economic return on the political state's investment, however diminished it might be. In this context, could faculty and students in higher education be potential sources of resistance to neoliberalism in higher education?

Let's consider that in the neoliberal university faculty are entrepreneurial workers who participate in a competitive marketplace over research funding with other faculty. Faculty participation in an entrepreneurial marketplace is motivated by the desire for personal prestige and institutional rewards. To participate in the marketplace faculty must identify with neoliberal principles which confound individual choice and freedom with externalized reward systems. The faculty's *sense of being* is closely associated with a university's identification of a system for distributing rewards and status. In the neoliberal university, faculty are *alienated*, to use the term loosely, from their being and selves because of their dependence on externalized reward systems. Unsurprisingly, in the neoliberal university, faculty are highly adaptive to a changing system of institutional management over their knowledge production. One might even observe that higher education, especially faculty, have been colonized by neoliberal practices (See Apple, 2006; Giroux, 2010; Slaughter & Rhoades, 2004).

In contrast to faculty who have long-term, even lifetime, institutional relationships, students in the neoliberal university are primarily consumers in the processes of knowledge production and distribution that occur in higher education. The students' institutional relationship is not comparably as long-term as that of faculty, but rather it is short-term with a 4–6-year lifetime. We suggest that based on their short lifetime institutional relationship, students may have a high propensity to pursue strategies that resist neoliberalism in higher education. We are not suggesting that faculty are not capable of strategizing efforts to resist neoliberalism. Instead, we are suggesting that students may be more adaptive to a discourse for developing strategies capable of transforming the neoliberal university into a socially democratic society, much as the Students for a Democratic Society envisioned.

Faculty and Student Activism

There is a history of faculty and student activism in higher education focused on social justice and the defense of academic freedom usually attended by repression by universities and the state. The Students for a Democratic Society was perhaps one of the most influential organizations of the last half century, along with the Student Nonviolent Coordinating Committee and the Freedom Riders. Among faculty, most activism has been at the individual level, although in the 1960s faculty in sociology and history began to organize themselves to support the embattled students in the Free Speech Movement and the Anti-War Movement. Long before that, however, individual faculty members had stood publicly on social issues and were dismissed from their university employment.

On October 8, 1917, Charles Beard, a noted historian, resigned from Columbia University to protest the firing of two fellow faculty members who, as pacifists, had voiced their opposition to America's involvement in the war with Germany. Professor Beard supported the war but resigned to protest the repressive actions taken by the administration and the trustees, referring to the latter as "visionless and reactionary" (Beard, 1917). In April 1918, Professor Beard made it clear that the issue was that of academic freedom. Two years prior to his resignation, the American Association of University Professors was founded to protect academic freedom in response to numerous firings, resignations, and censures of faculty, especially radical political economists.

Although the 1920s were relatively quiet on the nation's college campuses, in the 1930s students who were to become what has been called the "Old Left" became active in response to the economic crisis that was set in motion by the stock market crash in 1929. Organized under the American Student Union, their activities primarily focused on anti-militarism and peace. In 1934, they organized the first national student strike in the nation's history. This was a time when a quarter of the labor force was out of work and labor and unions gained key footholds in advancing the rights of workers. It was also a time when socialist ideas became widespread. During the 1930s, the Farmer-Labor Party promoted the rights of workers and farmers in Minnesota and became the most successful third party in the country. Edgar Hoover, Director of the Federal Bureau of Investigation, was authorized to investigate subversive activity and organizations at universities and labor unions. In 1931, the State of Washington passed legislation requiring a loyalty oath by teachers and faculty members. By the end of the 1930s, WWII was emerging as a geopolitical shift in history.

Progressive activism diminished during the early part of the 1940s as the impulse of the nation turned to patriotism. In the years following the second world war, the political climate shifted to anti-communism. In 1947, President Harry Truman issued Executive Order 9835 requiring a loyalty investigation of persons entering employment with federal agencies, and in 1949 the Cantwell Committee of the Washington State Legislature began calling suspected communist faculty to testify before its members. Earlier that year, three faculty members at the University of Washington were dismissed by the university's president, Dr. Raymond B. Allen, for suspected ties with Communists. California's own un-American Activities Committee was also investigating faculty suspected of advocating communism as a social and political agenda. In 1950, the Regents of the University of California enacted a policy requiring a loyalty oath by employees.

During the 1950s, Senator Joseph McCarthy began raising the specter of communism inside federal agencies and across the nation's universities. During this decade hundreds of faculty members were subpoenaed to testify before the U.S. House on Un-American Activities Committee. In 1953, Helen Lynd, a sociologist and student of Marxism at Sarah Lawrence College, testified before the U.S. Senate Subcommittee to Investigate the Administration of the Internal Security Act and Other Internal Security Laws, of the Committee on the Judiciary, also known as the Jenner Committee, and denied knowing any Communists on the faculty. One outcome of McCarthyism was the dismissal of an unknown number of faculty from their posts at colleges and universities.

The nation's political climate during the 1960s was deeply polarized. Elements of that polarization were evident in colleges and universities where students and young faculty debated the role of values in the social sciences and questioned their role in society. Influenced by Robert S. Lynd's book, *Knowledge for What?*, published in 1939, and the works of C. Wright Mills, Irving Horowitz, and other sociologists, they questioned the objectivity and value-free stance of the social sciences. In 1968, a number of them organized the New University Conference at the University of Chicago to develop strategies for "challenging the established structures of the disciplines and the prevailing practices of academic life" (Flacks, 1988, p. 10). A few weeks after the conference and three weeks after the assassination of Dr. Martin Luther King, Jr., 1,000 students at Columbia University commandeered five buildings on campus demanding an end to its relationship with the Institute for Defense Analyses, which had ties to the Department of Defense. Although the student revolt lasted a week and was quashed by law enforcement, its principal goal was achieved, and it sparked a series of student revolts across the country. A byproduct of the event was the linking of sociology graduate students and faculty at Columbia University with the New University Conference faculty which led to the Sociology Liberation Movement, a short-lived effort to make sociology a "vehicle for human enlightenment" (Flacks, 1988, p. 18).

As this brief history of activism in higher education shows, students and faculty have formed alliances to promote progressive ideas. They have repeatedly been met by repressive forces internal and external to universities. Like participants of other social movements, they have placed their careers and, in many cases, their lives on the line. For example, Dr. Staughton Lynd, a young professor of history at Yale University and a former organizer of Freedom Schools in Mississippi, was fired and blacklisted for visiting North Vietnam in 1965 with Tom Hayden and Herbert Aptheker. During this period hundreds of students were expelled and suspended from colleges and universities and many faculty members were dismissed from the positions. Today, the transformation of neoliberalism requires the same courage and commitment as those who came before us.

Historically, academic freedom has been at the center of student and faculty activism. That is the case in today's neoliberal order which has taken on the features of neoliberal nationalism. The conservative and well-coordinated assault on academic freedom is focused on Critical Race Theory, a framework for uncovering the systemic features of White Supremacy in America. The assault, which is part of a rising New McCarthyism (Schrecker, 2005), has been framed as an anti-racism movement, but it is in fact an attack on the anti-racism movement spearheaded by the Black Lives Matter Movement. Legislation has been passed in several states prohibiting the teaching of Critical Race Theory in public schools. The freedom to teach and to study all aspects of the world around us is at stake.

In this context, both students and faculty can rally and mount a defense of academic freedom. It does not matter if they are liberals, conservatives, Leftists, or radicals, academic freedom should be of concern to all. Williams (2006) has noted that because faculty tend to attract the most attention in studies of neoliberalism in higher education, comparatively little attention has been focused on neoliberalism's effect on students. However, students have as much at stake as faculty when the content of their studies is limited by politicians. Like the members of the student movement organizations of the 1960s, students have a vested interest in the acquisition of transformative frameworks via the curriculum that allow them to question the commodification of education and their roles in the commodification process in higher education (Saunders, 2007; Saunders & Ramirez, 2017).

For example, in the neoliberal university race has been eliminated in student admissions processes, scholarships have shifted from need-based to merit-based, and student financial aid packages have become dependent on loans instead of grants, especially for students from low-income families (Rhoades, Wagoner, & Ryan, 2009). This shift reproduces both institutionalized racial barriers in access to higher education and patterns of inequality in society. While some may say that students have been "tamed" by the exigencies of neoliberal policies and practices, there is always the promise for change inherent in the development of critical thinking skills and perspectives emphasized in the teachings of faculty even as conservatives seek to suppress such perspectives as Critical Race Theory.

In fact, college student activism has been increasing since the late 1980s at institutions of higher education in the United States (Elin, 2016; Giroux, 2002). College student activism has resulted in sites of resistance in the neoliberal university focused on social and racial justice (Cahill, 2011; Rhoads, 2016), as seen in the recent student protests of Israel's mass killing of Palestinian civilians. These sites of resistance have the potential of transforming the neoliberal depiction of students as passive consumers into students who see themselves as stakeholders in imagining post-neoliberal higher education (Cahill, 2011; Cole & Heineke, 2020). According to Cole and Heineke (2020, p. 104), "Student activism in higher education has been a significant indication of resistance and rollback to neoliberalism, a reflection of a vision or social imaginary about a post-neoliberal society…".

When it comes to activism, students embody a capacity to challenge neoliberalism and avoid the Faustian relationship which most faculty have forged with neoliberalism. That is, the commodified relationship faculty have developed via neoliberalism deters them away from strategizing on how to challenge neoliberalism. This is especially the case in a context grounded in a history of academic repression of faculty. Student as consumers, however, can strategize to challenge the neoliberal practices that externalize them in the university. Comparatively speaking, the prestige and rewards most faculty enjoy under neoliberalism are obstacles in their ability to challenge the conditions that determine their academic existence. In contrast, students are consumers of a product (an education crowned by a degree) for which they pay, and payment for services can situate them as overseers of how neoliberalism operates in higher education.

Conclusion

Neoliberalism is deeply embedded in the nation's public colleges and universities. It has transformed the role of higher education in society from promoting the public good through social democratic values to a private good that must be paid for by individuals and which promotes competition as a universal value and practice. Historically, faculty have avoided acting on social values, believing that science must be objective and value-free. There is, however, a growing disenchantment among some faculty with the widget model of research production that prevents time to think broadly and deeply about critical social issues. Students are increasingly becoming aware of the assault of conservative forces on the academic culture and its core values and beginning to raise important questions about the costs of a college education and the depth of social inequalities that characterize today's America. Social justice concerns are evident among both some students and some faculty. The conditions that precipitate social movements around higher education issues are intensifying. Whether it is students or faculty who set in motion a movement around academic freedom and the role of education does not matter, what matters is that they mobilize and form alliances, as those before them did, that will save the university from the neoliberal practices and the New McCarthyism of our day.

References

Aguirre, Jr., A., Eick, V., & Reese, E. (2006). Introduction: Neoliberal globalization, urban privatization, and resistance. *Social Justice, 33*, 1–12.

Apple, M. W. (2006). Understanding and interpreting neoliberalism and neoconservatism in education. *Pedagogies, 1*, 21–26.

Beard, Charles. (1917). *Charles A. Beard Resignation Letter, October 8, 1917.* Retrieved from https://edblogs.columbia.edu/histx3570-001-2014-1/readings/charles-a-beard-resination-letter-october-8-1917/

Cahill, D. (2011). Beyond neoliberalism: Crisis and the prospects for progressive alternatives. *New Political Science, 33*, 479–492.

Cole, R. M., & Heineke, W. F. (2020). Higher Education after neoliberalism: Student activism as a guiding light. *Policy Futures in Education, 18*, 90–116.

Daniel, M. C. (2016). Contingent faculty of the World Unite! Organizing to resist the corporatization of higher education. *New Labor Forum, 25*, 44–51.

Donoghue, F. (2008). *The last Professors: The Corporate University and the fate of the humanities.* Fordham University Press.

Elin, A. (2016). Meet the new student activists. *New York Times*, February 9.

Flacks, D. (1988). The sociology liberation movement: some legacies and lessons. *Insurgent Sociologist, 15*(2), 9–18.

Gildersleeve, R. (2017). The neoliberal academy of the Anthropocene and the retaliation of the lazy academic. *Cultural Studies/Critical Methodologies, 17*, 286–295.

Giroux, H. A. (2002). Neoliberalism, corporate culture, and the promise of higher education: The University as democratic public sphere. *Harvard Educational Review, 72*(4), 425–464.

Giroux, H. A. (2010). Bare pedagogy and the scourge of neoliberalism: Rethinking higher education as a democratic public sphere. *The Educational Forum, 74*, 184–196.

Ingleby, E. (2015). The house that Jack built: Neoliberalism, teaching in higher education and the moral objective. *Teaching in Higher Education, 20*, 518–529.

Jeffress, D. (2008). *Postcolonial resistance: Culture, liberation, and transformation.* Toronto University Press.

Kandiko, C. B. (2010). Neoliberalism in higher education: A comparative approach. *International Journal of Arts and Sciences, 3,* 153–175.

Lynd, R. S. (1935). *Knowledge for what? The place of social science in American Culture.* Princeton, NJ: Princeton University Press.

Martinez, R. O. (2018). "Neoliberalism and the context of Public Higher Education for Latinos." In A. G. de los Santos, L. I. Rendón, G. F. Keller, A. Acereda, E. M. Bensimon, & R. J. Tannenbaum (Eds.), *Moving forward: Policies, planning, and prompting access of hispanic college students* (pp. 95–114). Bilingual Press, Hispanic Research Center.

Olekenko, R., Molodychenko, V., & Sheherbakova, N. (2018). Neoliberalism in higher education as a challenge for future civilizations. *Philosophy and Cosmology, 20,* 113–119.

Olsson, M., & Peters, M. (2005). Neoliberalism, higher education and the knowledge economy: From the free market to knowledge capitalism. *Journal of Education Policy, 20,* 313–345.

Phipps, A. (2017). Speaking up for what's right: Politics, markets and violence in higher education. *Feminist Theory, 18,* 357–361.

Rhoades, R. A. (2016). Student activism, diversity and the struggle for a just society. *Journal of Diversity in Higher Education, 9,* 189–202.

Rhoades, R. A., Wagoner, R. L., & Ryan, E. (2009). The American Community College and the Neoliberal State: A critical analysis of the case of California. *Education and Society, 27,* 5–33.

Saunders, D. (2007). The impact of neoliberalism on college students. *Journal of College & Character, 8,* 1–9.

Saunders, D. B., & Ramirez, G. B. (2017). Resisting the Neoliberalization of higher education: A challenge to commonsensical understandings of commodities and consumption. *Critical Studies-Critical Methodologies, 17,* 189–196.

Schulze-Cleven, T., Reitz, T., Maesse, J., & Angermuller, J. (2017). The new political economy of higher education: Between distributional contexts and discursive stratification. *Higher Education, 73,* 795–812.

Schrecker, E. (2005). The new McCarthyism in academe. *Thought and Action, 21*(Fall), 103–117.

Seal, A. (2018). How the University became Neoliberal. *Chronicle of Higher Education, 64*(4), 28–56.

Shahjahan, R. (2021). From 'no' to 'yes': Postcolonial perspectives on resistance to neoliberal higher education. *Discourse: Studies in the Cultural Politics of Education, 35,* 219–232.

Slaughter, S., & Rhoades, G. (2004). *Academic capitalism and the new economy: Markets, state, and higher education.* Johns Hopkins University Press.

Steck, H. (2003). Corporatization of the University: Seeking Conceptual Clarity. *Annals of the American Academy of Political and Social Sciences, 585*, 66–83.

Students for a Democratic Society. (1962). *The Port Huron Statement- Draft.* Retrieved from https://www.sds-1960s.org/PortHuronStatement-draft.pdf

Venn, C. (2020). *After Capital.* SAGE.

White, K. (2016). Black lives on campuses matter: The rise of the black student movement. *Soundings: A Journal of Politics and Culture, 6*, 86–97.

Williams, J. J. (2006). The Post-Welfare State University. *American Literary History, 18*, 190–216.

6 Neoliberalism, Neopopulism and the Assault on Higher Education[1]

RICHARD VAN HEERTUM

Introduction

An extraordinary number of books, articles and chapters have been published over the past 30 years detailing the scourge of neoliberalism at the economic, political and cultural level. A not insubstantial subset of this work has homed in specifically on its impact on higher education. One fair question to ask at this point is whether there is a point in continuing to catalogue the problem? Another is whether enough has been written on viable solutions to address its shortcoming?

I think a third important question to pose is whether we are witnessing the complete collapse of the neoliberal consensus in the past few years, as exemplified by Brexit, the election of Donald Trump and other populist leaders, the consolidation of power of Putin, Xi, Orbán, Erdogan and others and the resultant push against globalization and toward nationalism, xenophobia and protectionism (Ágh, 2018). In fact, I believe the rise of neopopulism is a direct reaction to the failures of neoliberal globalization and the resultant increased inequality, accelerating destruction of planet earth and dramatic increase in transnational migration it has wrought. The shifting landscape has also altered the nature of reforms in higher education, though I will argue there are surprising parallels between the neoliberal and neoconservative agendas.

I follow my detailing of those parallels with the argument that professors need to move from the often arcane and cloistered confines of the Ivory Tower back into the public sphere to openly combat the attacks on science, reason, truth and education that neopopulism (and neoliberalism) have entailed. This is made more vital by the three key threats we face today: global climate change, dramatic and increasing economic inequality and the withering of democracy across the globe.

While this chapter will focus on policies in the United States, there are even more pronounced instantiations of these reforms evident across the globe, whether in the Russian shift toward the entrepreneurial university with an emphasis on optimization and marketing (Nureev et al., 2020), neoliberal reforms that have dominated higher education in Latin America for decades, the neoliberal underpinnings of the Bologna Process in the European Union (Štech, 2011). China's 1+X program that combines traditional college curriculum with vocational training (Ross, 2019), quality assurance reforms in Italy that began in the 1990s (Capano, 2014) or David Cameron's draconian funding cuts to higher education in England (Mason & Adams, 2019).

State of Play in Higher Education

While the true battles today are over equality across multiple lines of demarcation, addressing the growing costs and perils of global warming and fortifying democracy against multiple lines of attack, one can rightfully argue that all these fights begin in the arenas of culture and meaning. Increasingly, as McLuhan (1965) predicted almost 60 years ago, we have moved from a world built on the foundation of the scientific method to one predicated on group think, received knowledge and retribalism, where ideological membership and in-group bias are the primary arbiters of epistemological positionality. Put more simply, rather than looking for evidence to support one's position, one's position is all the evidence necessary for what many believe. Or as Errol Morris put it, believing is seeing, particularly in a world of hyperpartisanship and insularity where indignation appears to be the most common political stance.

This battle over meaning is fortified by an attack on the legitimacy of any and all social institutions that can counteract the ideological manipulation and sculpting of reality entailed by both neoliberalism and neopopulism. We see this in attacks on the "liberal" media, in the nature of corporate and conservative political framing, in the social media world of "fake news" and viral attack ads and, of course, in attacks on education (Hetherington & Ladd, 2020). It is most obvious in continued beliefs around the "real winner" of the 2020 election, over battles around coronavirus, vaccines and masks and those still willing to doubt the reality of global warming even as heat waves and extreme weather surround and endanger them. We also see it specifically in the concerted efforts of corporations and conservatives to undermine the broader goals of higher education, replacing them with a more instrumentalized, constricted and vocationalized version of post-secondary education that seriously circumscribe its deeper goals and attachment to democracy, social justice and freedom (Newfield, 2016).

Given their success in delegitimating the media, the law, the state and schools, many see the university as the last bastion of hope, besides the streets, to combat the neopopulist turn and its attempt to establish authoritarianism in the U.S. (Van Heertum, 2021). This is made particular dire by the multiple attempts to undermine higher education from not only conservatives but liberals as well. Their collective goal, from opposite poles, appears to be the shuttering off of the channels of critique and dissent, returning us to the age of spirituality, mythology, faith and received knowledge. Tied into this shift is the current state of insular political and social life, where individuals are free to subsist in a world of news, socializing and interaction that largely serves to reinforce what they already believe, unencumbered by inconvenient facts and truths (Halpern, 2017). In the end, it is a new cynicism that is resistant to the idea of honest, reasoned debate, a vibrant public sphere and the power of democracy to improve our lives (Van Heertum, 2009).

These trends emerged with the advent of neoliberalism, which was the dominant global ideology from the early 90s until quite recently, and still governs world affairs across much of the developed and developing world, even as neopopulist movements are certainly challenging neoliberalism's push for market liberation, government retrenchment and dismantling of the social safety net (Van Heertum & Torres, 2009). Free trade and free markets were the dual call to arms of neoliberalism and even as the victory of Brexit, neopopulist movements across Europe and the truculent anti-trade rhetoric of the Trump administration challenged the global détente, Africa has just signed their most comprehensive free trade agreement ever as China builds a modernized silk road to further exploit its abundant supply of cheap labor and advanced technology.

Freire (1998) was among the first to offer a profound critique of neoliberalism and its tendency to undermine critique and define itself as the inevitable culmination of historical progress. He argued that the very nature of neoliberal educational policy scuppered the radical potential of education, instead leading it to surreptitiously serve the interests of the powerful. The paradigm centers this perspective of education around a rather astounding claim, as Lois Weiner pointed out in reviewing a 2004 World Bank Draft Report, "unions, especially teachers union, are one of the greatest threats to global prosperity" (Weiner & Compton, 2008). While surprising on the surface, a deeper examination of these 13 words gets to the heart of the neoliberal project—which is to privatize public goods, shrink the size and scope of governmental oversight and regulation and thus allow the free market to mediate domestic and global relations unfettered by the institutions that dominated modernism. In attacking teachers and teachers' unions specifically, they sought to solidify the process of transforming schools to serve primarily economic aims of training and sorting future workers.

At a deeper level, it can be argued that the neoliberal agenda attacks schools as ideological institutions that could challenge the discourses and rationality behind neoliberalism itself. This would explain the move to weaken the power of teachers and establish teacher-proof curriculum, to calls for neutrality and apolitical classrooms all the way through to the university and to standardize curriculum and use high stakes testing to all but erase time for education outside its vocational and job training facets (Nichols & Berliner, 2007).

Alongside the push toward standardization, instrumentalization and professionalism are three additional shifts in higher education: an increased focus on vocational education and the needs of commerce in teaching methods and content, the infusion of business models and rationality into the relationship between schools and students and an increasingly close relationship between universities and the private sector in research. For instance, with regard to accreditation and universalization, major efforts are underway not only in the United States, but across the globe to reform academic programs through accreditation processes and strategies that produce increased homogeneity across national boundaries, tying education to outcomes that redefine "success" in learning (Van Heertum et al., 2013).

When we consider these reforms within the broader context of a changing higher education landscape, where state and federal funding cuts place a growing financial burden on schools, it is not surprising that many have turned to corporate models and corporate funding to remain solvent. This has included increased branding and salesmanship, resources reallocated to athletics and other perks and experiential elements of the school over broader educational goals. It has included huge influxes of cash from private and corporate donors for new projects, which often come with influence over teaching, priorities and research. And it includes a broader focus on serving student interests, that alter the nature of the relationship between schools and "student-consumers" often moving away from rigor and well-rounded education toward pursuit of the satisfaction of those consumers (Tuchman, 2011).

The funding shift has also allowed the corporate world to wield increased influence on the overall direction and focus of academic institutions. The rhetoric and discourse of economics and business culture have become common in higher education, centered on the "bottom line," "efficiency" and "serving the business community." Corporate models of governance have been adopted and many leaders of business have risen to the top of the university power structure. This has increased dramatically in the two decades since, as funding cuts push universities to seek funding and undertake research that is most likely to fill funding gaps and increase revenue (McCluskey, 2017).

Today, research that incorporates ethical considerations and underlying structural problems is often ignored or marginalized. As Giroux (1983) argued as this trend emerged, "theory and knowledge are subordinated to the imperatives of efficiency and technical mastery and history is reduced to a minor footnote in the priorities of 'empirical' scientific inquiry" (p. 87). Today questions of what *should be* or *is* tend to dominate those of what *can be* undermining the radical potential of knowledge to empower students and improve the human condition (Van Heertum, 2005). On top of this, the nature of tenure and advancement decisions in our top universities appears to disincentivize engagement in the public sphere, which too often has no positive, and even sometimes negative, impacts on both.

In a broader sense, the cuts to funding that have occurred as a result of neoliberal policy force universities to seek alternative sources of revenue, that pushes them to make a series of decisions that arguably undermine the broader goals of the university, including: (1) hiring and promoting professors and researchers who bring in the most money, thus putting a huge focus on income generation and thus the funders with the most money, (2) disadvantage those doing research without any serious opportunity for funding before or additional revenue after, (3) as previously argued, allowing the further infusion of corporations and the elite into the university by both taking over administration and offering necessary funding with a concomitant increase in the influence they can bring to bear over not only research but curricular decisions, and (4) Realigning higher education employment away from a balance between research and teaching to a teaching force predominantly comprising part-time, low pay educators who are ultimately answerable to student evaluations, often at the cost of creativity and rigor (Mintz, 2021).

More instrumentalized notions of post-secondary education have influenced the liberal arts and smaller liberal arts colleges quite profoundly as well. Regarding the former, as revenue and funding cuts demand cuts in programs, the liberal arts have often been the first on the chopping block and the most profoundly hurt over time. And in regard to the latter, we have seen the shuttering of a number of liberal arts colleges, the reduction in enrollment at others, the merging of still others and a change in focus on those that have survived (Harris, 2018; Jaschik, 2019). The overarching theme that emerges from these attacks on the liberal arts and humanities is the devaluing of knowledge not directly tied to market activity and future employment (Slouka, 2009; Stover, 2018).

Before moving on to deconstruct neopopulist higher education "policy," it is important to first define what I mean by neopopulism, particularly as the term remains highly contested. Taggart (2000) condensed down to six common characteristics: (1) hostility to representative politics; (2) idealization of the "heartland"; (3) populism as an ideology lacking core values; (4) a reaction to the crisis; (5) populism as containing fundamental dilemmas that makes it self-limiting; (6) a context-dependent phenomenon. Rooduijn (2015) extracts four minimal features out of twelve commonly associated to populism: (1) the emphasis on the central position of the people; (2) criticism against the elite; (3) conception of the people as a homogeneous entity and (4) the conviction of living in a period of serious crisis. And De Cleen et al. (2018) use the work of Laclau and other post-Marxists to define populism more simply as, "a form of reason that centres around a claim to represent 'the people', discursively constructed as an underdog in opposition to an illegitimate 'elite'." At its core, neopopulism encapsulates movements defined by uber-nationalism, xenophobia, trenchant masculinity, a redefining of elites as the well-educated within social and creative industries, a push toward authoritarianism and suspicious of all forms of diversity, while wholly supportive of capitalism.

Since neopopulism is a relatively new instantiation of a movement that goes back at least as far as the 1890s, it is difficult to ascertain the exact contours of their plans specific to higher education, particularly given the reality that they have differing and often soft ideological commitments, but three cases can provide a frame to hypothesize the place where their rhetoric meets policy. The first is the dire situation of the Alaska University system after dramatic cuts from the Republican Governor put state higher education on the cusp of collapse (Hazelrigg, 2019). The second is the rhetoric and action of the Trump administration and Betsy Devos during his four years in office. And finally, is the Wisconsin University system under the tutelage of right-wing darling, and ex-Governor, Scott Walker.

In the case of Alaska, the Koch-Brothers funded Republican Governor Mike Dunleavy's decision to veto parts of the proposed state budget cut funding to a number of public institutions and initiatives in the state including a massive 41 percent cut in state funding to the University of Alaska ($135 million). In the wake of this decision, the Board of Regents voted 10 to 1 to declare financial exigency, a move that generally precedes layoffs and program elimination, Moody's downgraded their credit rating and they were in danger of losing their accreditation, before a compromise was reached that halved the cuts to $90 million and spread them over several years. In the Trump administration, Devos made it harder for international students to study in the U.S., targeted affirmative action programs, tied research funding to free speech and barred schools received federal funding from certain types of diversity training. The administration also tried to push short-term job programs and pressure higher education to align its goals more closely with business needs. Finally, the ex-Governor of Wisconsin Scott Walker, heavily funded throughout his political career by the Koch brothers, waged and unprecedented assault on higher education during his eight years in charge, largely dismissing the value of a four-year degree, questioning the public role and work ethic of faculty and even trying to end the "Wisconsin Idea" of the state system to "extend knowledge and its application beyond the boundaries of its campuses and to serve and simulate society." He sought to change the spirit of the larger goal by replacing the "search for truth" with "meet the state's workforce needs;" possibly the greatest literal example of the neopopulist push as it relates to education. He cut hundreds of millions of dollars in funding and then increased tuition, pushing the financial onus onto students and their parents. And he successfully undermined the tenure system, a bête noir of conservatives for decades.

Combining the three together with other anecdotal evidence, a picture emerges of the neopopulism vision for higher education, including: (1) cut funding to schools and push for the restoration of the broad for-profit model that both instrumentalize and vocationalize knowledge while often targeting poor and minority students with a substandard education, (2) work to increase student loan debt load and limit the options for reducing that debt through public service or needs based, lower interest loans, (3) following the lead and legacy of David Horowitz's Academic Bill of Rights, attack progressive educators, progressive ideas and progressive education in general in service of circumscribing the curriculum, most recently with attacks on critical race theory, (4) attack PC culture in all perceived forms, using the extremes of the higher education culture to solidify their position as champions of an atavistic return to a mythological past of white male rule while redefining "elites" as those highly educated individuals that champion progressive politics (Kronman, 2019), (5) heavily related to the former two, use higher education to advance their anti-feminist agenda through the support, for example, of those charged with rape over the victims of sexual violence and other attempts to diminish feminist movements, (6) attack sciences and research based on the scientific method, particularly as relates to global climate change, instead focusing on suspect research fed through conservative media outlets, (7) attacking tenure, to take away Academic Freedom and hold professors hostage to an increasingly hostile school administrations, and (8) Fund university research themselves, thus partially controlling the contours of what kinds of research are undertaken (and, by extension, those that are not).

In fact, recent research has highlighted the ways in which the richest families in America are behind many of the most successful attacks on science, knowledge and truth, as well as the nativist movement that ultimately put Trump in the White House. *Kochland* (2019) highlights the Koch brothers' role as the key architects of the global warming skepticism movement, among other ways they have circumvented and undermined democracy to further their corporate interests. Walsh (2019) provides a comprehensive list of corporate influence over higher education including by the Walgreen and Olin Foundations and the Federalist Society, among others pushing conservative and free market ideologies. And a recent *New York Times* profile highlighted the role Cordelia Scaife May, an heiress to the Mellon family's banking and industrial fortune, played as the most important donor to the modern anti-immigration movement during her lifetime (Kulish & McIntire, 2019).

It appears the rhetoric and material effect of the conservative critiques of higher education have paid dividends with their base, with a Pew Research study finding that between 2015 and 2017 alone, Republicans belief that higher education has a positive impact on the country fell from 58 percent to 36 percent, while 58 percent now claimed it has a negative effect (Kaufman, 2017). In 2019, the numbers were even worse, with only 33 percent believing college has a positive effect and 59 percent claiming the obverse. Overall, only half of all Americans see higher education as good for the country while 38 percent believe it has an overall negative impact, up 12 percentage points from 2012. In the study, those who had a negative perception of higher education cited admissions decisions, free speech constraints on campus and a general suspicion about their role and benefits (Parker, 2019).

Bringing the two ideas together, a surprising alignment emerges between the neoliberal policies that dominated higher education for decades and more recent neopopulist efforts. Neoliberalism attempts to accomplish it aims through a firm commitment to epistemological positivism and economic determinism, while supporting modern globalized capitalism and codifying the status quo indirectly. Neopopulism instead focuses on epistemological skepticism and cynicism as methods to take advantage of the increasing political insularity and retribalism of our age, spoon feeding ideology to a largely uncritical audience without worry of critical investigation, critical analysis or even rationality sneaking in to challenge their narrowing worldview.

Both seem committed to profoundly circumscribe both the teaching, research and learning done at universities and colleges, placing all three in line with corporate and economic interests or their skewed worldview. Both seem intent on expanding the intrusion of corporate ideology into our colleges and universities and allowing the logic of business to become the logic of higher education (Hunt, 2018; Tuchman, 2011). Both, for differing reasons, appear poised to continue pushing for the end of tenure and less job security for already underpaid faculty, controlling academic freedom through job insecurity. And both seem intent on starving postsecondary institutions of the funding necessary to meet any broader goals or aims beyond those of training workers for their future careers, while undermining the cosmopolitan consciousness and multiculturalism that once oriented many teacher education programs and the broader discourse within universities.

In both cases, there is essentially an attack on the broader goals of higher education, on its ability to inculcate students with the knowledge, skills and confidence to challenge entrenched power and the status quo, to push students to contest conventional wisdom and seek out their own truth, to confront and overcome the power of hegemony to perpetuate social reproduction and to build a foundation for a more ecumenical, balanced and tolerant view of the world. The overarching aim of both seem heavily invested in undermining the left and progressive politics through a process of imposing myopic epistemology on the public and instrumentalizing education. And, as many have argued, including Labaree (1997), instrumentalizing education within the popular consciousness makes many of the other changes we have outlined here unnecessary, as it creates a mindset in many students that education is merely a route to their future economic success (or at least survival).

In the end, it is a new cynicism that is resistant to the idea of honest, reasoned debate, a vibrant public sphere and the power of democracy to improve our lives and only highlights the importance of reinvigorating the progressive public intellectual to combat these trends. Without the intervention of educators across the globe at all levels, these trends will only strengthen over time, pushing future generations further to the brink of a new world order for the few.

Educators as Public Intellectuals

In the introduction, I argued that we must move beyond critique to reimagine how we can combat the neoliberal and neopopulist movements. To accomplish this shift, I believe a multi-pronged approach is necessary that includes a shift in political discourse toward more positive, forward looking rhetoric;

a reaffirmation and commitment to alternative media and to actively engage in the space of social media to combat the motivated "fake news" models that have become so successful in massive propaganda campaigns; civics education instituted across all years of schooling and more targeted attempts to fight conservative reigns on curriculum. It includes continued experimentation in more progressive modes of popular, proportional and direct democracy, methods to fortify protections against another coup attempt, particularly with more and more conservatives seemingly intent on killing the nearly 250-year experiment in American democracy based on a lie and a nod toward authoritarianism as superior to popular rule.

Chenoweth (2021), in her extensive and unparalleled research into effective popular movements against authoritarianism has found four strategies that have proven most effective in enacting progressive change: (1) mobilization of mass popular participation, (2) defection of people in authority (including elites, security forces and even opposition party members), (3) moving beyond mass demonstrations to include noncooperation (e.g., strikes and boycotts), and (4) staying disciplined, even in the face of increased repression. Looking at this list, beyond activists, NGOs, nonprofits and organizers, that there is a huge role for educators to play. But what does that look like? My argument is that educators dedicated to social justice and democracy must dedicate themselves to intervening in the classroom and the public sphere, and that means becoming public intellectuals themselves. This includes:

1. Finding ways to do research in service not just of social justice but democracy as well and disseminate that research outward through channels of the public sphere, like newspapers, popular Internet sites, the mainstream media and, maybe, most importantly, engaging in social media sites like Facebook and YouTube that can reach broad audiences most susceptible to fake news.
2. Working to educate and empower students to become civically engaged themselves. I don't believe this entails teaching them about their own oppression or working to get them to think like we do, but instead creating the space to allow them to find their own place in the world and their own positions of interest.
3. Safely engaging in political action ourselves. As Freire highlighted so often, we must be leaders not through our words alone, but our actions.
4. Modeling democracy by being authoritative rather than authoritarian in the classroom and inviting democratic participation whenever possible.

5. Teaching not just tolerance, but empathy and embrace of difference, most effectively by allowing students to see through other's eyes and not judging them, even if you disagree with their perspective. This does not mean to forgive or excuse bad acts, but to start with the question of why, rather than with judgment.
6. While I love *Pedagogy of the Oppressed* (1970) and his other work, I think the most practical advice Freire provides in all his writings is his last book, *Pedagogy of Freedom* (1998). It is a guide to being a good teacher working to fight the cynicism at the heart of neoliberalism. While neopopulism is arguably the much bigger threat today, I believe there is a different version of the same cynicism, maybe even deeper in this case, and that education is even more central in the new environment.

Freire believed that teachers should be public intellectuals, working to empower students and provide them with the critical thinking skills, creativity and knowledge necessary to fight for a better future. Having taught in U.S. colleges and universities for 13 years, what I find the most striking is a persistent cynicism among college students believing that politicians are corrupt as a rule, that things are likely to stay the same rather than change in positive ways and a blindness to the positive change even within their own lifetime. And I think this is a key area where professors can have a huge impact, by inspiring students to believe in hope and the possibility of change.

Broader reforms in higher education could also help educators to play a more active role in the public arena, for example the move away from traditional tenure has already established a model that can incorporate service as a component of advancement, thus providing a space to engage in the community and more public research rather than relying solely on academic journals and publications that rarely cross over into the public view. Professors must also work collectively to reassert their power over institutional decision-making, including—whenever possible—vetoing hiring decisions that further ensconce corporatization into governance. At the more basic level, they must work to redress both the attacks on tenure and the ways administration has weaken faculty senates. And they must work to reaffirm their academic freedom, particularly in the wake of a number of high-profile firings or tenure decisions that appear to have political undertones. More generally, professors should work to combat the attacks on the humanities and arts and attempts to commodify higher education as the training ground once charged to the corporate world itself.

Conclusion

The commodification and instrumentalization of knowledge together with the rightward shift in popular discourse has created an environment that is arguably antithetical to reasoned debate and notions of thick democracy. Leaders across education and the public sphere must confront the trenchant common sense and work at the local, national and international levels to provide viable alternatives to the new world order. I believe ample examples exist inside and outside the United States of building effective collaborations between universities, educators and social/community organizations. And I believe it is the responsibility of activists, intellectuals, educators and scholars dedicated to social justice to seek out opportunities to work in collaboration with others to get their research and knowledge out to the public, toward altering the nature of debate and discourse in the public sphere.

Yet how do we make this work within an environment that appears to be moving in the opposite direction? As dictates of a prescribed and proscribed curriculum increasingly infiltrate higher education, how is one to navigate the wrought space of administrative oversight, particularly if not protected by tenure? I believe here it is a question of not only content but pedagogical strategies themselves. I have found that active learning creates the trust and engagement necessary to spark truly critical and creative thinking. This includes project-based approaches (like running a campaign for political office) that are iterative in nature, in-class debates, simulations (on conflict resolution, creative development and the like), small group assignments both inside and outside class, flipping the classroom (when possible) and other course specific approaches to be incredibly effective at creating a deeper engagement with material, a more group-oriented classroom and opening a liminal space where students are more likely to share personal experiences that can resonate with others. At the core level, it means ensuring that you provide a safe space for students who disagree with your perspective, build mechanisms to increase empathy among students and fortify their belief in democracy and social justice as worthy goals.

This must be coupled with efforts to move beyond research within your field to engage with the public whenever possible. Many professors have become effective communicators of complex ideas to the public by capitalizing on social media sites like Facebook or YouTube. Others have made themselves available to news outlets, working to correct the tendency of media to sensationalize or oversimplify complex issues and research. Educators can also go directly to elected officials with their research or seek out community collaboration that can go beyond simply researching and reporting on problems to actively working to solve them, in a collaborative process of participation-based research. Finally, educators can simply open the door for students to think differently and challenge their own deeply held beliefs simply by showing them how easily we fall into the trap of believing something because of who told it to us or through the power of ritualization and social reproduction.

Intellectuals like Mike Rose, Jeannie Oakes, Jonathan Kozol, Paul Krugman, Jeffrey Sachs, Joseph Stiglitz, Henry Giroux, Thomas Piketty and Emmanuel Saez, Ta-Nehisi Coates, Masha Gessen, David Autor, Slavoj Zizek, and Diane Ravitch, among others, have all been effective at bridging the gap between the sometimes-insular world of academia and the larger public debates on key issues of our times. They have done so by moving from the top-down approach of organic intellectuals of the past to engaging in public dialogue and conversation, becoming immersed in the marketplace of ideas. We need to build alliances and solidarity among groups and organizations to ensure that the next wave of intellectuals can continue to fight for the principles of democracy, equality and social justice.

The central point is that professors have specialized knowledge, access to multiple channels to disseminate that knowledge and providence over the most radical space of possibility left in society—a college classroom with the door closed. Educators in higher education must reaffirm the importance of science and the scientific method to their students, reinforce the culling process necessary to truly use the Internet as a meaningful source of useful information and help students to understand how to adapt knowledge to real life situations. In the miasmic cloud of skepticism that now fogs our world, it is imperative that we reassert the importance of legitimation and justification for truth claims and the power of hope and imagination to improve the world in the future.

Notes

1 Parts of this chapter have been previously published in the following book chapters: Van Heertum, R. (2020). Neoliberalism, neopopulism, and democracy in decline: The university under attack on multiple fronts. In K. Roth & Z. Ritter, *Whiteness, power, and resisting change in US higher education: A peculiar institution* (pp. 103–127). Palgrave Macmillan, and Van Heertum, R. (2022). The American university and the struggle for democracy. In Roth, Ritter Kumah-Abiwu & Camacho, *What Can Be: Emancipatory Changes in U.S. Higher Education*. Palgrave MacMillan, 2022.

References

Ágh, A. (2018). The long road from neoliberalism to neopopulism in ECE: The social paradox of neopopulism and decline of the left. *Baltic Journal of Political Science*.

Capano, G. (2014). The re-regulation of the Italian university system through quality assurance. A mechanistic perspective. *Policy and Society, 33*(3), 199–213. https://doi.org/10.1016/j.polsoc.2014.08.001

Chenoweth, E. (2021). *Civil resistance: What everyone needs to know*. Oxford University Press.

De Cleen, B., Glynos, J., & Mondon, A. (2018). Critical research on populism. Nine rules of engagement. *Organization, 25*(5), 649–661.

Freire, P. (1970). *Pedagogy of the oppressed*. The Continuum International Publishing Group, Inc.

Freire, P. (1998). *Pedagogy of freedom*. Rowman & LittleField Publishers, Inc.

Giroux, H. (1983). *Theory and resistance: A pedagogy for the opposition*. J. F. Bergin.

Halpern, S. (2017). How he used Facebook to win. *The New York Review of Books*. https://www.nybooks.com/articles/2017/06/08/how-trump-used-facebook-to-win/

Harris, A. (2018). The liberal arts might not last the 21st century. *The Atlantic*.

Hazelrigg, N. (2019). Alaska's new path. *Inside Higher Education*. https://www.insidehighered.com/news/2019/07/23/alaska-president-offers-new-plans-following-vote-financial-exigency

Hetherington, M., & Ladd, J. (2020). Destroying trust in the media, science, and government has left America vulnerable. *Brookings*. https://www.brookings.edu/blog/fixgov/2020/05/01/destroying-trust-in-the-media-science-and-government-has-left-america-vulnerable-to-disaster/

Hunt, J. (2018). *University Nike: How corporate cash bought American higher education*. Penguin Random House.

Jaschik, S. (2019). Private nonprofit college closures, 2016-present. *Inside Higher Education*. https://www.insidehighered.com/news/2019/06/13/list-private-colleges-have-closed-recent-years

Kaufman, E. (2017). The next right-wing populist will win by attacking American education. *The National Review*. https://www.nationalreview.com/2017/07/right-wing-populism-next-target-american-higher-education/

Kulish, N., & McIntire, M. (2019, August 14). In her own words: The woman who bankrolled the anti-immigration movement. *The New York Times*.

Labaree, D. (1997). Public goods, private goods: The American struggle over educational goals. *American Educational Research Journal, 34*(1), 39–81.

Leonard, C. (2019). *Kochland: The secret history of Koch industries and corporate power in America*. Simon and Schuster UK.

Mason, R., & Adams, R. (2019, May 30). May urges Tories to cut tuition fees and revive student grants. *The Guardian*. https://www.theguardian.com/education/2019/may/30/may-urges-tories-cut-tuition-fees-revive-student-grants

McCluskey, M. (2017). Public universities get an education in private industry. *The Atlantic*. https://www.theatlantic.com/education/archive/2017/04/public-universities-get-an-education-in-private-industry/521379/

McLuhan, M. (1965). *Understanding media: The extension of man*. McGraw-Hill.

Mintz, B. (2021). Neoliberalism and the crisis in higher education: The cost of ideology. *American Journal of Economics and Sociology, 80*(1), 79–112.

Newfield, C. (2016). *The great mistake: How we wrecked public universities and how we can fix them*. JHU Press.

Nichols, S., & Berliner, D. (2007). *Collateral damage: How high-stakes testing corrupts America's schools*. Harvard Education Press.

Nureev, R., Volchik, V., & Strielkowski, W. (2020). Neoliberal reforms in higher education and the import of institutions. *Social Sciences, 9*(5). https://doi.org/10.3390/socsci9050079

Parker, K. (2019). The growing partisan divide in views of higher education. *The Pew Research Center*.

Rooduijn, M. (2015). The rise of the populist radical right in Western Europe. *European View, 14*(1), 3–11.

Ross, J. (2019). China embraces '1+X.' *Inside Higher Education*. https://www.insidehighered.com/news/2019/07/11/new-chinese-model-higher-education

Slouka, M. (2009). Dehumanized: When math and science rule the school. *Harper's Magazine*. https://harpers.org/archive/2009/09/dehumanized/

Štech, S. (2011). The Bologna Process as a new public management tool in higher education. *Journal of Pedagogy, 2*(2), 263–282.

Stover, J. (2018). There is no case for the humanities: And deep down we know our justifications are hollow. *The Chronicle of Higher Education*. https://www.chronicle.com/article/there-is-no-case-for-the-humanities/

Taggart, P. (2000). *Populism*. Open University Press.

Tuchman, G. (2011). *Wannabe U: Inside the corporate university*. University of Chicago Press.

Van Heertum, R. (2005). How objective is objectivity? A critique of current trends in educational research. In *Interactions: UCLA Journal of Education and Information Studies, 1*(2).

Van Heertum, R. (2009). *The fate of democracy in a cynical Age: Education, media & the evolving public sphere*. ProQuest, UMI Dissertation Publishing.

Van Heertum, R. (2021). Neoliberalism, neopopulism, and democracy in decline: The university under attack on multiple fronts. In K. Roth & Z. Ritter, *Whiteness, power, and resisting change in US higher education: A peculiar institution* (pp. 103–127). Palgrave Macmillan.

Van Heertum, R., Arnove, R., Berman, E., Keating, J., Preston, R., & Burke, P. (2013). Educational reform in Australia, England and the United States. In C. A. Torres, R. Arnove, & S. Franz, *Comparative education: The dialectic of the global and local*. Rowman & LittleField Publishers, Inc.

Van Heertum, R., & Torres, C. A. (2009). Policy and domination: Uses of critical theory in the public arena. In G. Sykes, D. Plank, B. Schneider, & T. Ford, *Handbook of education policy research*. Routledge.

Walsh, D. A. (2019). *Conservative philanthropy in higher education*. https://www.urban.org/sites/default/files/2019/06/27/conservative_philanthropy_in_higher_education.pdf

Weiner, L., & Compton, M. (2008). *The global assault on teaching, teachers, and their unions: Stories for resistance*. Palgrave Macmillan.

7 Life Lessons Learned (L³) Inside a Neoliberal Capitalist Educational System

Victor M. Mendoza

What Was Going on in Nature

My current ride through the higher levels of education have been serendipitous, as a hard determinist Radical Anarchist in criminology, my self-narrative remains that the education system has always remained part of that trip called, my Life. My foray into the American education system began in the early 1970s, when Juan Crow was a lingering miasma, and the school system did not allow children of Mexican descent to speak West Texican dialects in the school. Porter (1998) wrote an article claiming people whose original language was not English wanted English-only for their kinds. Porter definitely does not speak for me and almost a decade later Mitchell (2019) contradicted this. Just as descendants of 19th century Germans in Wisconsin remained Germanically monolingual into the 20th century, monolingual West Texican people in my barrio could still function, work and progress in the late 1960s and early 1970s in West Texas. Prior to the 1920s researchers found that acceptance of multiple languages for communication and education existed in the US, yet not all languages were accepted equally, and people in Indigenous, Asian, and Mexican communities found their languages systemically segregated and disparaged (Bybee, Henderson, & Hinojosa, 2014).

For about fifty years, into the early 1970s, English immersion, (aka sink or swim) policies governed instruction for children who began and lived life with a non-Ameringlish language, schools provided few or no remedial services, retaining children in the same grade level until enough Ameringlish was mastered. Lyndon Johnson who had taught at a Juan Crow school in Cotulla, Texas in the 1920s helped pass the Bilingual Education Act (BEA),

Title VII of the Elementary and Secondary Education Act in 1968, even if funding was premised on the belief that Mexican-based bilingual students were deficient (Bybee et al., 2014). In 1974 a landmark US Supreme court case, *Lau vs. Nichols*, decreed educators needed to provide affirmative remedial efforts for linguistically deprived children, which is how many of the young West Texicans in my school ended up in "special ed." Conservatives and reactionaries began to immediately attack this progress using similar reasoning used against people of African descent of separate but equal, yet that did not guarantee a right to bilingual education, and four years later in *Castañeda v. Pickard*, the Court devised a three-prong test. Bilingual educational programs must be "based on sound educational theory," they must be "implemented effectively with resources for personnel, instructional materials, and space," and after a trial period, the program must prove effective in overcoming language barriers/ "handicaps." While a Federal mandate for English-only never caught on, at least 23 states have adopted "Official English" legislation (Bybee et al., 2014).

Practical Knowledge—What Are We and How I Got Here?

My behavior seems outlier behavior from the onset, an acquaintance of mine once labelled me as an intrepid child, this was a subjective view from a third party. My youth was typical in that two parental units raised me in a West Texian barrio, in a town populated by white supremacists of all colors and flavors, it would be years before the structural racism endemic to neoliberal capitalism would become obvious to me. The neoliberal public school of my formative years taught the wasp Western canon, focusing on reading, writing and rithmetic, the fundamentals of an American education which focused on dead white males and their supremacy. During my formative years in the educational system my rebellious streak pushed me away from the rigid structure of school or attempting to seriously compete scholastically with the other bipedal featherless primates. The Texas school system from 1980 to 1985, my years of High School, used a state legislated and mandated testing program, called the Texas Assessment of Basic Skills (TABS), for students in grades 10, 11, and 12, known by students as achievement tests (Kruse, 1985).

TABS became a way for students across the state to take a standardized test, and this allowed individual students, parents, and teachers to receive mastery information for each basic skill (8 to 12 per test). Classroom summaries were dismissed, but TABS data about campuses and districts were made public which allowed for comparisons between districts and allowed public attention on student learning to a rare degree; the results appeared dramatic

(Kruse, 1985). Local school officials could identify which methods appeared to be successful instructional strategies and use them in a way that seemed to increase student achievement statewide, with overall student performance increasing, and differences in student performance between minority and majority subpopulations decreasing. In 1980, only 70 % of grade 9 students mastered the mathematics portion, by 1985 the mathematics portion was mastered by 84% of grade 9 students, and mastery of the reading portion improved from 70 to 78% in the same six years (Kruse, 1985). TABS started with the usual conservative resistance to change associated with such large scale educational efforts, that is just part of the natural human condition in the unfolding, developing Universe we find ourselves in.

Certain teacher groups fought the idea of a "state program" standardizing the needs of different types of students, supporters of TABS believed it was "basic" skills that were being monitored, for all educators and students (Kruse, 1985). School administrators did not like the idea of comparing schools because of student populations with diverse ethnic composition, family wealth, and limited Ameringlish proficiency, even if reporting strategies for TABS included demographic information as a part of reporting student performance. Standard reports for every school district included three separate aggregations, including one for all students, one for limited Ameringlish proficient students, and another for non-limited Ameringlish proficient students and certain minority organizations closely monitored the TABS program. For those times most people tried to ensure that TABS tests were free from bias, and the results of those efforts were made public and transparent, with even critics agreeing that because of this push for equity results of minority groups improving at a faster rate than majority students appeared apparent, which helped overcome what little opposition was left (Kruse, 1985).

Did the TABS program succeed and become widely accepted, even decades later the answer remains nuanced, but it must be remembered that the entire program was tied to state monies, which were given to school districts on the basis of eligibility for free or reduced priced meals. That law also required those districts to use the funds to create and use appropriate remedial programs for the students who faltered on the basic skills measured by TABS, using the perspective of a "needs assessment" strategy for state monies (Kruse, 1985). Supporters of TABS, including educators and public policy makers, also wanted documentation of educational needs and empirical evidence of educational improvement when it occurred, by the end of the program, no organized group offered public opposition to TABS (Kruse, 1985). The true evaluation of the program should probably be based on what happened during the Reagan era, in 1984, a special session of the Texas

Legislature, passed one of the most comprehensive educational reform laws in Texas public education, House Bill 72 which altered not only the way the State Board was constructed, but it radically altered the way education was financed, requiring students to make 70 or higher to pass regular school classes, while also using it to curtail participation in school sports, known as the "no pass, no play" rule in Texas schools, it even required teachers to pass "competency" tests and ultimately revised the TABS program. The TABS language was moved from the compensatory education section of the Texas Education Code to a separate section of its own, creating a bloated new program, the Texas Educational Assessment of Minimum Skills (TEAMS) which tested every student in grades 1, 3, 5, 7, 9, and 11, approximately 1.6 million students annually (Kruse, 1985).

What Was Going on in Nurture (Anti-Thesis)

My foundational real life lessons learned were transmitted through the primary West Texican language of the late 1960s/early 1970s and it would not be until about 1974 that formalized American would start to become my secondary language. The propaganda model, taught even among Anarchists, is usually a neoliberal ideological model that we live in a *nation* called the United States of America, that began when some intrepid, pink-skinned people made a voyage across the sea and arrived on Turtle Island to find it "abandoned." Allow me to define some terms, people in the US donot speak English, they speak American (or Ameringlish), English people speak English, just like only people from Spain speak Spanish (Castellano), everyone else outside these cultures speaks an amalgam or polyglot language, and therefore my primary language was West Texican, a blend of Spanish, Indigenous, Texian and American. School in the early 1970s in West Texas was still under the "English" immersion ideology, done under the penalty of corporal punishment, if children spoke their primary native language instead of "English-only," we would be beat on the bum with a wooden paddle of some kind.

The school was funded by a tax base of West Texas petrodollars which remained local in those years and not long after my graduation from High School, a billionaire named H. Ross Perot began a wealth transfer from wealthier districts to special interests using the Select Committee on Public Education (SCOPE), and HB 72 became known as "Robin Hood," by 1990 (ADP, 2009). The claim was that monies from wealthier districts would be given to the State who would then redistribute it to the poorer districts, but through the plutonomy of the kakistocracy the wealthier and larger districts have gamed the system to take a larger share. But that was all in the future, in my time local taxes paid for local schools and they were flush with West Texas petrodollars, which afforded me what some have labelled as an upper middle class educational experience. The school district provided the students not only a low student-to-teacher ratio, but teachers who had years of experience teaching their subjects, because the district could afford to pay petrodollar wages. Children, who chose, could get a well-rounded education not only in the white western canon, but music, sports and multiple extracurricular activities, which the school paid for, through the local tax base. While my family was relatively poor for the town, my father who was without formal education, illiterate and only spoke West Texian, earned well above the national average in the petroleum mines. And while much can be said about reinforcing the neoliberal capitalist system through the school, a vein of critical thinking was imparted along with the tales of Greek mythology and dangling participles. Seemingly there was no explicit education about Revolución, for the masses there was conformity, but there was an underlying current of subversive critical thinking for individuals such as myself. The fundamentals that were imparted to me at the Primary and Secondary level of education is the reason for this paper, "The same boiling water that softens the potato hardens the egg. It's about what you're made of, not the circumstances," at least according to a current anonymous meme. This may seem anathema to people of a Revolutionary bent, but a current reading of Robert Sapolsky will confirm what neuroscience is beginning to understand, we are products of Nature and Nurture (Sapolsky, 2017).

There is a memory of my mother being upset because a West Texican went to the school board and protested that not allowing children to speak their primary non-Ameringlish language was discriminatory. This ideology partially drove my mother, even if she never wanted me to become a yo no sabo malparido, in fact until my father and mother passed, we only spoke West Texican, never in Ameringlish. Unfortunately, my mother was wrong for believing that we should accommodate the ubiquitous wasp culture, after all we didn't land on Plymouth Rock. Fortunately, my parents were just smart enough not to assimilate and turn me into a yo no sabo malparido, so like all the people around me in Airport Additions and beyond, my primary language was West Texican. Currently when encountering another speaker of polyglot Spanish, that becomes my primary language of immediate communication, this is done consciously as an act of Revolución, Delgado reminds us that "Mexicans were lynched for 'acting too Mexican' – speaking Spanish too loudly or reminding Anglos too defiantly of their Mexicanness," (2009, p 299).

The problem with white supremacy is that it remains insidious and eventually even those with melanin begin to identify with the melanin-deficient and their white supremacist ideology, developing a white supremacist false consciousness, meaning they believe they can get in and fit in. After the school allowed us to begin speaking West Texican in the schools, the act lost subversiveness, but neoliberalism is nothing if not resilient and the fundamentals had been laid down since the integration of Juan and Jim Crow, (Mahoney, 2020). While neoliberalism has accommodated teaching of the historical narrative of white supremacist practices of Jim Crow laws, Rodney E. Hero writes that "Less studied are the impacts of these discriminatory practices regarding Latinos/as, especially in the Southwestern United States," (Mahoney, 2020). According to the denotative explanation given in the *Oxford Learner's Dictionary*, schools in America provide a good education, which is "the process of receiving or giving systematic instruction, especially at a school or university," or as Gatto (1992) writes "The truth is that schools don't really teach anything except how to obey orders." Gatto was just echoing Godwin who wrote that the State "will not fail to employ it [state sponsored schooling] to strengthen its hands and perpetuate its institutions" (2013, p. 399). Goldman wrote that children in public schools were a "delicate human plant in a hothouse atmosphere, where it can neither breathe nor grow freely," (1906, n.p.) and plants that grow in hothouses normally donot survive in real world conditions. Goldman wrote that school no matter if "public, private, or parochial...is for the child what the prison is for the convict and the barracks for the soldier—a place where everything is being used to break the will of the child, and then to pound, knead, and shape it into a being utterly foreign to itself," (2009, n.p.) The reader should understand that the current American society is ruled by a kakistocracy that serves its own plutonomy even if the neoliberal ideology blathers on about capitalism, free markets and free will and this shapes how and what children/adults are taught.

My hometown a few years ago had been in a bit of a brouhaha concerning what had started out as a whites-only school and plans to demolish it, because of asbestos issues, while the other school buildings had been renovated. The Jim Crow school on the other hand was converted into a school system warehouse, even with "asbestos" issues, while the Juan Crow school was unceremoniously sold to a West Texican church who eventually tore it down to build a new church building. The first West Texican mayor of our town told me the story of the Juan Crow school at a cookout around 2014, because he had actually gone to that school along with other West Texican children in the 1950s, eventually the school was demolished with no hullabaloo from even the West Texican citizenry. The whites-only school, which was my Middle School, is the current Administration Building for the school district and the legacy of the Juan Crow school is just a memory that none of the yo no sabo malparidos went and protested *against*, like they did *for* the legacy of the white-supremacist school.

Several years ago, while on a day trip through West Texas to test my car, my cousin and me stopped in Iraan, Texas at the Alley Oop Park and Museum and in one of the rooms was a stack of school yearbooks. Iraan, like many West Texas towns had sundown laws, not just for people of African descent, but for the predominantly large population of people of Mexican descent who had lived here hundreds, if not thousands of years, due to our indigenous lineage. The yearbooks went back into the 1950s and there was an obvious pattern; up until the early 1960s only white people went to a school with yearbooks, which to an individual of Mexican descent such as myself was a glaring discrepancy. When West Texican children did begin appearing in the yearbooks circa the mid-1960s only children from the first to fourth grade (Primary School) appeared, with fifth through eighth being Middle School and ninth through twelfth being High School. It must be understood that winning the "hearts and minds" of the children creates a subjugated population, this was understood by Louis Hubert Gonzalve Lyautey as part of his strategy to counter the Black Flags rebellion along the Indochina-Chinese border as early as 1895 (Porch, 1986) or as US cavalry captain Richard Henry Pratt, who opened the first Native boarding school in Carlisle, Pennsylvania stated,

> A great general has said that the only good Indian is a dead one, and that high sanction of his destruction has been an enormous factor in promoting Indian massacres. In a sense, I agree with the sentiment, but only in this: that all the Indian there is in the race should be dead. Kill the Indian in him, and save the man. (Pratt, 1892, p. 46)

The reason for including only children from fourth grade down was to indoctrinate them early and "save the man" with neoliberal capitalist white supremacist ideology that has always plagued American education.

Synthesis

Here is a critical race theory for you, when did history in this geographical location begin, if you went to an American school, "prehistory" is the 20,000 plus years that indigenous people lived here, which is typically relegated to one chapter of most elementary American history books. Glorification of white supremacy, American and otherwise, takes up the other twenty-four chapters of the book, even if it's only been about 300 years of the 10–20 thousand years of people living on this continent. As West Texicans we are an amalgam of arriviste blood, mixed with the much older genetics of the First peoples who arrived tens of thousands of years ago, yes tens of thousands, which gives us dibs on blood and soil. This remains a determinist Anarchist critique of the current system that most people buy into, not just in America, but worldwide, the system typically named neoliberal capitalism, which in a more nuanced form is a kakistocracy run plutonomy and influences the entire edifice (Baraza, 2015). While there is much credit to be given to revolutionary thinkers in general, what Radicals saw and philosophized on at the inception has evolved, even if they believed that they were addressing the human condition in general, the times they are a changing.

Much of what has been discovered about people and how their central nervous systems work has radically changed just in the last forty years, with the ability to measure the individual and their brain, growing exponentially. From a determinist perspective people just repeat behaviors they sense around themselves and the neurochemical payoff from communal sharing drives many of the motivators, in plainspeak, "monkey see, monkey do," (Sapolsky, 2017). So, this tendency to conform is human, as many studies will show, even for those of us who believe ourselves to be non-conformists, again determinist behavior is limited by the options available in the natural environment that immediately surrounds the individual, no man is an island. The modern method of inculcating and indoctrinating individual people was not created by neoliberal capitalists, they just happen to be a dominant mindset which influences the individual life forms we call human. These individual people maneuver themselves into influential positions within the current structures, not only do they get in so they can fit in, but they perpetuate these thought forms, manifesting them. Here the Catechism of youth remains appropriate, "For we wrestle not against flesh and blood, but against principalities, against powers, against the rulers of the darkness of this world…," (BH, 2021, n.p.) in other words, we wrestle against our own individual mindsets which is assailed by the propaganda of the principalities. Practitioners of late stage capitalism understand this, that most human beings are lazy, possess a conformist mindset and subliminally desire to be part of the in-group and this synergizes the inculcation and indoctrination that passes for education in America and the world.

What we seek are trends to understand why entire swaths of people tend to blow in one direction or another and the recent studies of people and neurology seem to favor physics and the Laws of Conservation, it therefore becomes easier to go with the flow, which in this case is neoliberal capitalism or for those paying attention, the plutonomy of the kakistocracy. While pursuing a PhD in criminology it has become apparent that most people in this field are conformist to the neoliberal capitalist mindset and those that are slightly more critical of the field often become reformist. It has been my experience that even people of African descent in historically Black Colleges and Universities such as the one attended by me, refuse to attack neoliberal capitalism, because fundamentally they believe that reform is better than Revolución, and that if "they" get the chance "they" can improve the neoliberal capitalist structure from the inside. We are all conformists, but some of us just don't conform to the norm, which is currently neoliberal capitalism.

Do better ways to educate people, especially children exist, than the current neoliberal capitalist model of indoctrination and inculcation, por su puesto, to quote Anton Ego "In the past, I have made no secret of my disdain for Chef Gusteau's famous motto: Anyone can cook. But I realize, only now do I truly understand what he meant. Not everyone can become a great artist, but a great artist can come from anywhere" (PizzaDewd, 2011). Along with this idea is the idea of Harry Callahan, "A man's got to know his limitations," (Movieclips, 2014) the fact is no matter how much you want it, Nature did not imbue everyone to swim as fast as Michael Phelps, run as fast as Usain Bolt or give birth to babies. My natural inclinations were the limitations of my education, genetic predisposition and the alignment of several forces acting upon and within me, coupled with parents who allowed me to be my bad self which pushed me in a critical, skeptical direction, which has served me both ill and well. Having spent almost two decades under bales and hatches in a monastic environment, self-education became an important part of my Life, but it would not have been possible had it not been for the fundamentals taught by neoliberal capitalist schools. Even while in the belly of the beast, my nature impelled me to seek out reading and educational material suitable to my temperament, and that is what we are mentally conversing about here. The current educational system is designed to produce slaves, but not all of us take to the conformity and this leaves a gap in understanding how to create a better system of learning that would be more beneficial to the masses and society. My current field of focus is criminology and how this became my pursuit was primarily due to Natural events, not so much individualism, but more of a determinist push, with heavy doses of chaos and complexity theory thrown in, "We don't invent our mission; we detect it," (Frankl, 1959).

My educational experience under a neoliberal capitalist framework in this particular corner of the world allowed me to later perform an informal ethnography, evaluate and compare, individuals from my hometown, with a cross-section of people from across the state between the years 1985 and

1994. Contrary to criminological belief, not all prisoners are morons as propagandized (Herrnstein & Murray, 1994) while there may be statistically more anti-social or asocial individuals in prisons, the same can be said for the volunteer military and policing. Texas prisons may be heavily weighted statistically with people of African and Mexican descent in proportion to the majority white population in Texas, yet that truly made no difference in evaluating the results of how well educated people were in the basics, depending on their places of origins. My metric for intelligence as a result of education is fundamental; the ability to critically learn information, shift the paradigm and act on it, so the quicker an individual can perform these steps the more intelligent they are. Regurgitating information as given, going to a certain school or passing standardized exams with high marks, in and of themselves, are not metrics of high intelligence, yet in the neocapitalist capitalist educational system these badges of conformity supposedly equal high intelligence. Another low sign of intelligence that is touted by the neoliberal capitalist as a badge of honor is patriotism for the state and many prisoners actually embrace this one fully, along with the laughable idea of "street knowledge."

The current focus is how does the current system of schooling perpetuate neoliberalism on a systemic level related to capitalism and how schools are constructed into stores where professors are products and students are consumers (corporate schooling). Also how on a social level schooling fosters selfishness, exploitation of individuals/groups, opportunism, careerism, and how standardization of curriculum, syllabus, assessments, and evaluations are exploited in the name of fairness and equality. The examination of neoliberalism promoting standardization, rubricization because of the influence of the factory (academic industrial complex) Taylorism capitalist model were focal points in 1980s/1990s Anarchist zines. Rubricization is the conditioning of students to behave the same and become dependent on rubrics for behavioral cues, which in short is the 2.0 of standardization, taking "monkey see, monkey do," to the next level. Revolutionary literature is rife with this systematic systemic analysis, much of which was made available to me through zines like *Factsheet Five*, during my monastic state-funded existence in the late 1980s/early 1990s, much of which arose out of the radical student movements of the 1960s. It was the same "radical" students in America who now sit in neoliberal positions that helped stifle and recuperate any radical revolutionary changes in the schooling systems, and this is what seems missing in the analysis. Much like the people of African descent who teach criminology at the HBCU attended by me for a PhD, the desire is not so much to uplift their masses and society, but to uplift members of their immediate tribe to positions using false consciousness and neoliberal capitalist realism.

What Is My Job

A professor of mine used this common meme "Complaining about a problem without proposing a solution is called whining," which is derived from a speech by Theodore Roosevelt, claiming my radical critical criminology without solutions was whining. My Atheism notwithstanding, studying world religions of all kinds was a focus for some years and so this analogy arose as a response to the professor, which did not seem to sit well with his Judeo-Xian belief system. In the Hindu religion and my personal understanding of Trimurti allows that the cosmic functions of creation, preservation, and destruction are personified as a triad of deities, typically Brahma the creator, Vishnu the preserver, and Shiva the destroyer. My life mission is neither to preserve the current schooling methods of the neoliberal capitalist nor to create a new one in its place, my life mission is to continuously assail structures invented by people to suit their personal agendas. While it seems obvious, the current neoliberal capitalist system of schooling is designed to create and maintain slavery.

My writings offer no solutions to the questions posed, what it does is give some explanation of how my journey allowed me to have a more critical, radical and revolutionary mindset in spite of the fact that my schooling took place inside of the same neoliberal capitalist institutions we are attacking. By no means is this supportive of neoliberal capitalist statist systems or ideologies, so my question to the readers is how many of you arrived at your current ideology because of an alternative school system and how many of you actually went to a neoliberal capitalist school? Yet here we are and how did we get here, with everything geared to turn us into slaves, how much is nature, how much is nurture, can you capture the lightning in a bottle that created your life circumstances? My outlook is not meant to be all things to all people, nor to serve as confirmation bias for your ideology or an interpretation of ideology, it remains an explanation of my experiences on this third rock from the Sun, in my current lifeform incarnation. It remains biased by the impressions made upon my organisms' neurochemical net by the cosmic subatomic existence it finds itself inside of and the deterministic patterns created by the interplay between the larger externalities, to the self-contained internalized structure that manifests as me. Lastly, a society should be judged by the way it treats its most vulnerable and we live in a society, Revolution is the only solution to the political pollution of the institution.

References

American Diploma Project (ADP) Network. (2009). *Taking root: Strategies for sustaining the college- and career ready agenda*. Achieve. Retrieved from https://www.achieve.org/files/Texas-SustainabilityCaseStudy_0.pdf

Baraza, P. (2015). "Kakistomoboplutocracy." *iampeterbaraza*. Retrieved from https://iampeterbaraza.wordpress.com/2015/10/24/kakistomoboplutocracy/

BH. (2021). "Ephesians 6:12." Bible Hub (BH). Retrieved from https://biblehub.com/ephesians/6-12.htm

Brett Koeshall. (2013, September 24). *The Octagon (1980)*. [Video]. Retrieved from https://www.youtube.com/watch?v=eQZSx-0z_Z0&t=3545s&ab_channel=BrettKoeshall

Bybee, E. R. Henderson, K. I., & Hinojosa, R. V. (2014). "An overview of U.S. bilingual education: Historical roots, legal battles, and recent trends." *Faculty Publications*. BYU Scholars Archives. 1615. pp. 138–146. Retrieved from https://scholarsarchive.byu.edu/cgi/viewcontent.cgi?article=2627&context=facpub#:~:text=In%201924%2C%20the%20Meyer%20v,private%20schools%20in%20the%20state.&text=Linguistic%20segregation%20continued%20in%20Texas,y.

Delgado, R. "The law of the Noose: A history of Latino Lynching." (2009). *Harvard Civil Rights – Civil Liberties Law Review* (CR-CL). U of Alabama Legal Studies Research Paper No. 2533521. Vol. 44., pp. 297–312. Retrieved from https://scholarship.law.ua.edu/cgi/viewcontent.cgi?article=1457&context=fac_articles

Frankl, V. E. (1959). "*...trotzdem Ja zum Leben sagen: Ein Psychologe erlebt das Konzentrationslager*:(*...Nevertheless saying 'Yes' to Life: A Psychologist Experiences the Concentration Camp*)." Beacon Press

Gatto, J. T. (1992). *Dumbing us down: The hidden curriculum of compulsory schooling*. New Society Publishers.

Godwin, W. (2013). *An enquiry concerning political justice* (Oxford world classics), ed. Mark Philip. Oxford University Press

Goldman, E. (1906). "The child and its enemies." *Mother Earth*. Vol. 1, No. 2. Retrieved from https://theanarchistlibrary.org/library/emma-goldman-the-child-and-its-enemies

———. (2009). "The social importance of the modern school." *The Anarchist Library*. Retrieved from https://theanarchistlibrary.org/library/emma-goldman-the-social-importance-of-the-modern-school

Herrnstein, R. J., & Murray, C. A. (1994). *The bell curve: Intelligence and class structure in American life*. Free Press.

Hero, R. E. (2000). *Faces of inequality: Social diversity in American politics*. Oxford University Press.

Kruse, K. L. (1985). "A brief history of testing policies in the State of Texas." The Office of Technology Assessment Congress of the United States. Pp. 267–275. Retrieved from https://www.princeton.edu/~ota/disk2/1987/8724/872430.PDF

Mahoney, M. G. A. (2020). "The new Juan Crow: Modern-day consequences of historic racial discrimination against Latino/a Americans." Honors Theses at the University of Iowa. Pp. 1–25. Retrieved from https://ir.uiowa.edu/cgi/viewcontent.cgi?article=1476&context=honors_theses

Mitchell, C. (2019). "'English-only' laws in education on verge of extinction." *EducationWeek*. Retrieved from https://www.edweek.org/teaching-learning/english-only-laws-in-education-on-verge-of-extinction/2019/10

Movieclips. (2014, February 6). *Magnum Force (10/10) Movie CLIP – A Man's Got to Know His Limitations (1973) HD*. [Video]. https://www.youtube.com/watch?v=uki4lrLzRaU&ab_channel=Movieclips

Nietzsche, F. (1998). *Beyond good and evil*. Dover Publications.

PizzaDewd. (2011, February 5). *Ratatouille Ego's Review* [Video]. https://www.youtube.com/watch?v=Ih6jcKd7VwU&ab_channel=PizzaDewd

Porch, D. (1986). "Bugeaud, Gallieni, Lyautey: The Development of French Colonial Warfare." In Peter Paret (Ed.), *Makers of modern strategy: From Machiavelli to the Nuclear Age*. Princeton University Press.

Porter, R. P. (1998). "The case against bilingual education." *The Atlantic*. Retrieved from https://www.theatlantic.com/magazine/archive/1998/05/the-case-against-bilingual-education/305426/

Pratt, R. H. (1892). "The advantages of mingling Indians with whites." In *Proceedings of the National Conference of Charities and Corrections*, ed. Isabel C. Barrows. Nineteenth Annual Session held in Colorado. Retrieved from https://play.google.com/books/reader?id=dpJIAAAAYAAJ&pg=GBS.PA46&printsec=frontcover&output=reader&hl=en

Roosevelt, T. R. (1910). "The man in the arena." "Citizenship in the Republic" speech. Retrieved from theodorerooseveltcenter.org/Learn-About-TR/TR-Encyclopedia/Culture-and-Society/Man-in-the-Arena.aspx

Sapolsky, R. M. (2017). *Behave: The biology of humans at our best and worst*. Penguin Press.

8 Triple Helix: The Intertwining Strands of Biology, Ideology and Policy in the Neoliberal Revolution

Laura I. Schleifer

Introduction—Neoliberalism: An Evolved Social Darwinism for the Post-Modern Era

In 2013, the Mont Pelerin Society, the original neoliberal think tank, discreetly held a special conference at The Universidad San Francisco de Quito (USFQ) on San Cristóbal in the Galapagos Islands. Perhaps the location's significance might have escaped many, but for those familiar with Darwinism, eyebrows raised. After decades of denial, it appeared neoliberals might be openly embracing their long-suspected Social Darwinist leanings. The conference brazenly announced its intention to connect, "evolution to freedom, reinforce the debate that opposes classical liberal society and statism using biology and anthropology as theoretical foundations, and to understand cultural evolution of open societies in order to escape the tribal order" (Society & Mont Pelerin, 2013). Eliminating lingering doubts, the Society then addressed their location choice:

> During this world summit, natural and social science scholars will discuss the evolution of and current challenges to freedom. Galapagos provides a unique environment for this; it inspired Charles Darwin, over one hundred fifty years ago, to make his groundbreaking contributions to the biological sciences. (Society & Mont Pelerin, 2013)

Adding to the Social Darwinist vibe was speaker Charles Murray, F. A. Hayek Chair Emeritus in Cultural Studies at the American Enterprise Institute neoliberal think tank and co-author of *The Bell Curve* (Herrnstein & Murray, 1995), which argued that IQ is intrinsic to race. Murray's latest book, *Human Diversity: The Biology of Gender, Race, and Class* (Murray, 2020), claimed that race and gender are not constructs but are biologically rooted, and explained inequality not through historical power imbalances, but through biology.

It would be tempting to write off Murray, and the conference organizers and attendees overall, as cranks trying to revive long-disproved nineteenth-century ideas. However, the Mont Pelerin Society is not some marginal organization; it is the birthplace of the premiere socio-economic ideology today. Starting in the 1970s, and expanding in the 1980s with Reagan and Thatcher, neoliberalism became the dominant force economically, politically, and in every other area of life. Yet, most people have neither heard of nor can define neoliberalism (Monbiot, 2016). It is like pollution: silently pumped out by corporations until it poisons everything, but undetectable.

While there is no single definition, Oxford dictionary defines neoliberalism as, "A political approach favoring free-market capitalism, deregulation, and government spending reduction" (Oxford University Press, 1992). It may seem odd that such a pro-corporate organization would hold a conference on natural and social sciences, but neoliberalism is an economic system/ideology that promotes environmental deregulation while also justifying its existence through supposedly aligning with nature. Other conference speakers further reveal how conceptions of nature intertwine with neoliberal ideology. Among them were Robert Boyd, a University of California in Los Angeles (UCLA) Anthropology Professor focusing on sociobiology, evolutionary psychology, genetics and ethology; Richard Wrangham, Harvard Biological anthropology professor; Peter Whybrow, Semel Institute for Neuroscience and Human Behavior Director at UCLA; David Kohn, Drew University Oxnam professor emeritus of Science and Society and general editor of the DarwinDigital Library of Evolution; Stewart Kauffman, University of Pennsylvania biochemistry professor emeritus and author of *At Home in the Universe: The Search for Laws of Self-Organization and Complexity* (Kauffman, 1996); Robin Dunbar, evolutionary psychology professor at Oxford; and Leda Cosmides and John Tooby, University of Santa Barbara psychology and anthropology professors and co-founders of evolutionary psychology. These speakers appeared alongside those who oppose democracy (Minogue, 2012), promote Capitalist Christianity (Sirico, 2012), and even promote scientific racism (Murray, 2020).

The Galapagos conference raises a question of whether evolutionary psychology, evolutionary biology, sociobiology, ethology, and other disciplines related to the 1970s genetics revolution have been influenced by neoliberal philosophy/ideology. This question is salient for several reasons. First, both neoliberalism and the genetics revolution gained prominence in the 1970s–1980s. Second, both promoted a certain worldview that seemed to mutually reinforce itself through these two movements. And third, a key neoliberal strategy has involved corporations coercing academics into conveying information that advances a pro-business agenda through strings-attached funding. Corporate sponsorship has influenced economics, political science, humanities, philosophy, social science and scientific curricula and research by lobbying for cuts to higher education public funding, then filling that gap themselves by providing funding in exchange for universities promoting pro-business ideas, as well as recruiting and sponsoring scholars willing to promote neoliberal ideology in their discipline (McClusky, 2017). Thus, the question is whether direct collaboration has occurred between the evolutionary sciences and pro-corporate forces seeking to naturalize neoliberalism by shaping public conceptions of nature, or whether neoliberal ideology has shaped scholars' perceptions of nature and humanity, themselves.

Copy the Socialists, Convert the Intellectuals

From its onset, neoliberalism was an economic movement seeking an epistemology. This quest was largely driven by one of its founders, Austrian economist Friedrich Hayek, who realized that for an economic ideology to influence the public and affect government policy, it first had to captivate the intellectual class. Although Hayek considered socialists deeply misguided, he admired how they inspired intellectuals with a revolutionary Utopian vision. In his essay, "The Intellectuals and Socialism" (Hayek, 1949), Hayek described an ideological landscape at once trans-historical and also specific to that time and place. Hayek described intellectuals as "second-hand idea dealers" who didn't necessarily have expertise nor experience in matters they spoke about. Yet, these generalists acted as the "sieve" through which the public was exposed to new ideas. Thus, their support was essential for transforming a society's ideology. According to Hayek, specialists and pragmatists with real world experience often despised and dismissed intellectuals, but underestimating the influence of intellectuals was a mistake, for they alone could transform public opinion, and once enough of them reached a consensus, their position would eventually become the mainstream perspective. Moreover, intelligent and good-willed intellectuals were the most likely to be socialist, for idealists flock to Utopian ideas and balk at reformist limitations and practicalities. Thus, university faculties were filled with socialists influencing upcoming generations—something Hayek believed was the route to tyranny, or as he put it in his most famous book, *The Road to Serfdom* (Hayek, 1944).

Liberalism, in contrast, was in an epistemological crisis. Hayek claimed that since liberalism had long-since formed its ideology, its maintenance had become the task of functionaries.

Philosophically, it was a dead-end. Having more institutional influence than socialists actually stunted liberals by making them fear what they might lose by venturing too far out of the box. Thus, all the radical energy was propelling socialism, while liberalism had become the status quo. Hayek believed that to win the long game, neoliberals had to complement their economic agenda with a radical philosophy that would intrigue intellectuals. Otherwise, even hyper-Capitalist America might become socialist within a few generations (Hayek, 1949).

From a contemporary neoliberal-era vantage point, it is difficult to imagine socialism potentially taking hold in Western society. Yet, the circumstances of Hayek's time were in many ways an inversion of today. World War II had just ended; fascism had (supposedly) been defeated, and the newly-socialist U.S.S.R. had emerged a global superpower. Eastern Europe and half of Germany had also just turned socialist. Socialism was also internationalist, grounded in ideas of permanent revolution and "workers of the world uniting." The year Hayek wrote "The Intellectuals and Socialism," Mao Zedong had just taken power in China. Moreover, the West had become aware that classically liberal laissez-faire capitalism had led to the stock market crash, Great Depression, and rise of European fascism. Thus, socialism held widespread appeal because it promised protection from both mass poverty and social pathology wreaked by economic instability and inequality. Even those who opposed socialism admitted some degree of socialist-influenced policy was needed to rein in capitalism, because without such safeguarding capitalism's flame would spread uncontrollably and burn itself out, prompting a full-blown socialist revolution. During the Depression, U.S. Communist Party membership surged from just 20,000 to over 66,000, sparking fears of a Communist rebellion. Thus, social welfare policies were not only meant to protect the lower classes from predatory capitalism, but also to protect capitalism itself from capitalism, and from socialism—i.e., to promote the health and longevity of capitalism (Lipset & Marks, 2001). Much like a vaccine uses part of a virus to stimulate the immune system's ability to ward off infection by the whole virus, the Keynesian economic model that dominated the post-war period injected the existing capitalist system with aspects of socialism to ward off full-blown socialist revolt. Keynesian economics operates on the premise that capitalist societies require a social safety net, government regulation, a strong middle class, powerful trade unions, and nearly-full employment to economically flourish and maintain social and political stability. These ideas formed the UK postwar consensus and U.S. New Deal, which brought about the "Golden Age of Capitalism." Indeed, even Hayek himself proposed policies during that period that sound downright Leftist by today's standards. In the anti-socialist *The Road to Serfdom*, Hayek nevertheless advocated for government-provided housing, healthcare, and other benefits, prompting Ayn Rand to excoriate him as a "compromiser," "abysmal fool," an "ass," and a "vicious bastard" (Wapshott, 2012).

It was in this climate that neoliberals began discussing how to revive and remake classical liberalism. Their goal was to create a new liberalism, distinct from collectivism, but in 1944 Hayek published *The Road to Serfdom* in response to the growing possibility of global socialism, founded the Mont Pelerin Society in 1947, and the neoliberal movement was born.

Neoliberal Economists, and the Rich Men Who Fund Them

Upon publishing *The Road to Serfdom*, Hayek began attracting wealthy businessmen keen to implement his ideas. Of these, American Harold Luhnow and British Anthony Fisher were among the most ardent supporters. Hayek's first sponsor, Luhnow, had inherited his uncle William Volker's fortune. Volker, a German Evangelical Christian progressive businessman, likely never could have imagined his nephew using his poverty-relief fund to support right-wing economists and conservative intellectuals leading a movement to restructure U.S. higher education, defeat communism, slash social services and strengthen America's Christian heritage. Luhnow became enamored with Hayek's theories after reading a condensed version of "The Road to Serfdom" in *Reader's Digest* (Von et al., 1988), and commissioned Hayek to write an Americanized version of the text. While that never materialized, Luhnow's inheritance bought faculty positions for Hayek and fellow Austrian School economist Ludwig Von Mises, both of whom had previously been unable to find academic positions due to their controversial ideas, at the University of Chicago and New York University economics departments.

Within these universities and others, neoliberal economists spent the following decades plotting how neoliberalism would replace U.S. New Deal economics, supplant the postwar consensus in the U.K., and eventually stretch its tentacles worldwide. In large part, the Volker Fund paved the road to neoliberalism (McVicar, 2011).

The Volker Fund was unique at that time because while other conservative businessmen were funding anti-New Deal policies, they were not joining their efforts. Ironically, in addition to learning from socialists how to successfully build an ideological movement, neoliberals achieved their goals through collectivism. Luhnow decided to pool his resources with two other anti-New Deal magnates, William Regnery and E.B. Earhart, and Sun Oil, Chrysler and Dupont executives. The Volker Fund also began hiring academics like Columbia University economists Ivan Bierly and F.A. "Baldy" Harper.

Harper later created the Institute for Humane Studies at George Mason University, which recruits and platforms new generations of neoliberal academics. During this period, the Volker Fund connected conservative scholars through Symposia, a nationwide book distribution effort, and other networking opportunities. Using a multi-pronged approach to achieve ideological dominance, Volker Fund's Humane Series published 15 conservative volumes; created the National Book Foundation, which awarded several right-wing texts per year, placed rave reviews of the winning books in influential publications, and distributed thousands of copies to libraries nationwide; promoted new pro-corporate economists, including several Nobel Prize winners; and established the Foundation for Economic Education (FEE) in 1946, and the Intercollegiate Society of Individualists in 1953. These last two organizations widely spread the neoliberal gospel in academia. An early U.S. libertarian institution, the FEE's mission was to "conduct, encourage, promote and support research in economics and all branches of related social sciences" (McVicar, 2011, p. 11), and disseminate that information widely.

FEE founder Leonard Reed traveled cross-country on Volker's dime, distributing copies of *The Road to Serfdom* and *Economics in One Lesson* (Hazlitt, 1946) to business owners and anyone else who would read them. Yet again, the neoliberals copied the socialists, even naming The Intercollegiate Society for Individualists after the Intercollegiate Society for Socialists. Focusing on U.S. college recruitment, the Volker Fund promoted conservative commentator William F. Buckley as a Milo Yiannapolis-esque enfant terrible New Right dandy, funded his campus lecture tours, provided scholarships and research funds to right-wing students and faculty, and distributed additional reactionary reading materials (McVicar, 2011).

Meanwhile, Antony Fisher, whose fortune came from his battery-cage chicken operation that single-handedly brought factory farming to the U.K., started a neoliberal think tank, the Institute of Economic Affairs, in London. Ten years earlier, Fisher had asked Hayek whether to enter politics to help spark the neoliberal revolution. Hayek's response: "No. Society's course will only be changed by a change in ideas. Politicians will follow." Twenty-five years later, Margaret Thatcher thanked Fisher for "creating the conditions that made it possible for Thatcherism to win" (Freedman, 2011).

Another neoliberal economist, the Nobel Prize-winning James Buchanan of George Mason University, also attracted a devoted following among businessmen. Buchanan, who hailed from Jim Crow era-Tennessee, combined the neoliberal ideas of Hayek, Von Mises, Friedman, and their peers with the property supremacism of John Calhoun, a pre-Civil War U.S. Vice President who defended slavery on the basis of "state's rights" and "individual property rights." According to Calhoun, owners using their property at their discretion was a fundamental American liberty—even if that "property" consisted of actual human beings. Thus, any governmental interference in that process entailed the oppression of the property holder, and violated liberal values. Combining this idea with neoliberalism, Buchanan created Public Choice Theory, which claimed that societal freedom required the ability of individual citizens to override public-majority decisions. Thus, forcing any individual to pay taxes, obey public safety measures, or follow labor, environmental, or human rights laws would be discriminatory. In *The Limits of Liberty: Between Anarchy and Leviathan* (Buchanan, 1975), Buchanan unironically argued that protecting freedom might require despotism. To defend freedom from the threat of democracy, Buchanan advised a "constitutional revolution" to thwart democracy through privatization. After all, the federal government could force public schools to desegregate, but attempting that with privately-funded schools would violate the owners' rights. Buchanan was also the first to propose privatizing universities and ending tuition subsidization, thus increasing corporate control of research and development, weakening democracy by making higher education inaccessible to the poor, and discouraging student/youth activism by forcing students to cost-evaluate their education, work jobs while in school, and saddling them with debt. Bolstered by millions of dollars from Charles Koch, Buchanan and fellow Mont Pelerin Society-economist Murray Rothbard, of the Koch-founded neoliberal Cato Institute, designed a top-secret master plan for the business community to take back their country from Big Government (Tanenhaus, 2017). In the U.S., that plan was launched in 1971, when right-wing Supreme Court justice Lewis Powell wrote his infamous "Powell memo," an oligarchical call-to-arms commencing the corporate takeover of America (Moyers, 2021).

Roots of Neoliberalism: Eugenics and Social Darwinist Influence on Movement Founders

When examining how science and other academic disciplines have been used to naturalize neoliberalism, it is important to consider the historical era influencing its founders. Hayek, Luhnow, Von Mises, Friedman, Fisher,

Buchanan, Rothbard and their peers grew up during the height of Social Darwinism and eugenics in countries where those movements were most prominent. Hayek, whose aristocratic Viennese family included philosopher-mathematician Ludwig Wittgenstein, a University of Vienna botany lecturer father, and a grandfather who taught natural sciences and wrote renowned works on biological systematics, was fascinated with biology. Growing up, he helped his father with botanical work, read genetic and evolutionary works by Hugo de Vries and August Weissman, and studied the philosophy of anthropologist Ludwig Feuerbach (Klein, 2014). In later life, Hayek applied these ideas to culture and economics. Hayek promoted bottom-up rather than top-down economics, claiming that market economies, like ecosystems, work best without interference from above.

According to bottom-up economics, just as biological organisms develop through an increasingly complex self-directed process, so do individuals within economic systems. Each individual knows what is best for them--and only them. Hayek's chief complaint about top-down economics—i.e., socialism—was that any one individual or group could not see the entire market, only their piece, and thus, no individual or group should make decisions that affect the rest (Degrauwe, 2009). Instead, Hayek promoted spontaneous order, the idea that from apparent chaos, order emerges. While this theory typically describes natural phenomena, Hayek applied it to economics: the idea that individuals all acting independently out of self-interest, without consciously considering the common good, would nevertheless create a flourishing economy that more efficiently allocated societal resources than any central planning could achieve (Lubin, 2019).

Culturally, Hayek did not identify as a Darwinist, and criticized Social Darwinism for applying biological principles to social evolution. In Hayek's view, social/cultural evolution involved passing down developed traits, aka traditions, intergenerationally, whereas in biological evolution traits became prevalent through a process of elimination, i.e., natural selection. In this sense, Hayek's views more resembled the pre-Darwinian biologist Jean-Baptiste Lamarck's evolutionary theory, which postulated that advantageous traits an animal developed during its lifetime could be passed down to their offspring. In practice, this belief meant that Hayek was socially conservative, opposing the determinism he promoted economically on the grounds that what is natural in humans isn't necessarily good, and thus traditions, not instincts, should be followed. While it may seem like Hayek's cultural and economic views oppose each other, the common logic lay in Hayek's controversial concept of group selection, which posits that while all cultural groups are biologically the same, some develop traditions that evolutionarily advantage them over others. Thus, liberal conceptions of equality and meritocracy met Social Darwinist (and culturally supremacist) notions of evolutionary selection, minus the biological component (Zywicki, 1999).

Other neoliberal founders also had complex attitudes toward Social Darwinism, fascism and eugenics. Ludwig Von Mises, Hayek's Austrian school mentor, joined the Fatherland Front, a fascist, ultra-nationalist Austrian political party, during the Nazi era. It, too, rejected biological supremacist notions in favor of cultural supremacy. On the other hand, anarcho-Capitalist Murray Rothbard rejected the view that it is culture, not biology, that determines difference (and superiority), rooting his elitism in conceptions of natural law. In *Egalitarianism as a Revolt Against Nature and Other Essays* (Rothbard, 2000), he railed against the Lockean notion of the *tabula rasa*, preferring the standard bio-essentialist approach to Social Darwinism. Neoliberal financiers Antony Fisher and Harold Luhnow also had eugenicist/fascist leanings. After Luhnow's Christian awakening impelled him to demand everyone associated with the fund become Christian, the Volker Fund imploded. Luhnow's behavior drove away many of its members, who were subsequently replaced by overtly anti-Semitic Nazis and right-wing religious fundamentalists (McVicar, 2011, pp. 201-203). As for Fisher, his choosing Ralph Harris, a British Eugenics Society member who advocated against democracy, to run the Institute for Economic Affairs speaks volumes (Freedman, 2011).

Perhaps it is not coincidental that both Luhnow and Fisher were involved in animal husbandry, considering that eugenics was founded on the Darwinian premise that if humans were animals rather than divine beings created in God's image, they could be controlled and bred just like non-human animals. In Fisher's case, we can only surmise how his battery hen and failed turtle meat operations may have affected his ideas about humans, but Luhnow, a former cattle rancher who had studied animal agriculture in college, bluntly stated that everything he knew about humans he had, "learned from working with cattle" (McVicar, 2011, p. 196).

The Biology of Neoliberal Belief

The question of neoliberalism's relationship to the genetics revolution of the 1970s, and its subsequent fields of sociobiology, evolutionary psychology, and related disciplines, remains. On one level, the theories in those disciplines are a gene-based throwback to Darwinian/biologically-rooted notions of human nature, which opposes classic liberal concepts of meritocracy, individual free will and rationality, all of which are present in neoliberalism. On the other, as recent years have shown, the leap from neoliberal/free market libertarian to far right determinist is a short one (Lewis, 2017). There is also evidence of neoliberal economics directly influencing evolutionary science. For example, British biologist John Maynard Smith's Evolutionary Game Theory applies Rand Corporation mathematician John Nash's Game Theory, a pillar of neoliberal economics that claims humans act selfishly through engaging in a rational decision-making process (Rational Choice) that concludes that selfish actions will best serve their interests, to evolutionary science. The key difference is that in Evolutionary Game Theory, Smith replaced the reason-based human self-interest of economic Game Theory with an instinct-based self-interest in animals, who instinctively act in selfish ways because their genes seek to survive long enough to pass on genetic material. The classic text, *The Selfish Gene* (Dawkins, 1976) claims this biological behavioral drive also manifests in humans. Another theory of that period that has influenced the evolutionary sciences, along with ecology, psychology, sociology, political science and economics, is the Tragedy of the Commons (Hardin, 1968). It too presumes that humans are innately selfish in its assertion that if everyone was allowed unrestricted, equal access to natural resources, they wouldn't share fairly, causing chaos, conflict, environmental degradation and resource shortages.

Ironically, the solution its creator, the ecologist, zoologist and eugenicist Garrett Hardin, proposed was to either relinquish control of nature to governments, or privatize it. What connects these seemingly opposite solutions is the Hobbesian belief that commoners cannot control themselves, and thus need hierarchical management. It was the rare theory that both authoritarian socialists and neoliberal capitalists endorsed. In evolutionary biology, researchers began applying the theory to destructive phenomena in nature, theorizing that non-human individuals also destroy nature through innate selfishness (Rankin et al., 2007).

According to some within the field, the fact that conclusions drawn by scientists seemingly mirror right-wing political ideology is no accident. In *Not in Our Genes,* (Lewontin & Kamin, 1984) evolutionary biologists argued the sciences were used to rationalize hierarchy, inequality, competition, aggression, selfishness, dominance-seeking, territoriality, tribalism, xenophobia and related traits in response to feminists, Black activists, and other oppressed groups during the 1960s demanding egalitarianism. Citing influential texts like *Sociobiology;The New Synthesis* (Wilson, 1975) and *The Selfish Gene* (Dawkins, 1976), Lewontin and Kamin (1984) revealed how evolutionary science has been used to transform public consciousness about what is natural and thus justifiable, such as naturalizing human rights atrocities through claiming they are driven by a selfish gene that wants our genes, and those of our closest genetic relatives, to survive, even if that means killing everyone with competing genes. Subsequently, in the decades since the genetic revolution, the far right has used genetic science to justify ethno-nationalism, such as the British National Front claiming racism is "natural" because of our selfish gene (Lewontin & Kamin, 1984). Anthropologist Susan McKinnon (2005) also challenges the use of evolutionary psychology as a form of bio-essentialist determinism that naturalizes neoliberalism. While Lewontin, Rose and Kamin and anthropologist McKinnon all criticize science being politicized this way, their criticism differs in that McKinnon pinpoints this type of reasoning's flaw as its failure to distinguish between the behavioral motivations of humans and other species, while Lewontin, Rose and Kamin assert it is the interpretations of other animals/nature themselves that are both biased and off-base, not just applying those observations towards humans.

Another fierce critic of neo-Darwinian interpretations of genetics was evolutionary biologist Lynn Margulis, who rejected the idea of competing genes in favor of a theory of evolution based on symbiosis. Margulis did not hesitate to criticize the scientization of economics occurring during that era, describing some of her contemporaries as,"wallowing in a zoological, capitalistic, competitive, cost-benefit interpretation of Darwin" (Mann, 1991, p. 5). Another prominent evolutionary biologist, Peter Corning, is currently challenging the neo-Darwinian interpretation of gene science with his Synergism Hypothesis, which explores how genes cooperate to develop further complexity rather than competing, a process that occurs other arenas of nature, as well—including human nature. Thus, an economic system truly in alignment with nature would be based on fairness and social justice, not greed and selfishness, which are both destructive to nature, and are the opposite of how nature actually functions (Corning, 2012).

Finally, one of the sharpest critics of the Tragedy of the Commons theory, which sparked the 1970s ecology movement's neo-Malthusian depopulation rhetoric, justified privatization of nature, and reinforced the humans-are-innately-selfish ideology emerging from the genetics field, is Marxist Geographer and Anthropologist David Harvey. In "The Future of the Commons" (Harvey, 2010), he revealed how the theory misleadingly presents a small-scale situation—local farmers sharing a field— to represent global problems, thus flattening the power differential between local farmers vs huge multinational conglomerates. It is not simply humans who greedily swallow-up too many resources, but rather those whose systemic power over others enables them to exploit resources for personal profit.

Thus, Hardin's proposed solution--to relinquish resource control to those above—is not only not the cure, it's the source of the problem.

Harvey also critiqued similar themes in his essay, "Population, Resources and the Ideology of Science," (Harvey, 1974), stating that despite the scientific community's claims of neutrality, its framing of the global ecological crisis in terms of overpopulation revealed pro-Capitalist bias, and not- so-coincidentally appeared right in time to replace 1960s campus critiques of Capitalism. Moreover, Harvey claimed, insisting on science's ideological neutrality is, paradoxically, ideological, as scientists' fear of appearing biased ultimately impedes them from using their work to benefit humanity. This ideology of denying ideology also aligns with neoliberalism, for despite its founders' clear efforts to create an ideology, a central tenet of neoliberalism is its supposed lack of ideology, since unlike ideology-driven movements like communism, fascism or religion, neoliberalism has no uniting principle, only millions of autonomous individuals operating separately out of rational self-interest.

Psychological Effects of Neoliberal Ideology on Students and Beyond

Additionally, neoliberal self-interest ideology is being filtered through other disciplines, including sociology, philosophy, psychology, criminology/criminal justice, law, history, social work and political science (Vanberg, 2004). The negative psychological impact of university privatization- induced faculty salary cuts and job instability, labor outsourcing to adjuncts and grad students, tuition hikes, standardization, and other such policies on both students and faculty is compounded by the interweaving of neoliberal ideology into course curricula. Behavioral research studies done on economics students show that being taught humans are innately selfish leads students to become more paranoid about the selfishness of others, and subsequently more selfish themselves (Vedantam, 2017). The all-pervasive lessons of Rational Choice Theory, Spontaneous Economic Order, Game Theory, Public Choice Theory, the Tragedy of the Commons and related theories are reified by universities that function like for-profit organizations by exploiting staff, outsourcing labor, hiring administrators without teaching experience, turning students into consumers and faculty into temps, standardizing and rubricizing education in order to produce quantifiable results, depending on private funding that corrupts research integrity, pressuring faculty to apply for grants rather than focus on pedagogy, and coercing students into choosing pragmatic majors for fear their hefty investment won't ultimately pay off. Combined, these factors create a campus and society that is more selfish, short-sighted, risk-averse and conformist, and less socially conscious, creative, confident and forward-thinking. In his essay, "The Death of American Universities," world-renowned scholar Noam Chomsky reveals that this state of affairs exists by design. In the 1970s, the Trilateral Commission, whose members populated the Carter administration, pinpointed universities as the source of the civil rights, feminist, anti-war, environmental and anti-capitalist movements, and claimed universities threatened the future of American Capitalism by "failing to indoctrinate the young." Thus, they decided to foist neoliberalism on the unsuspecting public, and no sector of society had a bigger target on its back than academia (Chomsky, 2014).

Conclusion—Remaking Society and the Courage to be Utopian

Today, with neoliberalism—and liberalism itself—in crisis, record-high inequality, climate collapse, rising fascism and ethno-nationalism, and renewed interest in socialism, it is worth considering what we can learn from the neoliberal rise to power. Ironically, just as Hayek learned from socialists, socialists can learn from neoliberals. As Hayek himself realized, the road to societal transformation requires having the courage to be Utopian and risk ostracization by the status quo— something factory-style universities discourage in students and faculty alike. Critical pedagogue Henry Giroux stresses the importance of revolutionaries existing in a permanent state of quasi-exile, with "one foot in, and one foot out," of the system, critiquing it from within without being dependent on it (Giroux, 2016). In Hayek's time, socialists were gaining ground through this insider/outsider status.

Today's Left-wing academics and activists must conceptualize what that might entail in the current neoliberal paradigm of chronic precarity, wage deflation, high living costs, and other challenges.

Moreover, conceptions of nature, animal nature, and human nature are pivotal to creating the epistemological shift needed to foment societal transformation. Considering the neoliberal founders' strategic awareness of that, direct collaboration between neoliberal organizations and the evolutionary sciences to naturalize the values of neoliberalism through science may have occurred. However, it is also possible that scholars in those fields have merely been influenced by ideas in the zeitgeist, just as other intellectuals and the general public are. Since such ideas have the power to shape society, contemporary Leftists would do well to promote the theories of Margulis, Lewontin, Kamin, Rose, Corning, and others who have challenged the presumption that nature, and therefore, human nature, is competitive, aggressive, individualistic, selfish, hierarchical, and territorial by revealing nature as cooperative, egalitarian, interdependent, holistic, nurturing, and mutually beneficial.

Though Leftists lack the neoliberals' ample funding, they have one tool the early neoliberals couldn't have fathomed: the internet. Gone are the days when only those with money or institutional platforms had control of the message. Despite many challenges, grassroots intellectuals today have the potential to remake the world, and the time has never been more urgent than now.

References

Buchanan, J. M. (1975). *The limits of liberty: Between anarchy and leviathan*. Liberty Fund. Chomsky, N. (2014, March 3). The death of American Universities. *Jacobin*. https://www.jacobinmag.com/2014/03/the-death-of-american-universities/

Corning, P. A. (2012). *The fair society: The science of human nature and the pursuit of social justice*. University of Chicago Press.

Dawkins, R. (1976). *The selfish gene*. Oxford University Press.

Degrauwe, P. (2009, November 19). Top down vs. bottom up economics. *Top down vs. Bottom up Economics*. https://voxeu.org/article/top-down-versus-bottom-macroeconomics

Freedman, M. (2011). How chicken farming, murder and eugenics spawned the anti-environmental revolution. *Resilience Magazine*. https://www.resilience.org/stories/2011-04-14/how- chicken-farming-murder-and-eugenics-sparked-anti-environmental-revolution/

Giroux, H. (2016). *Exile as a space of disruption in the Ivory tower – Truthdig*. https://www.truthdig.com/articles/exile-as-a-space-of-disruption-in-the-ivory-tower/

Hayek, F. A. (1944). *The road to serfdom*. Routledge & Kegan Paul.

Hayek, F. A. (1949). The intellectuals and Socialism. *The University of Chicago Law Review*, 16(3), 417. https://doi.org/10.2307/1597903

Hardin, G. (1968). The tragedy of the commons. *Science*. https://www.science.org/doi/10.1126/science.162.3859.1243

Harvey, D. (1974). Population, resources, and the ideology of science. *Economic Geography*, 50(3), 256. https://doi.org/10.2307/142863

Harvey, D. (2010). The future of the commons. *Radical History Review*, 2011(109), 101–107. https://doi.org/10.1215/01636545-2010-017

Hazlitt, H. (1946). *Economics in one lesson: The shortest & surest way to understand basic economics*. Currency, a member of the Crown Publishing Group.

Herrnstein, R., & Murray, C. (1995). *The Bell curve*. Free Press.

Kauffman, S. A. (1996). *At home in the universe: The search for laws of self-organization and complexity*. Oxford University Press.

Klein, P. (2014, August 18). *Biography of F. A. Hayek (1899–1992): Peter G. Klein*. Mises Institute. https://mises.org/library/biography-f-hayek-1899-1992

Lewis, M. (2017, August 23). *The Insidious Libertarian to Alt Right Pipeline*. https://www.thedailybeast.com/-the-insidious-libertarian-to-alt-right-pipeline

Lewontin, R. C., Rose, Steven Peter Russell, & Kamin, L. J. (1984). *Not in our genes: Biology, ideology, and human nature*. Pantheon Books.

Lipset, S., & Marks, G. (2001, January 30). How FDR saved socialism. *Hoover Digest*.

Lubin, D. (2019). Cambridge University Press. https://doi.org/10.26226/morressier.60c8d83cbea1445efd9a1905

Mann, C. (1991). Science's unruly earth mother. *Science*. http://www.environmentalevolution.org/environmentalevolution.org/Fair_Use_files/Unruly%20Earth%20Mother_2.pdf

McClusky, M. (2017, April). Public universities get an education in private industry. *The Atlantic*. https://www.theatlantic.com/education/archive/2017/04/public-universities-get-an-education-in- private-industry/521379/

McKinnon, S. (2005). *Neo-liberal genetics: The myths and moral tales of evolutionary psychology*. Prickly Paradigm Press.

McVicar, M. J. (2011). Aggressive philanthropy: progressivism, conservatism, and the William Volker Charities Fund. https://diginole.lib.fsu.edu/islandora/object/fsu:209940/datastream/PDF/view

Minogue, K. R. (2012). *The servile mind: How democracy erodes the moral life*. Encounter Books. Monbiot, G. (2016, April 15). Neoliberalism; the ideology at the root of all our problems. *The Guardian*. https://www.theguardian.com/books/2016/apr/15/neoliberalism-ideology- problem-george-monbiot

Moyers, B. (2021, April 9) *The Powell memo: A call-to-arms for corporations*. BillMoyers.com. https://billmoyers.com/content/the-powell-memo-a-call-to-arms-for-corporations/

Murray, C. A. (2020). *Human diversity: The biology of gender, race, and class*. Hachette Book Group.

Oxford University Press. (1992). *The Oxford Dictionary*.

Rankin, D. J., Bargum, K., & Kokko, H. (2007). The tragedy of the commons in evolutionary biology. *Trends in Ecology & Evolution, 22*(12), 643–651. https://doi.org/10.1016/j.tree.2007.07.009

Rothbard, M. N. (2000). *Egalitarianism as a revolt against nature, and other essays*. Ludwig von Mises Institute.

Sirico, R. A. (2012). *Defending the free market: The moral case for a free economy*. Regnery Publishing.

Society, Mont Pelerin. (2013, June). *The Mont Pelerin Society special meeting June 22 to 29, 2013*. The Mont Pelerin Society Special Meeting June 22 to 29, 2013 | Universidad San Francisco de Quito. https://www.usfq.edu.ec/en/event/2013-06-22/mont-pelerin-society-special-meeting-june-22-29-2013

Tanenhaus, S. (2017, August 15). The architect of the radical right. *The Atlantic Monthly*.

Vanberg, V (2004). *Public Choice from the Perspective of Sociology*. Springerlink.

Vedantam, S. (2017, February 21). *Does studying economics make you selfish?* NPR. https://www.npr.org/2017/02/21/516375434/does-studying-economics-make-you-selfish

Von, H. F. A., Bartley, W. W., Kresge, S., & Klein, P. G. (1988). *The collected works of F A Hayek*. University of Chicago Press.

Wilson, E. O. (1975) *Sociobiology; the new synthesis*. Harvard University Press. Wapshott, N. (2012, August 27). The ryan paradox; rand & hayek? *Politico*. https://www.politico.com/story/2012/08/the-ryan-paradox-rand-hayek-080235

Zywicki, T. J. (1999). Was Hayek right about group selection after all? review essay of unto others: The evolution and psychology of unselfish behavior. *SSRN Electronic Journal*. https://doi.org/10.2139/ssrn.182509

9 Bad Education: President Obama and the Neoliberalization of American Education

RILEY CLARE VALENTINE

Introduction

President Barack Obama (2016) in his final State of the Union address states, "many of our best corporate citizens are also our most creative." Obama ended his presidency of hope and change with a continuation of neoliberalism without the neoconservativism of his predecessor President George W. Bush. Obama's presidency was an exciting divergence from the prior eight years of neoconservativism; however, he ultimately solidified neoliberalism in American politics. He optimistically tells his audience, all of America, that those corporate citizens' best practices will spread across the country. Obama states, "I believe a thriving private sector is the lifeblood of our economy. I think there are outdated regulations that need to be changed. There is red tape that needs to be cut...I want to spread those best practices across America." *Trust business* he seems to say. *Trust neoliberalism*. Obama's presidency was a moment when neoliberalism uncovered itself for all to see. Before millions of people, neoliberalism showed itself as a full-bodied ideology that stood for nothing—nothing except economization. That sentiment of neoliberalism as an adherence to economization over people arose from President Obama's decision to prioritize financial institutions over citizens in response to the Great Recession.

The Great Recession was a global economic crash resulting from early 2004 to 2008 market deregulation in which global financial systems began to bet upon individuals' debts. President Obama's response was to bail out financial institutions. He prioritized creditor rights, rather than addressing bankruptcy reform or debt relief (Watson, 2016). Obama's administration did not prosecute monopolies, and as *Washington Post* journal Matt Stoller (2017) notes, "Obama's administration let big-bank executives off the hook for their roles in the crisis. Sen. Carl Levin (D-Mich.) referred criminal cases to the Justice Department and was ignored." It was deeply unpopular, and the young president turned a public relations effort to regain his popular support (Stein, 2010). Vice President Joe Biden went on *The Daily Show with Jon Stewart* in 2010 to defend President Obama's bank bailout. *The Daily Show with Jon Stewart* was a television show largely popular with young Democrats, often seen as a news show rather than a comedy program. Jon Stewart held such cultural influence, that presidential candidates regularly came onto the show. During his appearance, Biden defended Obama saying, "if we did not bail them out, we would have been in a position where there was a literal depression, not a recession" (Stein, 2010). Meanwhile, as Biden spoke to Jon Stewart many citizens struggled to meet their needs as many lost their homes and livelihoods. Americans suffered, watching angrily as the wealthy continued to live their lives unscathed (Mirowski, 2013). A PEW Research Center report (2017) shows that the wealth among the upper classes increased, while the poor became increasingly impoverished.

Obama's presidency was a moment where neoliberalism's flaws were revealed, and despite that—it was saved. Colin Crouch (2011) refers to this moment as neoliberalism's "strange non-death." Crouch argues that this was the very moment in which the contradictions of neoliberalism were made evident. The extreme wealth divide was visible. The lies of trickle-down economics were *there*. Neoliberalism should not have survived. But it did. The American education system, which was already struggling from neoliberalizing measures such as charter schools, became characterized by Obama as *investments*. Obama's characterization of education as an *investment* highlights the replacement of the teacher student binary with that of the producer consumer binary. We see education transforming from an intimate relationship between students and teachers to that of a business model—including discussions of best practices and integrating the notion that we are human capital into education. This chapter examines the neoliberalizing of education through Obama's State of the Union addresses and his first address to the session of Congress in 2009. Neoliberalism is a political and economic ideology that seeks to marketize all of society. Obama's presidency and the Great Recession is a significant moment because it presented a crossroads. Would Obama take the path of President Franklin Delano Roosevelt who pushed for a highly regulated market and pushed for policies such as an Economic Bill of Rights, or would he pursue the path of President Ronald Reagan who introduced neoliberalism to America during the 1981 recession? We now see that Obama took the latter path.

Within all of this, we see the neoliberalization of education heightening in rhetoric. Neoliberals such as Gary Becker in *Human Capital* (1964) spoke on the importance of education in a society. It is an *investment*. The turn from classical liberal notions of education as a right and something that helps cultivate our capabilities as human beings, became cemented during Obama's presidency. Obama's Secretary of Education, Arne Duncan, actively pursued expanding charter schools and cutting funding for public schools (Mora & Christianakis, 2011). We see a movement towards education as something that citizens *must* have, and if they do not obtain a degree that they are failing the nation. Becker's discussion of education as human capital furthers significantly under Obama's presidency. Education loses both a deeply important function as something social, that helps us cultivate our*selves* as well as a political function. Wendy Brown (2015) pinpoints this as an end to the classical liberal Aristotelian theory of education in which it is seen as key for a person to learn ethics, deliberation, critical thinking, and the capacities necessary to be a political participant. Instead, education is now something to profit from.

The danger of neoliberalizing education to our politics has been discussed at length by Wendy Brown (2015, 2019). She contends that it chips away at democratic ideals and skills such as collective deliberation until it leaves us with only ourselves as products (2015, p. 30). The treatment of education as a method of production advocates for the utilization of standardized assessments, which reinforce capitalist neoliberal concepts of the self. In other words, education in the liberal arts tradition seeks to cultivate *skills* and encourage developing one's ethical thinking and engagement rather than depositing knowledge into the student as though they are a vessel rather than a person. The movement away from this conception of education furthers the neoliberal project and embeds it into an essential facet of society—education. Because of this, I focus on the danger of neoliberalizing education to our moral selves. By this, I mean that neoliberalism has changed what is seen as immoral and moral through marketized best practices. Neoliberalism prioritizes liberty above all political ideals, because of this we are all free to be unequal. We are all free to experience numerous inequities due to systematic biases and forms of oppression.

It's a Neoliberal World

Neoliberalism assumes that all individuals have access to the same amount of knowledge. It universalizes and collapses all individuals into one being—*homo economicus*. Michel Foucault (2008, p. 268) coined the term *homo economicus* defining it as a rational economic person who utilizes market reasoning across all political, social, and economic spheres. *Homo economicus* blurs the lines between these aspects of life until they become subsumed under economic life. Early neoliberalism, that of the turn of the 20th century, held closely to this model. Neoliberal figures such as Walter Lippmann avoided all mention on morality. However, post-World War II neoliberals such as Friedrich Hayek integrated morality into neoliberalism. Hayek argues in his seminal text *The Road to Serfdom* (2007) that government interference in the market is *immoral*. Considering this, contemporary neoliberal discourse presents the everyday person as both an economic rational actor and imbues their successes and failures with moral weight. Obama's insistence that dropping out of high school is quitting on yourself as well as the country shames individuals who drop out of high school. There is no consideration of what may cause a person to drop out of high school—there is no idea that a young adult may suddenly encounter precarity that upends their life. Instead, we see public shame—leaving high school is an immoral action. It is embarrassing. Neoliberalism flattens all individuals into the singular *homo economicus*, a figure subject held to be the standard for all people. *Homo economicus* reflects America's conception of *who* the everyday person is—they are white, middle class, able-bodied, and are free from marginalizations which may make school not an option for them. The application of *homo economicus* to all people holds individuals to a privileged standard. Obama, despite his acknowledgment of disenfranchised Americans, uses universalizing neoliberal logistics.

Neoliberal scholar Jessica Whyte (2019, p.8) asserts that neoliberals hold a deep, "belief that a functioning competitive market required an adequate moral and legal foundation." A good market necessitates that society and politics have *proper* morality. Obama describes progressive neoliberal morality as developing from a *better politics*. During his 2015 State of the Union, he states, "A better politics is one where we appeal to each other's basic decency instead of our basest fears. A better politics is one where we debate without demonizing each other, where we talk issues and values and principles and… spend more time lifting young people up with a sense of purpose and possibility, asking them to join in the great mission of building America." Better politics rests upon a moral appeal to Americans' decency, but it *also* appeals to shaping youth into *homo economicus*. A good political system is one in which individuals can deliberate over principles and values. Obama appeals to an idea of giving them purpose and possibility, which develops from our shared moral capability to engage with one another *for* a better future. A better politics will help young Americans economically succeed. A better politics reflects a morality inclined towards successful futures.

The Reckoning

During his first address to session of Congress in 2009, Obama criticizes politicians for allowing the Great Recession to happen—for allowing a fully unregulated housing market to create an impossible bubble. The Great Recession was triggered by the collapse of the housing market bubble in 2006, which led to the subprime mortgage crisis, resulting in the collapse and bailout of numerous banks and industries. Obama refers to the Great Recession as a "day of reckoning." But his criticisms are not just for politicians, the day of reckoning is also for Americans who have made poor decisions for their future. Obama (2009) asserts that while he will invest in education, it is the everyday person's responsibility to participate in it, "And dropping out of high school is no longer an option. It's not just quitting on yourself, it's quitting on your country, and this country needs and values the talents of every American." Dropping out of high school is not just a bad decision for yourself, it is also one that harms the nation—by investing in education, Obama contends that the government is investing in young Americans. If those same Americans leave the education system, then they have reneged on an implicit bargain. The rugged individualism that Obama points to is essential to neoliberalism. Neoliberalism separates us from one another, requiring us to seize onto a responsibility to invest in ourselves. It is, "the basic bargain that built this country: the idea that if you work hard and meet your responsibilities, you can get ahead…" (Obama, 2013). Americans have a responsibility for their own success, and the State has an obligation insofar as it comes to investing in the infrastructure necessary for it. If we refuse the terms of this bargain, we have failed ourselves and the nation. Failure to succeed on the market is a moral failure. Obama's political rhetoric is isolating. It turns collective struggles into individual ones—chipping away at group consciousness and developing a political vision in which we are all separate individuals.

Because education is a means to a positive economic end, educators are placed in the role of grooming and selecting students who will flourish. Obama describes the ideal citizens as ones who are inspired by ideas of fairness and who focus on the American identity. The ideal citizen is one who embodies national principles. It is the ideal *homo economicus*. Traditionally, the ideal citizen is seen as a white, straight, cisgender, man who adores his country. Obama expands this person to include marginalized people—bringing in all of us who live outside of this paradigm into being able to become the best neoliberal that we can be. He sees the future of the nation within these individuals, "I see it in the dreamer who stays up late at night to finish her science project and the teacher who comes in early, maybe with some extra supplies that she bought because she knows that that young girl might someday cure a disease" (2016). The futures that are possible are accessible if you can transcend the boundaries that neoliberalism, racism, sexism, and cisheteronormativity among other strictures. You transcend that as *human capital*.

We see in Obama's discussion of the relationship between teachers and students one that reflects this capitalist neoliberal idea of human beings as capital. Obama describes the relationship between the young student and the teacher as one of *investment*. The teacher sees the potential, she *knows* the student's potential, and because of that she provides the student extra assistance. The teacher and the student are both ideal citizens. They are engaged in the basic bargain of the United States that Obama outlines—if you put in the effort to invest in the future, you will be rewarded for that investment. Obama's educational philosophy requires that we move away from viewing the relationship of teacher to student as one that encourages students to develop themselves as thinking feeling beings. Instead, it transforms this intimate relationship to one of economic production. The educator does not assist her student because she cares. She *invests* in the student, transforming the relationship into one where both the teacher and student see education like a market.

Yet, there is complexity to Obama, because he does recognize marginalization and its impacts on American youth. Obama attends to the student as being a recipient of Deferred Action for Childhood Arrivals (DACA), telling us the student is an undocumented youth, who may lack the same resources as her peers. Obama is socially progressive, but he is fundamentally neoliberal. The State has little to no role in supporting this undocumented girl. The teacher steps in to provide supplies. The State's sole role is to fund educational systems. Disenfranchised individuals receive help, but it comes in the form of investing in that person's future. There is no incentive to help individuals who do have the possibility to becoming a success. A world in which this educator does not have to provide help because the State is doing so does not enter Obama's speeches. The State's role is nonexistent within this anecdote. Educators assume responsibility for their students' futures, and within this they are given the responsibility to select who *best* deserves their time—a task that harms both educator and student. By turning the classroom into a marketized space, the relationship between educator and student reflects an unfolding future in which the classroom is for capital, not for cultivating our innate capacities. Even though neoliberal logic can acknowledge marginalization, it cannot engage with justice and equality in a meaningful way, because those concepts are not found within market logistics.

Educational Best Practices

Neoliberal school reform politics rest on dialogues of teaching and leadership as discourses of efficiency, performance, and performance management. All of this is done for student performance. Reform politics are part of neoliberal morality. Pamela Rogers (2020) contends that education is consistently discussed as "never there." Schools and teachers are never at their pinnacle. Youth are never reaching their potential. The education system is trapped in a dialogue of *not yet*. The educational *not yet* is, of course, one of economic possibilities—as Obama states in his 2015 State of the Union, we must "spend more time lifting young people up with a sense of purpose and possibility." America's educational system will never reach its capacity. Because of this, Obama's presidential discourse on education is a consistent discourse of improvement. Neoliberal morality rests upon the importance of constant improvement. Individuals can *always* be more efficient and more productive. Likewise, systems can always be more efficient and productive. The educational system can always produce better students. Teachers can always be more efficient in their teaching.

The neoliberalization of secondary school systems pairs with the neoliberalization of higher education. Obama describes the connection in his 2013 State of the Union address:

> And we'll reward schools that develop new partnerships with colleges and employers and create classes that focus on science, technology, engineering, and math: the skills today's employers are looking for to fill the jobs that are there right now and will be there in the future. Now, even with better high schools, most young people will need some higher education. It's a simple fact: The more education you've got, the more likely you are to have a good job and work your way into the middle class.

The State aids schools that develop hirable students. Hirable students study STEM rather than a broad-based education, humanities, or social sciences. Higher education demands greater access to "good" students. Because of the demand for "good" students, high schools are pressured into developing these ideal students. Inevitably, good students join the middle class.

Obama's 2013 State of the Union address prioritizes the middle class. The middle class is every person's goal. If you succeed in school, then you have a chance succeeding in employment and thus class mobility is an option. Americans have a bargain with the State. Americans all hold "the idea that if you work hard and meet your responsibilities, you can get ahead" (Obama, 2013). This bargain, "encourages free enterprise, rewards individual initiative, and opens the doors of opportunity to every child across this great nation" (Obama, 2013). Simply put, the American Dream rewards individuals who work hard and meet obligations. As Obama (2009) states elsewhere, "dropping out of high school is no longer an option. It's not just quitting on yourself, it's quitting on your country." Our obligations are to treat ourselves as investments. We work hard and meet the responsibilities we have to ourselves—to struggle to be *better*. We achieve the American Dream through not "quitting" on ourselves or the country. We have a chance at joining the middle class so long as we do *not* quit on ourselves by sidestepping our responsibilities. We treat learning as not a space of growth and not as a life-long practice. Instead, it is something that is done for an economic goal. Thus, the ways in which American educational systems measure student progress or success, such as standardized testing, concretizes the notion that education's purpose is simply to deposit information rather than to encourage students' development as a person.

The neoliberalization of education extends into the family. Obama in his 2011 State of the Union address points out that, "responsibility begins not in our classrooms, but in our homes and communities. It's family that first instills the love of learning in a child…We need to teach them that success is not a function of fame or PR, but of hard work and discipline. Our schools share this responsibility. When a child walks into a classroom, it should be a place of high expectations and high performance." Schools, communities, and families *all* have responsibilities to students. Families and communities must come together and educate children that they must work hard to succeed. Likewise, schools should be spaces of excellence. Teachers, families, and community members all have a part to contribute to a student's success. Neoliberal morality places the onus of an individual's success onto them and their support structures. Wendy Brown (2015) refers to this process as *responsibilization*.

Responsibilization is an idea and practice, in which the subject is forced "to become a responsible self-investor and self-provider" (Brown, 2015, p. 84). Brown argues that to do so the subject must engage in "a particular form of self-sustenance that meshes with the morality of the state and the health of the economy" (Brown, 2015, p. 84). When it comes to education, we see responsibilization play out in the teacher who gives extra resources to a student who they see has potential. They participate in market-based speculation—bargaining on a future potential gain. Responsibilization highlights the diminishment of the State in society. The State no longer has a role in providing concrete goods for its citizens so that they can exercise their capabilities. Instead, the *community* must assume this burden. Obama, in his 2013 State of the Union address, compels Americans to ask themselves three questions, "How do we attract more jobs to our shores? How do we equip our people with the skills they need to get those jobs? And how do we make sure that hard work leads to a decent living?" Obama (2013) is clear that access to these jobs and much-needed skills come through education, "The more education you've got, the more likely you are to have a good job and work your way into the middle class." The onus for economic mobilization is placed upon educators. Educators must *provide* students skills they need to transcend boundaries such as class, race, immigration status, and disability among others. While protection for marginalized groups exist, within right to work to states individuals can be fired at will. Thus, an employer may not fire you for being transgender, but they may decide that your work is subpar. Because of this, responsibilization takes on the ultimate role—to ensure individuals have the capacity to succeed despite histories of exclusion. The morality of neoliberalism sees no race, no nationality, no creed beyond success. If you fail, it is you and your community's failure alone.

Neoliberal subjects are made within systems of oppression. Nonetheless—according to neoliberal logistics, they exist outside of these systems. Their failure is a reflection upon their own innate subpar-ness rather than any aspects of white supremacy, cisheteronormativity, and carceral thinking among other systemic harms. Because of this, our interactions matter *insofar* as they lead to economic success. The ways in which we demonstrate love and care for one another are less important because they do not necessarily fit into neoliberal morality. When we express care for others, we demonstrate an attentiveness to the ways in which society harms them. The care that we practice does not adhere to the belief that all individuals are strict rational actors who move through society utilizing best practices. Instead, care highlights an understanding of vulnerability. The educator meets the students' psychological and mental needs because they are a being in pain—not because they are an investment. The neoliberal model, places pressure on the student to displace their grief to succeed. The neoliberal model requires a loss of vulnerability.

It's a Material World

The loss of vulnerability comes with a movement away from a morality in which a meaningful life is one of flourishing. Obama outlines a good life, in his 2012 State of the Union address, "a country that leads the world in educating its people; an America that attracts a new generation of high-tech manufacturing and high-paying jobs; a future where we're in control of our own energy and our security and prosperity aren't so tied to unstable parts of the world; an economy built to last, where hard work pays off and responsibility is rewarded." Obama describes a good life in this moment. A good life comes from access to education, good jobs, sustainable energy, and independence. Human wellbeing connects to developing our capabilities which exist within the bargain that exists between the State and its citizens. Obama describes an accessible American Dream. It is not restricted to individuals by class, gender, race, or any other identity. A country that can provide this dream is "within our reach." Equitable access to a good life is a possibility.

Obama asserts, in his 2012 State of the Union address, that Americans historically have contributed to the promise of a good life, "if you worked hard, you could do well enough to raise a family, own a home, send your kids to college, and put a little away for retirement." The promise of happiness is an ongoing project. Obama (2012) states that fulfilling this promise is the "defining issue of our time." A good life intersects not only in the immediacy of good employment and education, but *also* in the future. A good life includes one in which you can have a family, a home, retire, and invest in your family's future. Obama centers his perspective of wellbeing around materialism. A good life is one in which there is material comfort.

The fundamental avenue towards material comfort is education. Education is the means by which individuals can move beyond class and place. A good future comes through a good education. Obama, in his 2010 State of the Union address, argues for the importance of education reform in the context of a good future:

> Instead of funding the status quo, we only invest in reform, reform that raises student achievement, inspires students to excel in math and science, and turns around failing schools that steal the future of too many young Americans, from rural communities to the inner city. In the 21st century, the best antipoverty program around is a world-class education…the success of our children cannot depend more on where they live than on their potential.

Obama condemns schools that perform poorly as stealing "the future" of young Americans. American politicians have a responsibility to ensuring that schools perform well so that youths can have a good future. Obama leans into a good education as "the best antipoverty program." A good future, in which individuals are not bound by poverty and economic failure, comes from educational success. Obama acknowledges that unfortunately individuals' futures may be limited by where they live. A school's quality is heavily dependent upon funding. Economic investment in schools opens potentials for youths' futures.

The future of schools *depends* upon good educators. Obama, in his 2011 State of the Union address, adopts patriotic language when it comes to working in schools, "to every young person listening tonight who's contemplating their career choice: If you want to make a difference in the life of our Nation, if you want to make a difference in the life of a child, become a teacher. Your country needs you." Obama utilizes language that is reminiscent of previous presidents such as Franklin Delano Roosevelt and his depiction of joining the industrial workforce during World War II as part of the patriotic war effort. The country needs *you*. Teachers shape the future. The nation needs teachers. Although Obama appeals to patriotism, he does not in kind develop respect for education as employment. Education is routinely disparaged as a position for "those who cannot do." American culture routinely refers to teachers as "heroes," and this was especially true during the COVID-19 pandemic (Manjoo, 2020). Teachers were heroized without taking into consideration that they were being asked to work at a time when vaccines were not in sight. America needs you to sacrifice yourself.

Educators are placed in a nebulous position in American culture. They are at once disposable and necessary heroes. They are individuals who could not hack it in their industry, and they have unique abilities to provide opportunities for marginalized students. Neoliberalism values those who can *do*, without seeing education as a career which is meaningful beyond cultivating future products. Because educators do not participate in industry jobs, but rather prepare students for that they are seen as incapable. America needs you, but it does not respect you. Much of what teachers do is provide emotional and mental support for students, finding ways to assist them as vulnerable individuals. Educators and students exist in relationships of human potential. Interactions matter in and outside of the classroom, and the mentorship opportunities can expand a student as a thinking caring being—not as a product. However, doing these things requires significant risk. It requires educators to refute institutional expectations, and it requires students to set aside the vision of them as a product aside. It creates a space that is antithetical to neoliberalism.

Conclusion

Neoliberalism conceives of justice as economic practices. Thus, by making education into something that no longer helps one flourish as a human being, we are chipping away at the belief that what we do has moral weight. Our interactions with one another matter. Presidential political rhetoric highlights the distance between us and moral considerations. Neoliberalism asks that we see as a market, interact with one another as marketized beings, and live as a market. I have sought to show that education is entrenched in neoliberal rhetoric and values. Because of this entrenchment, education has moved away from a place of cultivation of the self. By this I mean that education is no longer a space in which we develop critical thinking skills and caring skills by which to live in community. Instead, the classroom as a marketized space.

The ways we teach and learn are essential to developing a community that can grapple with the problems of neoliberalism. However, to do this we must counter standardization and rubricization, which require the classroom to become structured around a model of thought where they must check off boxes to succeed. A successful student can take 10s across the rubric, whereas an unsuccessful student consistently makes lower marks. Standardization and rubricization focus on quantitative *improvement*, often called "growth" within pedagogy. Growth is measurable. We can mark these changes in a student. However, these pedagogical forms confine students to viewing themselves as *human capital*. Education is fundamental to building and creating an anti-capitalist world. Because of that we must engage with anarchist pedagogy and critical pedagogy. We must ask ourselves—how can the classroom be a space of *unlearning*, in which we upend capitalism to make a new world possible.

References

Barack, O. (2010, January 27). *Address before a joint session of the Congress on the state of the Union*. Address Before a Joint Session of the Congress on the State of the Union | The American Presidency Project. https://www.presidency.ucsb.edu/node/287936

Barack, O. (2011, January 25). *Address before a joint session of the Congress on the state of the Union*. Address Before a Joint Session of the Congress on the State of the Union | The American Presidency Project. https://www.presidency.ucsb.edu/node/289120

Barack, O. (2012, January 24). *Address before a joint session of the Congress on the state of the Union*. Address Before a Joint Session of the Congress on the State of the Union | The American Presidency Project. https://www.presidency.ucsb.edu/node/299426

Barack, O. (2013, February 12). *Address before a joint session of Congress on the state of the Union*. Address Before a Joint Session of Congress on the State of the Union | The American Presidency Project. https://www.presidency.ucsb.edu/node/303424

Barack, O. (2015, January 20). *Address before a joint session of Congress on the state of the Union*. Address Before a Joint Session of Congress on the State of the Union | The American Presidency Project. https://www.presidency.ucsb.edu/node/308225

Barack, O. (2016, January 12). *Address before a joint session of Congress on the state of the Union*. Address Before a Joint Session of Congress on the State of the Union | The American Presidency Project. https://www.presidency.ucsb.edu/node/313186

Barack, O. (2009, February 24). *Address before a joint session of Congress on the state of the Union*. Address Before a Joint Session of Congress on the State of the Union | The American Presidency Project. https://www.presidency.ucsb.edu/node/286218

Becker, G. (2009). *Human Capital*. University of Chicago Press.

Brown, W. (2015). *Undoing the Demos: Neoliberalism's Stealth Revolution*. Zone Books.

Foucault, M. (2008). *The Birth of politics: Lectures at the Collège de France 1978–1979*. Picador Press.

Hayek, F. (2014). *The road to Serfdom: Text and documents*. Routledge.

Manjoo, F. (2020, July 15). *Please don't call them heroes*. The New York Times. https://www.nytimes.com/2020/07/15/opinion/schools-reopening.html

Mora, R., & Christianakis, M. (2011). Charter schools, market capitalism, and Obama's neo-liberal agenda. *Journal of Inquiry and Action in Education, 4*(1), 5.

Rogers, P. (2020) "Are we there yet? Neoliberal education and never-ending reform." *Our Schools, Our Selves*.

Stein, S. (2017, December 7). *Biden on the Bailout: 'Socialism for the rich and capitalism for the POOR' (VIDEO)*. HuffPost. https://www.huffpost.com/entry/biden-on-the-bailout-soci_n_361900

Stoller, M. (2019, March 1). *Democrats can't win until they recognize how bad Obama's financial policies were*. The Washington Post. https://www.washingtonpost.com/posteverything/wp/2017/01/12/democrats-cant-win-until-they-recognize-how-bad-obamas-financial-policies-were/

Whyte, J. (2019). *The morals of the market: Human rights and the rose of neoliberalism*. Verso.

10 Neoliberalism, Democratization, and the Re-Visioning of Education

STEVE GENNARO AND DOUGLAS KELLNER

Introduction

The matrix of technological revolution, globalization, and neoliberal capital has produced intense change, conflict, and upheaval in the worlds of society, culture, politics, and education throughout the 21st century. The recent events of the global COVID19 pandemic have only further increased the polarity between economic haves and have nots, while at the same time doubling down on education, and even more so public education, as the battleground for where neoliberalism must be confronted.

The centrality of globalization, technology, and neoliberalism in contemporary experience and the need for adequate conceptualizations and responses require critical theory and pedagogy to engage the conjuncture of technology and globalization in the context of neoliberalism in order to maintain their relevance in the present age. Critical educators need to comprehend the effects of globalization and technology on education over the last half century, work to democratize education in the present moment, and develop pedagogies adequate to the challenges of an age of neoliberal capital and corporate models of education that we need to contest and offer alternatives. In addition, the COVID19 pandemic has presented a challenge to the future of education at the same time as it has opened up an opportunity for contestation and transformation to make education serve the needs of students and teachers, opposed to neoliberalism that wants to commodify education and make it subservient to global capital and the ruling elites.

Globalization, Neoliberalism, and the Reconstruction of Education

In the face of expanding globalization and digital technologies of information and communication in the context of neoliberalism, critical educators continue to develop transformative educational strategies to understand and to counter the oppressive forces and effects of neoliberal globalization in conjunction with possibilities for democratization in order to empower individuals to understand and act effectively in a globalized neoliberal world, and to struggle for social justice.

The project of transforming education will take different forms in different contexts. For example, in the post-industrial or "overdeveloped" countries individuals need to be empowered to work and act in a high-tech information economy, and thus should learn skills of critical media and digital literacies to survive in the novel social environment. Traditional skills of knowledge and critique should also be fostered, so that students can name the system, describe and grasp the changes occurring in it as well as the defining features of the evolving neoliberal global order, and can learn to engage in critical and oppositional practice in the interests of democratization and progressive transformation. This requires gaining vision of how life can be, of alternatives to the present order, and the necessity of struggle and organization to realize progressive goals. Languages of competition in education, grading and success, must thus be supplemented by the discourse of critique, hope and praxis.

Critical media and digital literacy pedagogies presuppose access to digital technology and media. However, even as access to mobile technology continues to rise globally, the rates of growth and access are unequal. For example, while a 2019 PEW research report noted that more than five billion people have access to mobile devices and more than half of these are smartphones (Silver, 2019), recent work from UNICEF in April 2020 on pandemic education documented how despite 188 countries adopting a digitally-based continuation of education during the pandemic using technologies such as internet, TV, and radio, one-third of schoolchildren worldwide (over 463 million) could not be reached by the broadcast- and Internet-based remote learning policies (UNICEF, April 2020).

This poses different challenges for the project of transforming education in underserviced regions, such as the global south. In *How Many Children and Youth Have Internet Access* at Home UNICEF reported that two-thirds of children and young people aged 25 years or less (over 2.2 billion) are without a home connection to the internet. (UNICEF, December 2020). The data is startling. In West and Central African Nations, only 5% have internet access at home compared to the 33 percent global average. Differences are starker yet between rich and poor countries, with only 6 percent of children and young people in low-income countries having internet access compared to 87 percent in high-income countries. A progressive reconstruction of education that is done in the interests of democratization would demand access to emergent technologies for all, helping to overcome the so-called digital divide and divisions of the "haves" and "have nots" (see Kellner, 2002).

Expanding democratic and multicultural reconstruction of education forces educators and citizens to confront the challenge of the digital divide, in which there are divisions between information and technology "haves" and "have nots," just as there are class, gender, and race divisions in every sphere of existing of societies and cultures that require constant confrontation. Although the latest surveys of the digital divide indicate that the key indicators are class and education (though not excluding race and gender as impacting factors too) making smartphones and internet access a significant force of democratization in education and society will require significant investment and programs to assure that everyone receives the training, literacies, and tools necessary to properly function in a high-tech global economy and culture.

It is interesting that one of the earliest proponents of critical pedagogy, Paulo Freire, was positive toward media and technologies, seeing them as potential tools for empowering citizens, as well as instruments of domination in the hands of ruling elites. Freire wrote that: "Technical and scientific training need not be inimical to humanistic education as long as science and technology in the revolutionary society are at the service of permanent liberation, of humanization" (1972, p. 157).[1] Many critical pedagogues, however, are technophobes, seeing new digital technologies solely as instruments of domination. In a neoliberal world inexorably undergoing processes of globalization and technological transformation, one cannot, however, in good conscience advocate a policy of clean hands and purity, distancing oneself from technology and globalization, but must intervene in the processes of economic and technological revolution, attempting to deflect these forces for progressive ends and developing critical and oppositional pedagogies to advance the project of human liberation and well-being.

A critical theory of technology maintains that there is utopian potential in the information and communication technologies as well as the possibility for increased domination and the hegemony of capital. While the first generation of computers were large mainframe systems controlled by big government and big business, later generations of "personal computers" and networks created a more decentralized situation in which, ever more individuals own their own computers and use them for their own projects and goals. A current generation of now exists both physically and digitally in the world, through handheld smartphones and emergent social media platforms that finds 95% of American teenagers claiming access to a smartphone and almost half of all American teens claiming to be online "almost constantly" (Andersen & Jiang, 2018). The utopian potential for the current technology can be seen in the global networks of young people who are using smartphones as a tool to organize, mobilize, and contest the greatest challenges of their contemporary moment, such as climate change, degendering S.T.E.M and racial inequity with movements such as Black Lives Matter (Gennaro & Miller, 2020).

In relation to education, the spread and distribution of information and communication technology signifies the possibility of openings of opportunities for research and interaction not previously open to students who did not have the privilege of access to major research libraries or institutions. The Internet opens more information and knowledge to more people than any previous technology and institution in history, despite its many problems and limitations. Moreover, the Internet enables individuals to participate in discussions, to circulate their ideas and work, and to access material that was previously closed off to many excluded groups and individuals.

As a response to globalization and technological revolution, transformations in pedagogy must be as radical as the technological transformations that are taking place. Education should be reconstructed in the light of the importance of citizenship and participation, thus linking, a la Dewey, education and democracy. A public pedagogy involves teaching citizens what is going on in their and other democratic and nondemocratic societies, threats to democracy, and the demands of citizenship. Training individuals for citizenship involves training in rhetoric, public speaking, and the fundamentals of reading and writing. It also requires cultivating critical tolerance in a multicultural society that affirms respect and tolerance for all, while being critical of social institutions and groups that themselves promote fundamentalism and assault tolerance, or that use terrorism, militarism, and violence to promote their ends.

Tolerance should be linked with cultural cosmopolitanism that affirms the value of world culture and multicultures and that is not chauvinistic and noncritical toward one's own culture and society. While democratic patriotism can help cultivate respect for the positive features of a culture or society and help create solidarities in times of trouble, a blind nationalistic patriotism can lead to submission to aggressive and nondemocratic policies and practices of political manipulation.

Critical citizenship thus involves cultivating abilities to read and critique the text of one's own and other cultures, including political and media discourses, social media, television programming, popular music, advertising, and other cultural forms. Thus a public pedagogy articulates with critical cultural studies that together require critical educators to rethink the concepts of literacy and the very nature of education in any high-tech and rapidly evolving society. Literacy must be expanded to develop novel forms of cultural and technological literacy for at the same time that the world is undergoing technological revolution, important demographic and socio-political changes are occurring in the United States and elsewhere.

In other works, we have delineated the **critical multiple literacies** necessary to utilize and deploy information and communication technologies, including an expanded role for critical media and digital literacies, and multimedia literacies that provide literacy in reading, researching and producing in the evolving multimedia world (Kellner & Share, 2019; Gennaro & Miller, 2021). Yet radically reconstructing education requires a wide range of other literacies often neglected in the current organization of schooling.

Since a multicultural society is the context of education for many in the contemporary moment, innovative forms of social interaction and cultural awareness are needed that appreciate differences, multiplicity, and diversity. Therefore, an expanded **cultural literacy** is needed, one that appreciates the cultural heritage, histories, and contributions of a diversity of groups. Whereas one can agree with E.D. Hirsch (1987) that we need to be literate in our shared cultural heritage, we also need to become culturally literate in cultures that have been hitherto invisible, as Anthony Appiah, Henry Louis Gates and their colleagues have been arguing in their proposals for a multicultural education (1998).

Social literacy should also be taught throughout the educational systems, ranging from a focus on how to relate and get along with a variety of individuals, how to negotiate differences, how to resolve conflicts, and how to communicate and socially interact in a diversity of situations. Social literacy involves ethical training in values and norms, delineating proper and improper individual and social values (which may well be different in various regions and countries). It also requires knowledge of contemporary societies, and thus overlaps with social and natural science training. In fact, in the light of the significant role of science and technology in the contemporary world, threats to the environment, and the need to preserve and enhance the natural as well as social and cultural worlds, it is scandalous how illiterate some overdeveloped societies, like the US, are concerning science, nature, and even peoples' own bodies. An **ecoliteracy** should thus appropriately teach competency in interpreting and interacting with our natural environment, ranging from our own body to natural habitats, like forests, oceans, lakes, and deserts.

The challenge for education today is thus to develop multiple critical literacies to empower students and citizens to use emergent technologies to enhance their lives and to create a better culture and society based on respect for multicultural differences and aiming at fuller democratic participation of individuals and groups excluded from wealth and power in the previous modern society. A positive postmodernity would thus involve the creation of a more egalitarian and democratic society in which more individuals and groups were empowered to participate. A great danger facing us, of course, is that globalization and emergent technologies will increase the current inequalities based on class, gender, and racial divisions. Currently, men own 50% more of the world's wealth than women, and the 22 richest men have more wealth than all the women in Africa (Oxfam, 2021). Economic inequality has only increased during the pandemic. Francisco Fereirra noted recently for the International Monetary Fund "The severe impact of the COVID-19 pandemic is clearly seen in the numbers: more than 3.1 million deaths and rising, 120 million people pushed into extreme poverty, and a massive global recession. As suffering and poverty have risen, some data show an increase in another extreme: the wealth of billionaires." *Forbes* noted in April 2021 that "U.S. billionaires have gotten about $1.2 trillion richer during the pandemic." Another layer of center to this economic discrepancy are the industries that experienced this explosion in wealth: Facebook, Amazon, Google, Oracle, Microsoft, and Dell; eight of the ten richest billionaires, who experienced the greatest rise in wealth during the pandemic. came from technology and media organizations(Forbes, 2021).

Thus, the concept of multiple critical literacies and the postmodern pedagogy that we envisage maintains that it is not a question of either/or, e.g., either print literacy or multimedia literacy, either the classical curriculum or a new high-tech curriculum, but it is rather a question of both/and that preserves the best from classical education, that enhances emphasis on print literacy, but that also develops critical multiple literacies to engage the emergent technologies. Obviously, cyberlife is just one dimension of experience and one still needs to learn to interact in the "real world" of school, jobs, relationships, politics, and community. Youth—indeed all of us!—need to negotiate many dimensions of social reality and to gain a multiplicity of forms of literacy and skills that will enable individuals to create identities, relationships, and communities that will nurture and develop the full spectrum of their potentialities and satisfy a wide array of needs. Contemporary lives are more multidimensional than ever, so part of the postmodern adventure is learning to live in a variety of social spaces and to adapt to intense change and transformation (Best & Kellner, 2001). Education, too, must meet these challenges and both utilize new technologies to improve education and to devise pedagogical strategies in which technologies can be deployed to create a more democratic and egalitarian multicultural society.

In the light of the neoliberal projects to dismantle the Welfare State, colonize the public sphere, and control globalization, it is up to citizens, activists, and educators to create alternative public spheres, politics, and pedagogies. In these spaces, that could include progressive classrooms, students and citizens could learn to use information and multimedia technologies to discuss what kinds of society people today want, and to oppose the society against which people resist and struggle. This involves, minimally, demands for more education, health care, welfare, and benefits from the state, and to struggle to create a more democratic and egalitarian society. Yet one cannot expect that generous corporations and a beneficent state are going to make available to citizens the bounties and benefits of the globalized information economy. Rather, it is up to individuals and groups to promote democratization and progressive social change.

Thus, in opposition to the globalization of corporate and state capitalism, we would advocate an oppositional democratic, pedagogical, and cosmopolitan globalization, which supports individuals and groups using information and multimedia technologies to create a more multicultural, egalitarian, democratic, and ecological globalization. Of course, the emergent technologies might exacerbate existing inequalities in the current class, gender, race, and regional configurations of power and give dominant corporate forces powerful tools to advance their interests. In this situation, it is up to people of good will to devise strategies to use technologies to promote democratization and social justice. For as the proliferating technologies become ever more central to everyday life, developing an oppositional technopolitics in alternative public spheres and pedagogical sites will become increasingly important. Changes in the economy, politics, and social life demand a constant rethinking of politics and social change in the light of globalization and the technological revolution, requiring critical and oppositional thinking as a response to ever-changing historical conditions.

Notes

1. Freire also stated that: "It is not the media themselves which I criticize, but the way they are used" (1972, p. 136). Moreover, he argued for the importance of teaching media literacy to empower individuals against manipulation and oppression, and using the most appropriate media to help teach the subject matter in question (1972, pp. 114–116).

References

Anderson, M., & Jiang, J. (2018). "Teens, Social Media, and Technology". PEW Research Center. https://www.pewresearch.org/internet/2018/05/31/teens-social-media-technology-2018/#vast-majority-of-teens-have-access-to-a-home-computer-or-smartphone (accessed October 1, 2021).
Appiah, A. A., & Gates, H. L. (1999). *Africana: The Encyclopedia of the African and African American experience.* BasicCivitas.
Aronowitz, S., & Giroux, H. (1993). *Education still under siege.* Bergin & Garvey.
Barber, Benjamin. (1996). *Jihad vs. McWorld.* Ballantine Books.
———. (2003). *Fear's empire. War, terrorism, and democracy.* Norton.
Best, S., & Kellner, D. (1991). *Postmodern theory: Critical interrogations.* MacMillan and Guilford.
———. (1997). *The postmodern turn.* Routledge and Guilford Press.
———. (2001). *The postmodern adventure.* Routledge and Guilford Press.
———. (2003). "Contemporary youth and the postmodern adventure." *The Review of Education/Pedagogy/Cultural Studies,* 25(2), 75–93 (April–June 2003).
Boggs, C. (2000). *The end of politics.* Guilford Press.
Bowles, S., & Gintis, H. (1986). *On democracy.* Basic Books.
Burbach, R. (2001). *Globalization and postmodern politics. From Zapatistas to High-tech Robber Barons.* Pluto Press.
Castells, M. (1996). *The rise of the network society.* Blackwell.
Cohen, J., & Rogers, J. (1983). *On democracy.* Penguin.
Cvetkovich, A., & Kellner, D. (1997). *Articulating the global and the local. Globalization and cultural studies.* Westview.
Dewey, John. (1997 [1916]). *Democracy and education.* Free Press.
Dyer-Witheford, N. (1999). *Cyber-Marx. Cycles and circuits of struggle in high-technology Capitalism.* University of Illinois Press.
Foran, J. (Ed.). (2003). *The future of revolutions. Rethinking radical change in the age of globalization.* Zed Books.
Ferreira, F. (2021). "Inequality in the time of Covid-19". International Monetary Fund. https://www.imf.org/external/pubs/ft/fandd/2021/06/inequality-and-covid-19-ferreira.htm (accessed October 4, 2021).
Friedman, T. (1999). *The Lexus and the olive tree.* New York: Farrar Straus Giroux.

Fukuyama, F. (1992). *The end of history and the last man.* New York: The Free Press.
Gennaro, S., & Miller, B. (Eds.). (2021). *Young people and social media: Contemporary children's culture. Delaware:* Vernon.
Giroux, H. (1996). *Fugitive cultures: Race, violence, and youth.* Routledge.
———. (2000). *Stealing innocence. Youth, corporate power, and the politics of culture.* New Saint Martin's.
———. (2003). *The abandoned generation. Democracy beyond the culture of fear.* Palgrave Macmillan.
Giroux, Henry. (2004). "Cultural studies, public pedagogy, and the responsibility of intellectuals." *Communication and Critical/Cultural Studies, 1*(1), 59–79, March 2004.
Hardt, M., & Negri, A. (2000). *Empire.* Harvard University Press.
Harvey, D. (1989). *The condition of postmodernity.* Blackwell.
Hirsch, E. D. (1988). *Cultural literacy: What every American needs to know.* Vintage.
Jenkins, H. (1997). "Empowering children in the Digital Age: Towards a Radical Media Pedagogy." *Radical Teacher, 50*(Spring), 30–36.
Kahn, R., & Kellner, D. (2003). "Internet subcultures and oppositional politics". In D. Muggleton (Ed.), *The post-subcultures reader.* Berg.
Kellner, D. (1995a). *Media culture.* Routledge.
———. (1995b). "Intellectuals and new technologies". *Media, Culture, and Society, 17,* 201–217.
———. (1997). "Intellectuals, the new public spheres, and technopolitics". *Science New Political, 41–42*(Fall), 169–188.
———. (1998). "Multiple literacies and critical pedagogy in a multicultural society". *Educational Theory, 48*(1), 103–122.
———. (1999a). "Theorizing McDonaldization: A multiperspectivist approach". In B. Smart (Ed.), *Resisting McDonaldization* (pp. 186–206). Sage Publications.
———. (1999b). "Globalization from below? Toward a radical democratic technopolitics". *Angelaki, 4*(2), 101–113.
———. (2000). "New technologies/new literacies: Reconstructing education for the new millennium". *Teaching Education, 11*(3), 245–265.
———. (2002). "Technological revolution, multiple literacies, and the restructuring of education." In Ilana Snyder (Ed.), *Silicon literacies* (pp. 154–169). Routledge.
———. (2003a). *Media spectacle.* Routledge.
———. (2003b). *From September 11 to Terror War: The dangers of the bush legacy.* Rowman and Littlefield.
———. (2003c). "Postmodern military and permanent war." In Carl Boggs (Ed.), *Masters of war. Militarism and blowback in the era of the American empire* (pp. 229–244). Routledge, 2003.
Kahn, R., & Kellner, D. (2003). "Internet subcultures and oppositional politics". In D. Muggleton (Ed.), *The post-subcultures reader.* Berg.
Lash, S. (1990). *The sociology of postmodernism.* Routledge.

Luke, A., & Luke, C. (2000). "A situated perspective on cultural globalization". In N. Burbules & C. Torres (Eds.), *Globalization and education* (pp. 275–298). Routledge.

Males, Mike. (1996). *The Scapegoat generation*. Common Courage Press.

Mander, J., & Goldsmith, E. (1996). *The case against the global economy*. Sierra Club Books.

Marx, K., & Engels, F. (1978). *The Marx-Engels reader* (second edition), R. Tucker, ed. Norton.

McChesney, Robert. (1997). *Corporate media and the threat to democracy*. Seven Stories Press.

McChesney, Robert. (2000). *Rich media, poor democracy*. The New Press.

McLaren, Peter. (1995). *Critical pedagogy and predatory culture*. Routledge.

Moody, K. (1988). *An injury to one*. Verso.

———. (1997). "Towards an International Social-Movement Unionism". *New Left Review, 225*, 52–72.

Oxfam International. (2021). "5 shocking facts about extreme global inequality and how to even it up". https://www.oxfam.org/en/5-shocking-facts-about-extreme-global-inequality-and-how-even-it

Peters, M. (forthcoming). "War as globalization: The 'Education' of the Iraqi People." In *Education in the Age of Terrorism*.

Peterson-Withorn, C. (2021). "How Much Money America's Billionaires have made during the Covid-19 Pandemic". *Forbes,* April 30, 2021. https://www.forbes.com/sites/chasewithorn/2021/04/30/american-billionaires-have-gotten-12-trillion-richer-during-the-pandemic/?sh=5fef7cf557e1 (accessed on October 4, 2021).

Ritzer, G. (1993 revised edition 1996). *The McDonaldization of Society*. Pine Forge Press.

Silver, L. (2019) "Smartphone ownership is growing rapidly around the world, but not always equally". PEW Research Center. https://www.pewresearch.org/global/2019/02/05/smartphone-ownership-is-growing-rapidly-around-the-world-but-not-always-equally/ (accessed on October 4, 2021).

Stiglitz, J. (2002). *Globalization and its discontents*. Norton.

UNICEF. (August 2020). "COVID-19: Are children able to continue learning during school closures? A global analysis of the potential reach of remote learning policies". https://data.unicef.org/resources/remote-learning-reachability-factsheet/ (accessed on October 4, 2021).

UNICEF. (December 2020). "How many children and young people have internet access at home? Estimating digital connectivity during the COVID-19 pandemic". https://data.unicef.org/resources/children-and-young-people-internet-access-at-home-during-covid19/ (accessed on October 4, 2021).

Waterman, P. (1992). "International Labour Communication by Computer: The Fifth International?". *Working Paper Series* 129. Institute of Social Studies.

Watson, J. (Ed.). (1998). *Golden arches East: McDonald's in East Asia*. Stanford University Press.

11 Has The Last Bastion Fallen?

FRANK A. FEAR

Introduction

A *bastion* is an institution, place, or person defending or upholding deeply held principles, attitudes, or activities. I view education that way—and higher education, especially, which is my area of attention. But I also know that the bastion is under assault, and I worry that it has fallen or soon will.

I am not alone in that belief. This chapter's title is courtesy of my spouse, Kathleen Lucille Fear, a professor, and a former collegiate administrator. She began her career as an elementary school teacher, earned a doctorate, transitioned to faculty life, earned tenure, became a department chair, and ended her career as dean of a liberal arts faculty. Over a forty-year time frame, she and I saw higher education migrate from our vocational platform to a largely unrecognizable enterprise.

There is evidence all around, both outside and within The Academy. For example, the prevailing society-wide answer has changed to a fundamental question, "*What is college for?*" It used to be about learning and maturing, and about being able to engage responsibly—both professionally and as citizens—in a democratic society. Today, students specialize as quickly as they can, focusing on getting a job, often at their parents' urging. Likewise, college worth—and colleges, generally—are frequently evaluated in financial terms—Return on Investment (Carrns, 2021).

What is more, the public interpretation of higher education is increasingly political, as are so many other things these days. A study by Pew Research shows that Liberals/Progressives are overwhelmingly supportive, while Conservatives and Libertarians—many of whom see college as a breeding ground for leftwing political indoctrination—are pronounced in their negativity (Parker, 2019).

Life inside The Academy has changed, too. Today, it is a corporatized industry governed largely by Neoliberal boards and managed by like-minded administrators who conflate business objectives and peer standing with mission obligations. With money and peer standing reigning supreme, academic governance—a medium for faculty voice and engagement—has been largely neutralized, if not neutered (American Association of University Professors, 2021).

Higher education, in the throes of a decades-long disruption, has changed in ways that many thought would never change but has (Fear, 2017a). The free press has gone through a similar metamorphosis. Prominent among the changes are accusations of "fake news" coupled with a corporate-led compression. Since 2006, there are 2100 fewer newspapers nationally and 60% fewer staff (Kennedy, 2021). Straightforward news reporting has been displaced by opinion-riveted commentary. Many people *still* view this as "news," but it is not.

A democratic society cannot afford to have its primary truth-seeking institutions in jeopardy, especially if it is by way of an incursion executed by politically motivated, corporate-linked, and self-serving actors. A strong, persistent response is required to *name* what is happening, *disdain* its pernicious implications, and *proclaim* an alternative that values and advances what *should be* (and needs to be) for democratic society to flourish.

Scholar-Activism is Required

Higher education *must* be center stage in this work, and scholar-activism—once a choice—is now an obligation. All of us, irrespective of field and role, must speak out and act up. Otherwise, higher education may join other species that have migrated from endangered to lost. What makes scholar-activism challenging is the insidious ways that Neoliberalism, which I shall discuss later, has seeped into the body politic and institutional life spaces. I saw that happen, first, in the nonprofit sector, and I witnessed it creep into higher education. I, many colleagues, and a good share of the public did not recognize what was happening. Like the proverbial frog in the boiling pot, recognition (if it came at all) arrived only as the temperature rose to a deadly level.

What many of us believed was business as usual (with a twist here and there) was something else. It became "new business." Chris Lorenz (2012) calls it "The New Public Management," a way of operating that combines free-market economics and intense managerial control. The result "parasitizes the everyday meanings of efficiency, accountability, transparency, quality, and excellence—and simultaneously perverts their original meanings" (p. 600).

Lorenz also asserts that The New Public Management possesses similarities to other forms of centrally and strictly controlled operations, not unlike a Communist state (p. 600). Mark Seis (2020, p. 51), along with Debra Leigh Scott (2018), contends that there is "a new class of college administrators," namely, technocrats who instill regimes aimed at "centralizing and homogenizing" a variety of functions that were previously under faculty control but are now controlled administratively using metrics they exact and monitor. Thomas Kilkauer and Meg Young (2021) refer to the circumstance as a disease, *academentia*, a portmanteau that combines academia and dementia. Caused, they assert, by heavy doses of Managerialism and Neoliberalism, its symptoms include "a severe loss of touch with the scholarly reality" and results in a "toxic environment" (p. 1). "Academentia," they write, downgrades what once defined the very existence of a university—the academic faculty—into some kind of over-stressed, semi-academic factory workers" (p. 1).

Camille Kandiko (2010) sees three major trends—privatization, commercialization, and corporatization—that contribute to capitalist and corporate influence (p. 157). Christopher Newfield elaborates in his highly acclaimed book, *The Great Mistake* (2016). In it, he settles on privatization, which he sees as "mode of governance and a control mechanism. Specific effects that people bemoan, like administrative bloat, are the symptom, not the disease.... These practices (accumulate over time) and create a devolutionary cycle" (p. 26, 27). That position was acknowledged recently in an international conference keynote address delivered by distinguished sociologist Michael D. Higgins, who currently serves as president of the Republic of Ireland. Higgins issued this warning: "Academics everywhere should be alarmed at the ongoing corrosive attack that faces the university, even at its core conceptual level, that has already occurred and continues to occur in so many places, and which has led to little less than the degradation of teaching, learning and scholarship.... This does not simply endanger academic freedom; it has consequences for the freedom of all citizens. Indeed, it endangers democracy itself, in those countries where it exists, and the possibility of democracy in those countries where there is none" (O'Connell, 2021).

Heretofore Separate Propositions are Now Connected

Once a social institution, higher education (and education writ large) used to be *apart from*, rather than *a part of*, the commercial landscape. That is not the case today. Distance from broader, politicized social trends and perspectives is also not the case. Heretofore politicized circumstances, albeit sometimes dramatic in nature (e.g., Scopes Trial of 1925), happen with regularity today. For example, analysts have urged the University of California system to discontinue using standardized test scores in the admission process, concluding that the tests discriminate against low-income students, who are in many cases Black and Latino (Watanabe, 2021). Soon thereafter, *The Atlantic*—a high-profile and reputable national publication—carried an article authored by Caitlin Flanagan (2021) with the curious headline, *Why the University of California Is Lying to Us.* As John Warner (2021) put it in *Inside Higher Education*, "Because of the currents of our never-ending culture war, Flanagan's attack needs not be accurate or factual to be persuasive to many people in her audience." Warner believes that when a university acts in ways to disrupt the system that exists (as U Cal did in this case) it seeks *not* "to preserve the kind of competition that they (Flanaghan and others) think 'makes America great,' the kind of competition at which they themselves have been so successful." This example is one of many attempts to push America's educational system to the Right.

Three seemingly separate propositions—*running education like a business, having education serve business,* and *imposing right-leaning ways of valuing, thinking, and practicing on education*—are connected, "the culprits" of our age to use Newfield's language. That said, many people attribute words like *good, successful, strong,* and *exemplary* to administrators and institutions that operate just that way. Furthermore, long gone is the time when those in power sought to direct and control affairs in Tammany Hall-style without engendering public support. The goal today is to get the public to think similarly, and to endorse the elites' way of viewing the world, including how organizations and institutions should operate. That quest is being undertaken masterfully and in a manner that can be depicted as public relations on steroids, aided by a staff of letter-writers/memo-creators, brand-originators, social media mavens, and video producers. Image-making and attitude-shaping is a shared job description. It is working, too. Evidence is found in the messages the public is carrying to those in their social networks. Consider photos across the nation showing everyday people attending school board meetings and decrying the teaching of Critical Race Theory.

Institutional leaders are also getting plenty of help well beyond those involved in messaging and branding—even when those performing the tasks do not share their leaders espoused values and beliefs. Hegemonic and other means are employed so that employees benefit professionally and economically by securing positions and salaries that yield lifestyles many presumed were not possible—even in their wildest dreams. What I have just asserted does not apply here and there; it applies everywhere. The happy face explanation is that it enables more people to experience The American Dream.

Another explanation is that it is how *regimes* are established and sustained. And, just like any regime, a distorted view of reality emerges and is then promulgated to the public through seemingly benign means, including public relations, outreach, and branding. With onerous implications, the charade has extended into the higher education sphere (Vinsel, 2021).

Claims Require Scrutiny

The fundamental problem is that you never know what to believe. More than at any other period in my lifetime, *claims* are being made in a cavalier, pall-mall manner, often with little (if any) credible evidence of support. Princeton philosopher Harry G. Frankfurt (2005) interprets this behavior as *bullshit*, a phenomenon he interprets as more dangerous than lies. Claims often seem reasonable, tantalizingly easy to believe and accept (p. 47). The onus is on us to research, evaluate, and decide what is credible. Sifting/sorting through an endless number of claims is not easy, and evaluating dubious claims is tiring, but necessary. That is because we live in a time that clinical psychologist Bryant Welch (2008) refers to a "state of confusion" and an "assault on the mind." Welch sees it as "a battle to shape what Americans perceive as reality" (p. 8). Tactics, such as gaslighting (people are made to question their reality, memory, or perceptions), "exploits weaknesses in the human mind and has a debilitating effect on the victim's ability to think rationally and to function independently" (p. 10). And when that happens, Welch continues, it is "highly unlikely that (victims) will reconsider their beliefs, no matter what the consequence and no matter what the evidence to the contrary" (p. 7).

How dangerous that is, and how real it is, too. That is because spewing B.S. is anything but episodic or restrictive. Today, it is a public art. Consider this example. Recently I came upon a post as I scrolled through my *Facebook Feed*. Because of its look—text written on yellowed parchment—I decided to investigate. The post begins with an attention-grabbing statement: *"This is a clipping I found in my dad's safe. He read a lot with main interests being history & government."* That is Grabber #1. There is personal allure in the introduction; a family heirloom, preserved by an erudite relative, is shared publicly. Grabber #2 is the attribution to an academic source—in this instance to the late 18th-early 19th Century Scottish historian Alexander Tytler. Even though Tytler is neither widely known nor read by the public, a more important matter is that linking a claim to an academic source enhances its credibility. In this post, Tytler writes about what he sees as *democracy's challenge*. "A democracy will continue to exist up until the time that voters discover that they can vote themselves generous gifts from the public treasury," Tytler writes. "From that moment on, the majority always votes for the candidates who promise the most benefits from the public treasury, with the result that every democracy will finally collapse due to loose fiscal policy, which is always followed by a dictatorship."

Whether or not there is sufficient evidence to support Tytler's assertion is less important than something else that is going on. It is Grabber #3, a common bait-and-switch tactic, namely, starting with something many people care about irrespective of standing or persuasion (in this case, democracy), but then zeroing in one one—*and only one*—explanation of a complex phenomenon. Only *loose spending* is identified, and that is singled out with intent. The poster uses Tytler's work to make a political point—accusing Biden and Democrats of reckless spending and chastising the public for feeding at the trough. Hook set, one Facebook Friend wrote, "*Sounds current*" in the Comments section.

Grabber #4 is in play. The endgame is to get you to believe/endorse a promulgated political position. Cleverly done in this case, it is also devious and dangerous. To some people, per Welch, it is not only believable, but it is also worth sharing. And that is what happened in this case: the person on my Facebook Feed received the post from another source. I then went to the attributor's Facebook page and, there, I found revealing posts. The most recent post (at the time of this writing) declared that Trump had won the 2020 presidential election in both Pennsylvania and Michigan, and that state legislatures in both states should investigate. Another recent post included a photo of President Biden at a signing ceremony. But superimposed on that photo was another photo showing what Biden had on his desk. He did not sign anything, and that was the point. The photo showed Biden working on a crossword puzzle.

What does this example have to do with education and higher education? There was a day—and it was not that long ago—when I worried little about shenanigans like this. They would be detected quickly and dismissed. Today, I worry that education writ large is no longer fully committed to developing students' minds, including helping students analyze and evaluate claims and positions, and to develop defensible claims of their own. Instead, in today's environment, education is an integral part of the overarching *Academic-Industrial Complex* (Nocella II, Best, & McLaren, 2010). As Morrow postulates, "In the neoliberal model...education is ideally integrated into the system of production and accumulation in which knowledge is reduced to its economic functions and contributes to the realization of individual economic utilities" (Morrow, 2006, p. xxxi). As a feeder system to the marketplace, *schooling* (for jobs) has supplanted *education* (for expanding minds and developing habits of a lifetime). Arts programs are being eliminated at the secondary level, and the humanities and social sciences are under siege at the collegiate level. Schools today are less about learning in the classic sense, and more about what Anthony Nocella II calls *rubricization*, that is, emphasis on training-for-tasks and doing so efficiently and effectively. This Tayloristic approach to schooling means that today's students are more likely to be viewed and treated as cogs in a capitalist-driven model of education.

Impact of a Rightwing Movement

The metamorphosis I have just described is the result of a well-coordinated, -funded, and -networked effort among plutocrats, corporatists, elected officials, and others. They are conspiring to hijack education so that it serves their preferences, purposes, politics, and aspirations. For example, consider an important historic document, namely, a 7000-word memo written in 1971 to the American Chamber of Commerce by Lewis F. Powell (1971), the soon-to-be-appointed U.S. Supreme Court Justice. Popularly known as *The Powell Memo* or *The Powell Manifesto*, it serves as a call to arms and a road map to achieve what Powell interprets as important and worthy ends. Reading it explains why there is emphasis today on American Exceptionalism, why there is wealth inequality, how "spinning and branding" have gained widespread appeal, why there are Political Action Committees, how the Koch Brothers gained such prominence, how tax cuts and supply-side economics became the rage, and why gerrymandering became a political weapon. It is a long list, including how to hijack education, higher education, and the free press. The politics Powell preferred were all-inclusive and the backstory tells why.

Powell witnessed activism of the 1960s—citizens protesting the Vietnam War, engaging in the Civil Rights Movement, and expressing growing concern for the environment, among other things. He also felt that President Nixon was capitulating to "liberal interests" by taking unnecessary and problematic actions, such as establishing the Environmental Protection Agency. Powell believed a broad-based, comprehensive counterassault was needed, and that it should include a blueprint with an action plan. He articulated both, but he did not see himself as the leader of a movement that he hoped would emerge. Others would serve in that public role, and, within a decade, Ronald Reagan became the face of the movement in America and Margaret Thatcher played the same role abroad. The two collaborated forcefully, laboring under the banner of Thatcher's famous words, "There is no alternative!" (Berlinski, 2011). Despite Reagan's memorable portrayal of America as "that shining city on the hill," he did not declare *who* would/should live there. The answer was revealed in his policies. Thatcher, on the other hand, was far more declarative in what she said, including her headshaking proclamation that "There is no such thing as a society, only individuals and families" (Margaret Thatcher Foundation, 1987). Thatcher backed rhetoric with action. Tax cuts, austerity programs, welfare reforms, and other moves designed to serve the business community and privilege elites by giving them greater voice and more influence. All of this started in the late 1970s-early 1980s and it has continued to this day.

Powell got the ball rolling, largely because the time was right, and he was able to express himself in a way that spoke to millions—then and now. "His people" took note, and they organized, charted strategy, and acted—not just then, but through the years—long after Powell, Reagan and Thatcher were gone. Consider just some of what Powell wrote a half-century ago and then compare it to contemporary circumstances (list drawn from Fear, 2016).

- The economic system—the enterprise system—is the cornerstone of society.
- The media is left leaning, and we must act to counter that bias.
- The rich are being demeaned when, in fact, they should be hailed as job-creators and the engines of industry.
- The business community must become centrally involved in political affairs.
- Higher education's liberal bias must be addressed and countered, including generating materials and supporting faculty that embrace Conservative ideas and causes.
- The business and Conservative community, generally, must engage the public more expressly and directly by getting messages out to engender public affirmation and support.
- We must pay far more attention to the courts and judicial system, becoming activists, and promoting the candidacy of sympathetic judges.
- Our work must not be done exclusively in the name of economics. We must link it meaningfully to historic concepts of the Republic, including liberty, freedom, and the American way.

Higher Education Infiltrated

That is Powell's legacy. And, today, numerous Powell-like efforts are underway, all with the same goal—capture people and institutions so that "our way" becomes the American way. Take, for example, *PragerU* (2021). It is *not* an academic institution, but it seeks to elevate its standing by portraying itself as a university, just as Trump University did. It is a right-wing media corporation that produces material designed to undermine what Prager believes is America's liberal-leaning media and educational system. Launched with significant funding from billionaires Dan and Ferris Wilks, at *PragerU,* you will find essays, videos, and other online content that promulgate rightwing perspectives on social and economic issues of the day, including climate change, slavery/the Civil War, race, and tax policy. In each case, a storyline is shared that promotes a significantly right-leaning perspective of the way things were or are.

At the top of *PragerU's* list of offerings on the day I drafted this chapter was a video promoting the work of Thomas Sewell, a Stanford University fellow and the academic darling of Conservatives and Libertarians. The video entitled *The Great Thomas Sewell* (Riley, 2021) touts him as "one of the greatest social theorists America has ever produced." That "great social theorist" debunks the concept of systemic racism (labeling its promotion as "propaganda"), strongly supports free-market capitalism and charter schools, promoted the election of Donald Trump, and warned that electing Joe Biden to the presidency would finish America as we know it, comparing it to the end of the Roman Empire (DeSoto, 2020).

The video is hosted by Jason Riley, a senior fellow at the Manhattan Institute, a right-wing organization that produces materials supporting (among other things) supply-side economics and the privatization of public services. *PragerU* and The Manhattan Institute are not one-offs in the world of strongly right-leaning think tanks and foundations that are infiltrating America's educational and political systems. Included on the list are the Hoover Institution, Claremont Institute, Aequus Institute, Heritage Foundation, American Enterprise Institute, Hudson Institute, American Majority, Markus Foundation. DonorsTrust, Bradley Foundation, the Olin Foundation and, most notably, the Koch Network. These operations are networked in the quest for common causes.

The situation is especially problematic in public higher education, a sector that has experienced significant state-level funding cuts over the past fifteen years or so. Plutocrats have taken advantage—often in collaboration with elected officials who share their philosophy—by filling the public funding breach with billions of private dollars through a seemingly benign pathway, namely, *philanthropy*. Subject-matter priorities include promoting the primacy of free-market capitalism and safeguarding the ethic of American Exceptionalism. Recent efforts have focused on restricting teaching the legacy of racism in America, including rejecting Critical Race Theory (CRT) as a legitimate framework for interpreting U.S. history (Graff, 2021). Politically motivated philanthropy can also influence which faculty members get hired, promoted, and are awarded tenure.

Several instances came to light during the writing of this chapter. For example, the national watchdog organization, *UnKochMyCampus* (2021), released a report documenting coordinated efforts to oppose CRT and keep it from being taught in our nation's schools. "We reviewed the published materials of 28 think tanks and political organizations," *UnKochMyCampus* reported, "and (we) analyzed the rhetorical tactics deployed around CRT and the effort to ban it from public schools." The organization found "146 articles, podcasts, reports, and videos about CRT, produced by organizations including The Heritage Fund, FreedomWorks, and the Manhattan Institute ... (that were designed) to generate and spread talking points, brief state and federal legislators on policy, and mobilize grassroots support to denigrate CRT and keep it out of school curricula."

Just days after that report was released, Nebraska's governor urged his state university regents to "pass a resolution opposing Critical Race Theory...so that we ke*ep academic freedom alive and well at the University of Nebraska.*" He went on to say that *"(we) should consider it to be an honor to be listed on the American Association of University Professor's censure list alongside notable conservative institutions, including Brigham Young University, Catholic University, and Hillsdale College"* (Flaherty, 2021).

Direct attempts to influence partisan outcomes like the one just described include soliciting faculty to undertake funded research work that advances Conservative/Libertarian causes. Coming across my desk during the writing of this chapter was a "note of encouragement and offer of assistance" (words communicated to faculty) from a high-ranking university fundraising official. It was a Request for Proposals issued by the rightwing The Lynde and Harry Bradley Foundation. Rife with code words, the solicitation focuses on research pertaining to (using the Foundation's words) "The Constitutional Order, Free Markets, Civil Society, and Informed Citizens." Words of elaboration include "to reform and re-imagine systems and higher education," "promote the teaching of American Exceptionalism," and "work with state policy groups to promote public policies that reduce government dependency."

While a good share of the work associated with grant-making and Requests for Proposals is consistent with education's historic mission of free inquiry, lurking in the bushes is a concerted effort to push education to the Right. It is done by influencing what students learn, what faculty research, and what knowledge higher education produces and shares (Fear, 2021). Thankfully, academics across the country are responding to these pernicious activities, including Professor Isaac Kamola of Trinity College. Kamola's article, *Where Does the Bizarre Hysteria About CRT Come From? Follow the Money* (2021), documents the scope of the problem. He writes: "Between 2005 and 2019, the Charles Koch Foundation has spent over $485 million at more than 550 universities." With money comes influence. For example, Kamola notes that "Conservative megadonor Walter Hussman, Jr. lobbied hard to deny the Pulitzer Prize-winning journalist Nikole Hannah-Jones a tenured professorship at the University of North Carolina Chapel Hill journalism school that bears his name." When framed nationally, Kamola concludes that "political actors with political motivations and a well-funded infrastructure are behind (what he characterizes as) "an onslaught." Kamola's book co-authored with Ralph Wilson (2021), *Free Speech and Koch Money: Manufacturing a Campus Culture War,* reveals how. The co-authors examine how the Koch donor network funds university student groups, think tanks, litigation organizations, and right-wing media outlets.

Rightwing funding is often targeted to support specific programs, faculty members, and academic units, especially at schools with sympathetic administrative officers, board members, and faculty. Perhaps the most notable example is what some assert as the Conservative/Libertarian takeover of Florida State University's economics department (Kotch, 2017). But sometimes the scope widens and a school writ large is the focus of attention. George Mason University, a public university in suburban Washington, DC, arguably holds the status of America's most politically infiltrated university (Stripling, 2016). Examples include external gifts totaling $30 million to rename the law school as the Antonin Scalia Law School, the C. Boyden Gray Center for the Study of the Administrative State, and the Mercatus Center, a unit that specializes in Neoliberal thought and promotes its practice. Professor Bethany Letiecq, a GMU faculty-activist, serves on the university's Faculty Senate and is president of the campus chapter of the American Association of University Professors (AAUP). Letiecq has also partnered with student leaders to expose undue donor influence at GMU, and she has challenged the privatization of presidential searches and working conditions of contract workers during COVID.

Letiecq (2019) describes the situation in her article, *George Mason University's Donor Problem, and the Fight for Transparency.* She writes: "Relationships between universities and private donors can be fraught with conflicts of interest and challenges to academic independence, especially when private gifts come with strings attached." In her GMU work, Letiecq found a situation that exists at other universities (e.g., SUNY at Buffalo), namely, a university foundation that is "off-limits to public scrutiny." At issue is whether the GMU Foundation is subject to the Virginia Freedom of Information Act, an objective made more difficult considering a 2021 U.S. Supreme Court ruling that struck down a California law. National Public Radio phrased the ruling this way: *"The Supreme Court Throws Out a State Law Requiring Nonprofits to Name Rich Donors"* (Totenberg, 2021).

Neoliberalism as Cultural Imperialism

While it would be easy to conclude that all of this is happening selectively across the country, I believe that a more prudent path involves recognizing, naming, and understanding an underlying and pervasive pattern. For that, I turn to a concept undergraduate students learn in introductory social sciences courses. *Cultural imperialism* (Tobin, no date) refers to the concerted effort to take over a culture as executed by a powerful and persistent outside force. The concept is useful for understanding the behavior of nation-states—the British Empire is an example. It applies equally well to circumstances when a power source seeks to render a deep change in a culture—a change that reflects the imposer's philosophy, preferences, and objectives. Grubbs (2000), for example, elaborated this way of thinking in his investigation of organizational change, concluding that "from this perspective, we may understand the deleterious human, social, and cultural consequences of organizational expansionism."

With that in mind, an epochal transition from old rules to new rules took root in the 1970s, grew in the 1980s, and became well-entrenched worldwide by the 1990s. It has a variety of names, and *Neoliberalism* is the nomenclature I prefer (Fear, 2020). Coined as a term over 80 years ago, Neoliberalism's genesis is the socio-politics of the 1930s, most notably with Nazism, Communism, and strong central government control in the U.S. during the New Deal years. Concerns emerged about how the world might look if any of those systems became pre-eminent. But the counterforce—conjoining capitalism and morality in an amalgam of money, markets, and traditional values (e.g., freedom)—evolved into something beyond a response to excessive state control. By the late 1970s and early 1980s, Neoliberalism began influencing national public policy in Great Britain, America, and other countries. What Neoliberalism wrought was smaller government, deregulated financial and capital markets, antagonism toward organized labor, rejection of progressive taxation, reduction of the public social safety net, the rise of the nonprofit sector (responsibility shifted from the public sector), the privatization of public programs, and other related policy preferences. As Neoliberalism evolved, it also morphed. Berkeley's Wendy Brown (2019) contends that by the 1990s Neoliberalism became a "saturating reality principle," and that its tenets expanded into the sociocultural domain.

Neoliberalism emphasizes the overarching value of *the individual* (vis-a-vis the collective), *competition* (the ultimate measure of success), *personal rights* (outweighing public responsibilities), and the belief that *all institutions* should be managed, led, and governed *using corporate-style practices*. In Kuhn's terms (Kuhn, 1996), Neoliberalism evolved into the dominant paradigm of our age. Strangely, though, Neoliberalism was rarely named as such. It either carried other names (e.g., Corporatism) or had no name at all. Stealth-like in nature, but powerful in application and impact, Neoliberalism became the contemporary version of Adam Smith's "invisible hand." In his widely read article, George Monbiot (2016) defined it this way: "Neoliberalism sees *competition* (italics added) as the defining characteristic of human relations." William Deresiewicz (2015) wrote "Neoliberalism is an ideology that *reduces all values to money values* (italics added). The worth of a thing is the price of the thing. The worth of a person is the wealth of the person." The Neoliberal ethic—a way of thinking, valuing, and acting—drifted into individual mindsets (what people valued and affirmed) and into public spaces, including the way public and non-profit institutions are governed and administered.

The corporate business model reigns supreme, including its preferred ways of structuring, operating, and evaluating. Language followed and sealed the deal—e.g., market share, chain of command, and Return on Investment. Very importantly, because corporate elites play oversized roles as executives, board members, and donors in the public/nonprofit sectors (including higher education), *those spaces became extensions of corporate culture*—led, managed, and operated in ways with which corporate elites are familiar and accustomed. Put another way, nonprofits and public enterprises are extensions of the corporate culture. Those who embrace alternative ways of thinking and approaches are often displaced or replaced by those with financial, corporate, and/or political connections. I saw that happen in my volunteer food bank work, an enterprise that is best depicted today as the food bank *industry*. It has happened in higher education, too.

All of what I have just described is a form of *cultural imposition*, that is, imposing a new way of thinking and operating *on* a culture. But imposition is not enough to exact culture change. For that to happen, *cultural expansionism* is required. Expansionism takes place when ad hoc and episodic impositions turn into multiple, persistent, and deep-cutting incursions. Over time, the new way becomes the norm, the way we do things. Reinforcing that depiction is this way of thinking: it is not only the way *we* do things here, but it is also the way *business is done everywhere.*

Expansionism sets the stage for accomplishing the final objective, *cultural domination*, which is (in effect) cultural takeover. That, I believe, has already happened in the nonprofit sector, and it is well on its way to ending the free press's standing as The Fourth Estate of the Realm. Higher education, as I see it, is in a late-stage struggle. The end-stage will reveal what it means to say *higher education* and ask, *"What is higher education (and college) for?"*

As Neoliberal preferences became embedded in society as the paradigm of our age, it showed what can happen when a social and economic force is permitted to go too far. In unbridled form, there is no major counterweight to keep it in line and, with that, it becomes too much and goes too far, pushing society, institutions, and people in extreme directions. That said, the culprit here is not Neoliberalism. It is *Capitalism*. Neoliberalism, after all, is nothing more than an enabling function for Capitalism to expand and deepen its hold—on people, social life, and institutions. As Mark Seis (2020) puts it, "Neoliberalism is a more aggressive form of capitalism designed to undo public collective values and replace them with a society of self-interested actors expressing their self-worth through the accumulation and consumption of wealth—all life boiled down to market-based, contractual relations leaving behind all other ethical frameworks for deciding the general welfare" (p. 43).

The problem, then, is what Monbiot (2016) called "the root of it all"— society's love affair with, and reliance on, Capitalism. Many Americans fear living without it, and many detest replacement options. The irony is that those perceptions hold despite the consistent record (empirically based) that America's standing in the world is falling and has been falling for some time. Consider the results of *The Social Progress Index (2020). The* Index measures performance across 163 countries using a system that analyzes data associated with 50+ social indicators selected from hundreds of possibilities. In 2020, the U.S. was ranked #28 in the world. In 2017, it was #18. It was #16 in 2015. In 2013 (the SPI's first year), America was ranked #6 (Fear, 2021a). Why is the U.S. falling in the rankings? The answer is lodged in what the system measures, namely, *Basic Human Needs, Foundations of Well Being,* and *Opportunity. The U.S. lags in those domains.* At #28, the United States is ranked in the middle of Tier 2, immediately following Greece and immediately before Singapore. The top ten countries (in order) are Norway, Denmark, Finland, New Zealand, Sweden, Switzerland, Canada, Australia, Iceland, and The Netherlands. Worse yet, it is where the U.S. stands vis-à-vis international peers, including Japan, Great Britain, and other G-7 countries.

Using 2020 SPI data, it is not possible to find *any peer country that underperforms the United States*. Those findings are not a one-off conclusion. The Commonwealth Fund (2021) recently issued a report on global health, and the U.S. ranked *last* among the eleven richest countries in the world on access to health care, equity, and health outcomes. Top performers were Norway, The Netherlands, and Australia. The Commonwealth Fund identified four reasons that separate the U.S. from top-performing countries: universal coverage, primary care systems equitably available to all people, administrative red tape, and investment in social services.

Of course, any time findings like those are announced, one response is inevitable: "One reason is that America's educational system is failing." But here is the problem with that explanation: you cannot have it both ways—high-impact social outcomes in an uber-strong Neoliberal/Capitalist system. The U.S. education system is doing *exactly* what Neoliberals prefer: it serves Capitalism. Focusing on the survival of the fittest in a highly competitive, economic feeder system based on the primacy of individual achievement and wealth creation, the result is a society of have's and have nots. Rampant inequality and privilege amid poverty defines America's reality, and it describes our educational system, too. Schools are *not* all the same; some are better than others, and it is not difficult to ascertain why. The standard approach in Neoliberalism is to protect elites' economic privilege and therein lies a huge systems-level problem.

In his well-researched book, *Winners Take All)* Anand Giridharadas (2018) calls it "the elite charade of changing the world." On the one hand, elites seek to control systems/structures that enable and sustain their privilege (e.g., tax policies in their favor). At the same time, they also seek to control response systems designed to assist those in need. In so doing, Giridharadas contends that elites replace the public square with private philanthropy funneled through nonprofit organizations they control. Elites, then, use money and influence to have it both ways—protect their advantage *and* direct how social welfare is managed. But in so doing, they address public problems through private means. Consequently, America—a victim of its own doing—lags internationally. America tinkers with alternatives to Neoliberalism, such as Progressive Neoliberalism (see Fear, 2017b; Fraser, 2017) and Progressive Capitalism (see Stiglitz (2019), but those approaches struggle to gain widespread appeal.

Clarion Call for Change

In the end, the problem is that too many of us accept the way things are, adjusting our behaviors accordingly to fit the system and culture that exists. Too few of us have come forward saying, "enough!" Even fewer follow up with sustained activism. While the public expresses outrage when *individuals* transgress, there is a shocking lack of outrage directed at problematic systems—even when it is widely acknowledged that things are seriously amiss (e.g., child abuse by Roman Catholic priests and the decades-long and widespread institutional coverup that followed). But non-response and inaction is inherently problematic—not only because it lets offending systems/institutions off the hook, but also because it implicates *us*. Our inaction *tamps down criticism, lessens calls for reform, and counteracts activism's impact.*

Amos Guiora (2020) studied the Holocaust and sexual assaults to understand why more people did not come forward in the face of those detestable behaviors. Two critical concepts emerged from his analysis. The *bystander,* Guiora explains, *"sees another in peril and chooses not to act,"* while the enabler *"is not a witness but decides not to intervene."* The implications are chilling because Guiora believes we do not have to be "perpetrators" directly to share responsibility. Enablement is especially widely shared, he contends, and that is why Guiora refers to enablers using a military metaphor—as "armies." Still, though, admitting *something is wrong means doing something, and that can be a heavy choice. Other options are often preferred, including denying* (e.g., it is not as bad as you are making it out to be), *deflecting* (e.g., "It's happening everywhere, not just here"), *and rationalizing* (e.g., times change, and we must change with the times). *Those who protest and act can be called moralizers and pontificators, and they can be characterized as disloyal.*

It is much easier to speak out and act from afar. Affiliates/insiders face a dilemma—personal risks associated with coming forward in protest and act. Fears of personal consequences can be high. Besides, coming forward effectively as an insider requires special skills that are not widely held. Debra Meyerson (2001) calls the capacity *tempered radicalism*—to act without being done in by one's activism. So, for those reasons and more, the path often traveled is to participate in change efforts that institutional leaders enact or endorse. While those efforts may begin with great promise, the politics of change often determine where things settle (Barr and Fear, 2005). Yeasty ideas get watered down as ideas and approaches are filtered carefully—some absorbed, others jettisoned in the clever quest to refresh a bit here and there—to change, but not change *too* much.

The problem today is that it is too late to take small steps and play political games. Incrementalism will not do. As I wrote at the beginning of this chapter, a *bastion strongly defends or upholds principles, attitudes, or activities*. As a bastion, education serves as a guardian of reason, a pathway to open inquiry, and an antidote to the adulterating effects of political manipulation. But that depiction is not where education seems to be trending and, if that is where it settles, I do not believe education is worth defending or upholding. That said, historic interpretations and practices of education *are*—to develop the mind, seek wisdom through understanding, cultivate a strong sense of personal and civic consciousness, and serve the public (not private) good. Education of that kind contributes mightily to lives worth living and a society worth extolling. Anything less cheapens what education is, and it also subverts—as well as perverts—education's central value in a democratic society.

That is why the stakes are so high. Silence is deadly. Complicity is surrender. Inaction is not an option. The Neoliberal scourge has gone on too long and it has gone too far. That is why I implore you to fight in some manner, shape, or form—irrespective of who you are, where you are, what field is yours, or what role you play. The future of society (not just education) is at stake. Richard J. White (2020) has put it well: "There is still time— *our time*—to revolt and re-claim the critical, inclusive, and public commons that will allow academia to flourish once more" (p. xvi). That said, President Higgins (quoted in O'Connell, 2021) reminds us that time is not on our side. "The academy is now in a 'winter,' as Max Weber, the great 19th-century social theorist, foretold. Weber spoke of the threat of a 'spring that would not beckon with its promise of new life,' but would deliver instead 'the threat of a winter of icy cold.' Weber prophesied 'an iron cage of bureaucracy within which conformity would be demanded' to that which no longer recognized its original moral or reasonable purpose."

Commit. Act.

References

American Association of University Professors. (2021, July). *The 2021 AAUP shared governance survey: Findings on faculty roles by decision-making areas*. Retrieved from AAUP.org: https://www.aaup.org/report/2021-aaup-shared-governance-survey-findings-faculty-roles-decision-making-areas

Barr, R. B., & Fear, F. A. (2005). The learning paradigm as bold change: Improving understanding and practice. In C. J. McPhail (Ed.), *Establishing and sustaining learning-centered community colleges* (pp. 13–31). Washington, DC: Association of Community Colleges.

Berlinski, C. (2011). *"There is no alternative": Why Margaret Thatcher matters* (2nd ed.). Basic Books.

Brown, W. (2019). *In the ruins of neoliberalism: The rise of antidemocratic politics in the west.* Columbia University Press.

Carrns, A. (2021, August 13). *Will that college degree pay off?* Retrieved from *The New York Times*: https://www.nytimes.com/2021/08/13/your-money/college-degree-investment-return.html

Commonwealth Fund. (2021, April 4). *Mirror, mirror 2021: Reflecting poorly. Health care in the U.S. compared to other high-income countries.* Retrieved from Commonwealthfund.org: https://www.commonwealthfund.org/publications/fund-reports/2021/aug/mirror-mirror-2021-reflecting-poorly

Deresiewicz, W. (2015, September). *The neoliberal arts: How college sold itself to the market.* Retrieved from Harpers: https://harpers.org/archive/2015/09/the-neoliberal-arts/

DeSoto, R. (2020, July 13). *Sowell: If Biden is elected, he could push the U.S. past 'point of no return,' like Roman Empire.* Retrieved from *Western Journal*: https://www.westernjournal.com/sowell-biden-elected-push-us-past-point-no-return-like-roman-empire/

Fear, F. A. (2016, March 24). *45 Years and counting: Sustaining power of 'The Powell Memo'.* Retrieved from LA Progressive: https://futureu.education/welcome-to-futureu/neoliberalism-comes-to-higher-education/

Fear, F. A. (2017, April 7). *Neoliberalism comes to higher education.* Retrieved from FutureU: Values and Change in Higher Education: https://futureu.education/welcome-to-futureu/neoliberalism-comes-to-higher-education/

Fear, F. A. (2017, April 7). *Neoliberalism's newest iteration: A progressive rip-off.* Retrieved from LA Progressive: https://www.laprogressive.com/progressive-neoliberalism/

Fear, F. A. (2020, December 5). *Neoliberalism: Marketing morals.* Retrieved from LA Progressive: https://www.laprogressive.com/marketizing-morals/

Fear, F. A. (2021, January 26). *Can Biden stop America's international decline?* Retrieved from LA Progressive: https://www.laprogressive.com/country-rank/

Fear, F. A. (2021, July 21). *Higher education faces big-time funding from rightwing plutocrats.* Retrieved from LA Progressive: https://www.laprogressive.com/university-donors/

Flaherty, C. (2021, July 28). *Nebraska's Critical Race Theory debate.* Retrieved from Inside Higher Education: https://www.insidehighered.com/news/2021/07/28/nebraskas-critical-race-theory-debate

Flanaghan, C. (2021, July 22). *The University of California is lying to us.* Retrieved from *The Atantic*: https://www.theatlantic.com/ideas/archive/2021/07/why-university-california-dropping-sat/619522/

Frankfurt, H. A. (2005). *On bullshit.* Princeton University Press.

Fraser, N. (2017, July 28). *Against progressive neoliberalism: A new progressive populism.* Retrieved from Dissent: https://www.dissentmagazine.org/online_articles/nancy-fraser-against-progressive-neoliberalism-progressive-populism

Giridharadas, A. (2018). *Winners take all: The elite charade of changing the world.* Vintage Books.

Graff, H. J. (2021, August 2). *Attacks on Critical Race Theory threaten democracy.* Retrieved from Inside Higher Education: https://www.insidehighered.com/views/2021/08/02/attacks-critical-race-theory-are-threat-american-democracy-opinion

Grubbs, J. W. (2000). Cultural imperialism: A critical theory of organizational change. *Journal of Organizational Change Management, 13*(3), 221–234.

Guiora, A. N. (2020). *Armies of enablers: Survival stories of simplicity and betrayal in sexual assaults.* American Bar Association Press.

Kamola, I. (2021, June 3). *Where does the bizarre hysteria about 'Critical Race Theory' come from? Follow the money!* Retrieved from Inside Higher Education: https:/www.insidehighered.com/blogs/just-visiting/guest-blog-where-does-bizarre-hysteria-about-%E2%80%98critical-race-theory%E2%80%99-come-follow

Kandiko, C. B. (2010). Neoliberalism in higher education: A comparative approach. *International Journal of Arts and Sciences, 3*(14), 153–175.

Kennedy, D. (2021, July 28). *Why we need federal assistance to save local news.* Retrieved from WGBH.org: https://www.wgbh.org/news/commentary/2021/07/28/why-we-need-federal-assistance-to-help-save-local-news

Kilkauer, T., & Young, M. (2021, July 28). *Academentia: The organizatinal insanity of the modern university.* Retrieved from CounterPunch: https://www.counterpunch.org/2021/07/28/academentia-the-organization-insanity-of-the-modern-university/

Kotch, A. (2017, January 30). *Investigation reveals the extent the Koch Empire is willing to go to take over a university.* Retrieved from Alternet: https://www.alternet.org/2017/01/koch-brothers-fsu/

Kuhn, T. S. (1996). *The structure of scientific revolutions* (3rd ed.). University of Chicago Press.

Letiecq, B. (2019, Spring). *George Mason University's donor problem and the fight for transparancy.* Retrieved from Academe: https://www.aaup.org/article/george-mason-university%E2%80%99s-donor-problem-and-fight-transparency#.YQrEXT-SnIU

Lorentz, C. (2012). Why are you under surveillance? Universities, neoliberalism, and New Public Management. *Critical Inquiry, 38*(3), 599–629.

Margaret Thatcher Foundation. (1987, September 23). *Interview for "Women's Own" ("no such thing as society").* Retrieved from Margaret Thatcher Foundation: https://www.margaretthatcher.org/document/106689

Meyerson, D. F. (2001). *Tempered radicals: How people use difference to inspire change at work.* Harvard Business Review Press.

Monbiot, G. (2016, April 15). *Neoliberalism—The ideology at the root of all our problems.* Retrieved from *The Guardian*: https://www.theguardian.com/books/2016/apr/15/neoliberalism-ideology-problem-george-monbiot

Morrow, R. A. (2006). Foreword—Critical theory, globalization, and higher education: Political economy and the cul-de-sac of the postmodernist cultural turn. In R. A. Rhodes, & C. A. Torres (Eds.), *The university, state, and market: The political economy* (pp. xvii–xxxiii). Stanford University Press.

Newfield, C. (2016). *The great mistake: How we wrecked public universities and how we can fix them.* Johns Hopkins University Press.

Nocella II, A., Best, S., & McLaren, P. (2010). *Academic repression: Reflections from the academic-industrial complex.* AK Press.

O'Connell, O. (2021, January 9). *Address by President Michael D. Higgins: 'On Academic Freedom' – Scholars at Risk Ireland/All European Academies Conference.* Retrieved from TogetherFM: https://togetherfm.com/address-by-president-michael-d-higgins-on-academic-freedom-scholars-at-risk-ireland-all-european-academies-conference/?utm_source=rss&utm_medium=rss&utm_campaign=address-by-president-michael-d-higgins-on-academic-freedom-scholars-at

Parker, K. (2019, January 30). *The growing partisan divide in views of higher education.* Retrieved from Pew Research: https://www.pewresearch.org/social-trends/2019/08/19/the-growing-partisan-divide-in-views-of-higher-education-2/

Powell, L. F. (1971, August 23). *Confidential memorandum to Eugene B. Sydnor, Jr., Chairman, Education Committee, U.S. Chamber of Commerce: Attack on the American free enterprise system.* Retrieved from Washington and Lee University: https://law2.wlu.edu/deptimages/Powell%20Archives/PowellMemorandumTypescript.pdf

PragerU. (2021, August). *PragerU.com.* Retrieved from PragerU: https://www.prageru.com/

Riley, J. (2021, August). *The Great Thomas Sewell.* Retrieved from PragerU: https://www.prageru.com/video/the-great-thomas-sowell/

Scott, D. L. (2012, October 16). *Here's how higher education was destroyed in 5 basic steps.* Retrieved from Alternet: https://www.alternet.org/2012/10/how-higher-education-us-was-destroyed-5-basic-steps/

Seis, M. (2020). Pondering the neoliberal public university with the ghost of Foucault. In E. Juergensmeyer, A. J. Nocella II, & M. Seis (Eds.), *Neoliberalism and academic repression: The fall of academic freedom in the era of Trump* (Paperback ed., pp. 43–57). Haymarket Books.

Social Progress Organization. (2020). *2020 Social progress index.* Retrieved from Socialprogress.org: https://www.socialprogress.org/static/8dace0a5624097333c2a57e29c2d7ad9/2020-global-spi-findings.pdf

Stiglitz, J. (2019). *People, power, and profits: Progressive Capitalism for an age of discontent.* W.W. Norton and Company.

Stripling, J. (2016, May 13). *How George Mason became Koch's academic darling.* Retrieved from The Chronicle of Higher Education: https://www.chronicle.com/article/how-george-mason-became-kochs-academic-darling/

Tobin, T. W. (N.D.). *Cultural imperialism.* Retrieved from Britannica: https://www.britannica.com/topic/cultural-imperialism

Totenberg, N. (2021, July 1). *The Supreme Court throws out a state law requiring nonprofits to name rich donors.* Retrieved from National Public Radio: https://www.northcountrypublicradio.org/news/npr/1004062322/the-supreme-court-throws-out-a-state-law-requiring-nonprofits-to-name-rich-donors

UnKochMyCampus. (2021, July). *Koch-funded moral panic: Ultra-right think tanks and Critical Race Theory.* Retrieved from UnKochMyCampus.org: https://static1.squarespace.com/static/5400da69e4b0cb1fd47c9077/t/60f97f1ef6b38207f741e44f/1626963747702/Koch+Funded+Moral+Panic+2021%281%29.pdf

Vinsel, L. (2021, July 9). *Marketing and PR are corrupting universities: The language of hype violates the language of truth.* Retrieved from The Chronicle of Higher Education: https://www.chronicle.com/article/marketing-and-pr-are-corrupting-universities

Warner, J. (2021, July 26). *'The Atlantic' owes UC a correction.* Retrieved from Insider Higher Education: https://www.insidehighered.com/blogs/just-visiting/%E2%80%98-atlantic%E2%80%99-owes-uc-correction

Watanabe, T. (2021, January 12). *UC should permanently eliminate all standardized tests for admissions, experts say.* Retrieved from the Los Angeles Times: https://www.latimes.com/california/story/2021-01-12/uc-should-permanently-eliminate-sat-and-all-standardized-tests-for-admissions-experts-say

Welch, B. (2008). *State of confusion: Political manipulation and the assault on the American mind.* Thomas Dunne Books, St. Martins Press.

White, R. J. (2020). Preface. In E. Juergensmeyer, A. J. Nocella II, & M. Seis (Eds.), *Neoliberalism and academic repression: The fall of academic freedom in the era of Trump,* (pp. xv–xvii). Haymarket Books.

Wilson, R., & Kamola, I. (2021). *Free speech and Koch money: Manufacturing a campus culture war.* Pluto Press.

BIBLIOGRAPHY \| 1033

12 Tied to the Loom: Alienation in the Neoliberal Academy, Anarcha-Feminism, and a Politics of Resistance and Care

CAROLINE K. KALTEFLEITER

Introduction

> The assault on the enterprise system was not mounted in a few months. It has gradually evolved over the past two decades. Although origins, sources, and causes are complex. There is reason to believe that the [university] campus is the single most dynamic source.
>
> Powell Memorandum, 1971

In August of 1971, Lewis Powell, an American lawyer and later appointee to the United States Supreme Court sent a confidential memorandum titled "Attack on American Free Enterprise System" to the US Chamber of Commerce. In this extensive missive, he argued that criticism and opposition to the US free enterprise system had gone too far that "the time had come for the wisdom, ingenuity, and resources of American business to be against those who would destroy it" (Powell Memo, 1971). Powell argued that individual action was insufficient, noting, "Strength lies in organization, in careful long-range planning and implementation, in the consistency of action over an indefinite period of years..." (Ibid.). David Harvey (2007) discusses Powell's argument as a full-frontal assault "upon institutions—universities, schools, the media, publishing, the courts—to change how individuals think about corporations, the law, culture, and the individual" (p. 43). Fifty years later, corporate influence over the United States educational system pervades, or as Chris Hedges (2018) asserts, "The blueprint for a corporate coup d'état is complete" (p. 19). Corporate power gains longevity from influencing young adults about to enter the workforce, and in the process, reshapes institutions of higher learning to prioritize such interests. Such thoughts lay the groundwork for us to consider the neoliberal university. Mark Seis (2020) notes that "Neoliberalism has become so ingrained in contemporary think that it is difficult to distinguish it as an ideology which now confronts most people as normalized discourse (p. 44).

Several studies about neoliberalism and the academy focusing on academic repression, entrepreneurialism, faculty productivity, and longitudinal learning outcomes exist (Newfield, 2010; Nocella, Best, & McLaren, 2010; Giroux, 2013; Hall, 2018). However, missing from these discussions is a more compelling examination of the physical and mental health of academic faculty in the accelerated university, now made more evident during the COVID-19 pandemic.

This chapter contributes to the field of critical university studies, wherein the university is "both a discursive and a material phenomenon, one that extends through many facets of contemporary life" (Williams, 2012). I turn my attention to the industrial pathology that degrades workers and academics and acknowledges that society, prefigured and reproduced by academic labor, is reliant and restructured through entrepreneurship, impact, excellence, rubricization, and student satisfaction. Further, I explore the corporatization of the university and link the contemporary work of academics to discussions of labor experiences and anatomical agency in textile mills during the Industrial Age.

Methodologically, I employ an approach that incorporates histography and (auto)ethnography that includes brief semi-structured interviews of narrators noted anonymously to protect their identity. My journey in the academy informs this essay, with attention given to recent acute debilitations attributed to accelerated academic productivity and self-alienation. Faithful to dialectical praxis, I examine how alienation in the academy connects to broader structural forms and offers suggestions for collective resistance. Here, I build upon my earlier work on anarcha-feminism with collectives of care (Kaltefleiter & Alexander, 2019). As such, I extend a clarion call for the recuperation of home, self, and care by underscoring anarchist values of autonomy, solidarity, mutual aid, and community.

Neoliberalism and the Academy: The Financialization of Everything

Recent economic constraints, changes in campus demographics, and dramatic changes in higher education are taking place around the world (Gill,

2009; Rottenberg, 2018). The pressure to perform across teaching, research, and service continues to compound with a focus on successful research and publication productivity scrutinized through algorithms, metrics, and output excellence frameworks.

The acceleration of academic life is grounded in the realities of neoliberalism and financialization, which as Catherine Rottenberg (2018) notes, "is not merely an economic system or a set of policies that facilitate privatization and market deregulation" (p. 7). In higher education, neoliberalism emerges as a dominant political rationality that recasts individuals as capital-enhancing agents. Faculty are atomized workers, monitored, assessed, reviewed, and rewarded by larger systems grounded in latent capitalism. College administrators create markets to commodify knowledge and harvest intellectual labor, not for the common good and society but rather a knowledge economy. Academic administrators become purveyors of packaged information and 21st-century skills (Kaltefleiter, 2020).

Neoliberalism's impact on public education is "widely recognized and well-illustrated by the growing budget crises plaguing public universities and colleges, and through changing structures of academia through the US and western world" (Seis, 2020, p. 44). These structural changes account for what Harvey (2007) describes as the financialization of everything. He articulates advancements in financial instruments and activity as central to the expansion of neoliberalism, Freed from the regulatory constraints and barriers and a wave of financial services that produced sophisticated global interconnection. Neoliberalization has meant, in short, the financialization of everything (Harvey, 2007, p. 33).

The emphasis on the financialization of everything provides an ideological framework to examine the assault on public education, and importantly, higher education. Financialization becomes part of the (re)organizational strategy of the academy. The decline of state funding for higher education creates a power vacuum where the organizational structure of the academy morphs with corporate modalities and in turn gives rise to a technocratic class of well-compensated high-level administrators who use financial austerity to "restructure the university to serve quantifiable, marketplace values, needs, and objectives" (Seis, 2020, p. 44).

Financialization and neoliberalism redefine higher education, charting a managerial and entrepreneurial culture that seeks to empty the universities from social justice discussions in the name of depoliticization and cost analysis. This cleansing of the curriculum becomes part of a wider attempt to transform civil society into an economic one while hollowing out of issues such as climate change, critical race theory, and vaccination science, advancing indifference to social and other forms of inequalities.

Neoliberalism provides an ideological foundation to redefine the nature of society, democracy, and its citizens in line with market logic and values, shoring up the influence of business and commerce of the public university. Students as consumers are the core of the marketization of higher education. Institutions hawk their wares as 'student-centered' and 'students first'. Universities are cultural malls with academic programs and faculty seen as stores and retail assistants, who neatly catalog and fold information about their programs into open house events, which place more emphasis on free college t-shirts and water bottles than on comprehensive curriculums designed to prepare the next generation of leaders and problem solvers.

In the neoliberal academy, state budget debates become ideological platforms where administrators, trustees, and wealthy alumni support the development of pre-professional programs while calling to eliminate liberal arts programs such as anthropology, modern languages, women's and gender studies, ethnic studies among others (Scott, 2018). Rhetoric calling for practical skills advances discussions to defund these disciplines. Seis (2020) notes, "These disciplines were not offering students the 'practical skills' needed for the job market—which was a powerful way to increase emphasis on what is now seen as vocational focus rather an actual higher education" (p. 48).

The corporatization of the public university is reliant on the idea of "manufactured consent" as articulated by Chomsky (1986). The removal of faculty, classes, and departments is a means to silence those engaged in critical pedagogy and analysis. As Scott (2018) asserts, "If you remove the classes and the disciplines that are the strongest in their ability to develop higher-level intellectual rigor, the result is a citizenry, more easily manipulated and less capable of deep interrogation and investigation of the establishment message."

The alteration of academia by neoliberal ideological policies relies on quantification, rubricization, and data collection to demonstrate accountability to federal and state agencies, and thereby heed the clarion call to advance neoliberal disciplinary regimes and create factories for societal indoctrination as articulated in the Powell memorandum,

> The ultimate responsibility for intellectual integrity on the campus must remain on the administrations and faculties of our colleges and universities. The Chamber should consider establishing a staff of highly qualified scholars in the social sciences who do believe in the system. (Powell, 1971)

The attack on the academy goes beyond local, state, and national politics. The cultural assault articulated by Powell (1971) takes place in the contemporary landscape, wherein the university becomes a glorified training center with the purpose to train future workers "for serving the needs of capital and markets without the ability to critique the established order" (Seis, 2020, p. 49). The focus on career readiness, student placement, and learning outcomes further obscures the manufacture of consent through capitalist production modes. Here, capitalism (re)distributes necessary labor and creates a value system cloaked in commodity fetishism (e.g., degree collecting and credentialing) that serves to obscure the reality of exploitative social relations and a culture of oppression. Seis (2020) eloquently asserts, "Refashioning the public university to serve the needs of capital and the markets is a grand-scale project aimed at reconfiguring the nature of knowledge, civic engagement, agency, and moral and social responsibility" (Ibid.).

In the end, the careful curation of the academy, replete with external control mechanisms of assessment turn faculty and students, into manageable subjects, "with limited curiosity and choice about the nature and structure of social reality" (Seis, 2020, p. 49). The financialization of the academy secures valves of commitment and strings of condition that ties faculty to a professionalized knowledge factory similar to women and children bound to looms in textile factories during the Industrial Age.

Looming Alienation: Weaving Together Interludes from Factories to Universities

> Fling wide the grain for those who throw
> The clanking shuttle to and fro,
> In the long row of humming rooms
> And into ponderous masses wind
> The web that, from a thousand looms,
> Comes forth to clothe mankind.
> - *The Song of The Sower,* William Cullen Bryant, 1871

Scranton, Pennsylvania, is two hours from where I live in Upstate New York. Scranton is home to not only the fictitious paper and office supply company Dunder Mifflin from the television show *The Office,* but also the historic Scranton Lace Company site, a factory that embodies the wreckage of industrial America. The factory's open rafters and rotting floorboards lay visible the abandoned looms of history where at the height of production, over 1200 workers worked on some of the largest looms ever built. The company closed in 2002.

The Scranton Lace Factory was a campus onto its own and creates an ontological link between textile workers and academic laborers. As Chris Hedges (2018) notes, "For more than a century, the factory included a café, gymnasium, auditorium, infirmary, and elegant clock town with the cast iron bell and large whistle that signaled shift changes" (p. 2). The factory was unionized and ensured workers were paid overtime and had medical care, pensions, and better working conditions than during the Industrial Age. Beyond the tangibles, Hedges (2018) elaborates, "The company gave more than a wage to the thousands of men and women who worked there. It gave them dignity, purpose, pride and a sense of hope, and self-esteem. All of that was gone and replaced by desperation, poverty, a loss of identity and crippling despair" (Ibid.).

The working conditions of early textile mills are well documented (Robinson, 1898; Flanagan, 2005). Factories were dangerous, dirty, and noisy. The work hours were long, often fourteen hours a day, six days a week; workers' wages were low. The "Iron Law of Wages" required all business people to keep wages low, hours long, and conditions dismal. Yet thousands of men, women, and children gladly accepted these jobs. One young mill worker described her experience—the deafening noise of machinery, the backaches, swollen feet, and sore limbs after long workdays (Dubois, 2004). Another mill girl wrote of wages and hierarchy of the factory, I was a 'little doffer until I became a drawing-girl...We drew in, one by one, the threads of the warp through the harness and read, and so made the beams ready for the weaver's loom. (Robinson, 1898)

Mill supervisors received rewards for the high production of their workers. Depending on the temperament of the supervisors, many children worked under pressure to work harder and faster to increase production. That often resulted in health problems for young children, pushed beyond their physical capacities (Ibid.) And yet, the intensity of the loom work brought a sense of purpose noted by several mill girls. "The discipline our work brought was of great value, teaching us taught daily habits of regularity and industry; it was a sort of manual training or industrial school" (Robinson, 1898). This higher calling or discipline underscore modernization, economic growth, and expansion, tying workers physically and metaphorically to their looms and work, alienated from their ontological selves.

The work experiences of mill girls intrigue me, having grown up in a legacy of textile workers. My connection to mill workers illuminates my ontological experiences as an academic, connecting mill supervisors to college administrators, all more apparent since the COVID pandemic. Like many faculty, I retreated to my home to teach my classes remotely for the entire academic year. While I was grateful for the opportunity to teach remotely, the change of instruction modalities added mental and physical stress to one's body. In a commissioned study, The *Chronicle of Higher Education* reports,

> Faculty members are experiencing high levels of stress, hopelessness, anger, and grief. They report heavy workloads and say their work-life balance has deteriorated. The pandemic has taken a significant toll on the lives of the faculty, with potentially profound implications for the future. (Chronicle of Higher Education, 2020, p. 5)

At my university, colleagues described physical ailments and mental fatigue. One colleague noted, "I have at least one cracked tooth as a result of stress-induced grinding. The cost of a root canal was too much, so I opted to have the tooth extracted." Another colleague described a heightened state of vertigo after teaching all of their classes online. I, too, experienced health issues from constant stress. I was teaching three seventy-minute courses twice a week. On alternating days, I fielded Zoom calls with students and meetings with faculty. This extended time on the computer contributed to several health issues. In March 2021, I was diagnosed with "Frozen Shoulder" from extensive hours working on the computer. The initial diagnosis set off subsequent ailments. I experienced excruciating pain and took prescription Ibuprofen which contributed to a stomach ulcer. I lamented my injuries to a colleague in the UK over Zoom. He likened the injuries to our bodies and academic selves to that of workers' mutilated bodies caught in machines during the Industrial Age. I began to see my body and mind, and that of my colleagues, soldered to the computer as the mill girls were tied to their looms. Despite a century's time difference, the impact, reaction to and management of these technologies have parallels to the present-day issues surrounding neoliberalism and academia, one that extends beyond the pandemic and is grounded in alienation and an unconscious state of being.

To further contextualize the fusion of the academic body with the machines of the neoliberal university, I return to Foucault's concept of biopower which is a form of political technology aimed at managing entire populations of humans utilizing institutional frameworks of society." (Seis, 2020, p. 47). Foucault (1980) notes that capitalism would not have been possible without the controlled insertion of bodies into the machinery of production and the adjustment of the phenomena of population to the economic processes" (p. 141). Foucault's biopower extends Antonio Gramsci's writings on the indoctrination of workers, "Capitalist states seek to keep workers unconscious because no worker under a capitalist system will receive the full amount for his or her labor" (as cited in Hedges, 2018, p. 18). Or as George Simmel

(1900) wrote, "The economic system of the world is assuredly founded upon an abstraction that is between sacrifice and gain" (p. 3). In turning to academia, we might then question whether academics are aware of their role in the reproducing systems of alienating oppression. The psychology of academic work and the privileges associated therein serve to obscure the degradation and alienation of the self. Tokumitsu (2014) argues this is critical for academics whose identities are fusing their work, "with a focus upon their subject and research, their students, and their status, such that they compromise their states of being and labor rights" (Hall, 2018, p. 5).

Today's capitalist market and the neoliberal academy is predicated on the notion that economic value is never inherent in the object itself, but instead is created through a politics of desirability, or as Simmel (1900) put it, the practicality of economic value is "conferred upon an object not merely by its own desirability, but by the desirability of another object" (p. 3). Such objectification of social relations leads to the cultivation of a false consciousness wherein workers become alienated from their own work and see their labor as merely a means to the attainment of other ends/material goods. The neoliberal university relies on those eager to enter the halls of academia, similar to girls lined up outside textile mills, to give of their whole selves and become part of the loom or knowledge machine in hopes of reifying one's self and social status in the pursuit of work that is intellectual, creative, and financially secure.

The illusion of the university and subsequent alienation of academics obscures how academic labor is increasingly proletarianized, and grounded in competition and performance management with outcomes that are standardized in rubrics and assessment plans. These transformations have catalyzed expressions of distress from those who work and study in universities. Such work points toward the sublimation and negation of the self because it identifies the ego with performance and subsequently leads to mental and physical exhaustion and, sometimes, bodily harm. Reports of overwork, mental health issues, self-harm, suicide, academic exodus now fill Twitter posts, blogs, and articles. Kilkauer and Young (2021) discuss managerialism in the academy and its impact on faculty under the term "Academentia." They note, "Academentia describes a state of organizational insanity in which academics no longer function as scholars." As such, managerialism destroys scholarly creativity and intellectual endeavors. And, as Kilbauer and Young (2021) continue, "Academentia downgrades what once defined the very existence of university—the academic faculty—into some kind of over-stressed semi-academic factory workers." Thus, the circuitry of alienation between mill workers and academic laborers becomes complete.

Workload issues contribute to the alienation and degradation of the faculty. Long before the pandemic, faculty reported an increase in workload. The line between work and home morphs together as faculty spend more time "doing work rather than living life." As I have written elsewhere, the strain on faculty to be productive scholars is part of the profession; however, the rise of new technologies, algorithms, and output metrics adds to the pressure to publish. The curation of citations acts as both cultural and professional capital to be monetized by individual scholars, academic institutions, and companies like Academia.edu or ResearchGate (Kaltefleiter, 2020). One untenured, early career researcher noted, "I feel like my work is constantly on review, and I am compared against all other junior faculty at my home institution and beyond. It's like my own version of the film *The Truman Show*." I feel like I'm always on and under surveillance" (Kaltefleiter, 2020, p. 185). Campus surveillance relies on learning management and student success systems such as Starfish, whose parent company, Hobsons tracks students starting in middle school.

Surveillance technologies enable the retraining of faculty and students to abandon values that contextualize historical and social processes and to embrace quantification and data fetishism, necessary to secure the neoliberal university. As Seis (2020) notes, "forcing faculty and students to think in terms of quantifiable outcomes requires an elaborate scheme of objectification. Knowledge has to be made tangible, measurable, and marketable" (p. 53).

In the end, faculty and students become tied to assessment plans and rubrics. Like the mill workers entangled with their looms, faculty stare at the computer, engaged in monotonous tasks that deplete their creativity and agency. The evisceration of intellectual work is noted as a contributing factor to suicidal thoughts and suicide among academics (Oswald, 2018). One faculty member, too young to retire, voiced the desire to "punch out" for the last time, an intertextual reference to "punching a time clock." On the ontological academic timeline, the compulsion to overwork and succumb to managerialism is a defense mechanism against fears of proletarianization, casualization, and precarity. Thus, the acceleration of university work becomes a crisis not only for the individual academic but for the greater society, serving as a clarion call for collective care and resistance.

Compounding Alienation: Anarchist Collectives of Care and Resistance

> Looking on the bright side of things is a euphemism used for obscuring certain realities of life, the open consideration of which might prove threatening to the status quo.
>
> Audre Lorde, The Cancer Journals 1997

Academia is exhausting and stressful, filled with efficiency frameworks, assessment rubrics, and publishing deadlines that invade the body like a cancer. A circuity of everyday alienation impacts academic faculty through narratives of productivity, excellence, impact, precarity, and casualization. Hall (2018) notes, "This feeds off our need to see ourselves in our work and to maintain our labor as the site of our identities, rather than enabling us to abolish that labor" (p. 3). In this context, the academic career ladder remains hierarchical and is pulled up to keep O/others from ascending and contributes to alienation in everyday life.

To disrupt this circuitry of alienation and to advance a dialectic of care, compassion, and commitment to values of creativity and social justice, I turn to anarchism, with a focus on anarcha-feminism and Post-Situationist anarchist thought. Positioning everyday life experiences becomes essential to politicize acts of resistance in the academy and counter traditional modes of organizing or, as noted on the CrimethInc. blog, *Your Politics Are Boring as Fuck*, "Make politics relevant to our everyday experience of life again. The farther away from the object of our political concern, the less it will mean to us, the less real and pressing it will seem to us, and the more wearisome politics will be" (Nadia, 1997).

As I have written elsewhere, to confront neoliberalism in the academy we must go beyond a radical feminist analysis, one that deviates from a traditional Marxian interpretation of alienation toward a framework that incorporates anarcha-feminist theory, intersectionality, and activism (Kaltefleiter, 2020). Here, I (re)investigate Post-Situationist analyses of alienation and agency. As Ruth Kinna (2005) suggests,

> Alienation is a theme linked to Post-Situationist anarchism. Though it is linked to exploitation, it describes the impact that the production process and the technology that it supports has on individuals rather than the mechanisms through which the capitalists make their profits. (p. 82)

John Zerzan (2008) illuminates alienation within an anarchist framework, suggesting that Marx defined the term too narrowly as a distinct separation from the means of production—that alienation creates estrangement from one's experiences and dislodges oneself from a natural state of being. Ruth Kinna (2005) distills this and states, "People are encouraged to think in terms of dreams but are frustrated by the impossibility of their achievement" (p. 83).

Zerzan (2008) elaborates on the essence of alienation, "People won't even notice there's no natural world anymore, no freedom, no fulfillment, no nothing. You just take your Prozac every day, limp along dyspeptic and neurotic, and figure that's all there is" (p. 80).

Zerzan's words struck me as prophetic, especially during the COVID-19 pandemic when many academic colleagues found themselves lost, tangled in looms of existence. Poignantly, they articulated a collective loss of the academy and estrangement from their academic selves. To make sense of these transformations, I began to theorize about what I refer to as "compounding alienation," a reference that incorporates financialization with neoliberalism and wherein individual interest(s) and alienation compound at intervals that give way to collective action and identities.

In response to the isolation and alienation of the pandemic, I helped initiate a collective of concerned teaching faculty that meet regularly on Zoom to share their experiences in response to administrative dictates involving performance reviews, assessment initiatives, curricular mandates, and public health updates. Communication exchanges allow for comradeship to develop and create bonds of solidarity and action. The digital platform creates spaces of support and collective self-care through intervals of resistance and agency.

Conclusion: Slow Down with Collective Self-Care to Save Academic Lives

As we consider synergistic modes of building alternative futures in the (Post)-COVID academy, we might think of individual and collective work stoppages, strikes, or slowdowns like textile mills strikes of the past. However, such actions must go beyond traditional union organizing. Here, the literature of the *Slow Movement* and activism of collective self-care confront the temporal modality of speed and acceleration in the academy. The notion of "slow scholarship" has been advocated as a valuable alternative to the logic governing academic life (Mountz et al., 2015). In spaces between publication targets, teaching courses, and promotion appeals, one might find ways to occupy spaces differently within the neoliberal academy and advocate to go slow or at one's own pace rather than sanctioned deadlines and assessment rubrics. For instance, the bi-weekly Zoom meetings with colleagues serve as a digital interval of resistance where colleagues support one another and advance mutual aid and direct-action projects such as food distributions, public health information, and medical leave donations. In our conversations, my colleagues articulate the need that preservation goes beyond the individual. An ethics of care reminds us to take care of the self and each other.

Sarah Ahmed (2014) decrees self-care as warfare on the neoliberal academy. She asserts, "In directing our care towards ourselves and intersectional spaces, relationships, and identities, we are redirecting care away from ideological objects/subjects" and institutions. This redirection focuses on the "ordinary, everyday and often painstaking work of looking after ourselves and looking after each other" (Ahmed, 2014). Such actions incorporate a scale of self-care, collective support, and resistance.

Neoliberal conditions can be challenged by calling attention to collective solutions to injustices by using one's position of power and connecting with others to confront interlocking systems of oppression. Such work calls into question the notion of self-responsibility by championing collectivity and solidarity through co-mentorships, co-authorships, and consciousness-raising groups to discuss the temporalities of accelerated culture and slow scholarship. Actions of intentionality contribute to an anarcha-feminism that counters neoliberalism by resisting hierarchies and (re)investing in communal agency and collective good.

In all, neoliberalism, coupled with financialization, has normalized new values and objectives by using institutional apparatuses to exert power in academe, which leads to academic estrangement and alienation. To counter, faculty engagement with concepts of estrangement and alienation allows for interconnected fronts of resistance. These actions go beyond awareness-raising and enable us to become awakened to the need for transnational networks of solidarity, re-organization, and reimagination. Hence, new methods for resistance, developed collectively, frame understandings of systematic oppressions and compounding alienation. A politics of collaborative care creates an intellectual space constituted by volunteerism, mutual aid, and direct action to be assembled within the corporatized university. In all, we must exert collective self-care as a radical act and create continuums of resistance that push to disentangle our human fibers from the neoliberal machine to free our academic minds and confined states of being.

References

Ahmed, S. (2014). Selfcare as warfare [Blog]. Retrieved 17 February 2019, from https://feministkilljoys.com/2014/08/25/selfcare-as-warfare/.

Chomsky, N. (1986). *The manufacture of consent*. Silha Center for the Study of Media Ethics and Law, School of Journalism and Mass Communication, University of Minnesota.

Chronicle of Higher Education. (2020). *On the Verge of burn out*. Chronicle of Higher Education and Fidelity. Retrieved from https://connect.chronicle.com/rs/931-EKA-218/images/Covid%26FacultyCareerPaths_Fidelity_ResearchBrief_v3%20%281%29.pdf

Foucault, M. (1980). *The history of sexuality, Volume I*. Vintage Books.

Flanagan, A. (2006). *The Lowell mill girls*. Compass Point Books.

Gill, R. (2009). Breaking the silence: The hidden injuries of neo-liberal academia. In R. Ryan-Flood & R. Gill (Eds.), *Secrecy and silence in the research process: Feminist reflections* (pp. 228–244). Routledge.

Giroux, H. (2013). *America's education deficit and the war on youth*. Monthly Review Press.

Hall, R. (2019). The Alienated academic. Palgrave MacMillan.

Harvey, D. (2008). *A brief history of neoliberalism*. Oxford University Press.

Harvey, D. (2011). *The enigma of capital and the crisis of capitalism*. Oxford University Press.

Hedges, C. (2018). *America, the farewell tour*. Simon & Schuster.

Kaltefleiter, C., & Alexander, K. (2019). Self-care and community: Black girls saving themselves. In A. Halliday (Ed.), *The black girlhood studies collection* (pp. 181–208). Canadian Scholars and Women's Press.

Kaltefleiter, C. (2020). Learning to labor (Anarcha) feminism, the myth of meritocracy, incivility, and resistance for Women in the Neoliberal Academy. In E. Juergensmeyer, A. Nocella, & M. Seis (Eds.), *Neoliberalism and academic repression*. Brill.

Kilkauer, T., & Young, M. (2021). *Academentia: the organization insanity of the Modern University* – CounterPunch.org. Retrieved 29 July 2021, from https://www.counterpunch.org/2021/07/28/academentia-the-organization-insanity-of-the-modern-university/

Kinna, R. (2005). *Anarchism*. Oneworld.

Lorde, A. (1997). *The cancer journals*. Aunt Lute Books.

Mountz, A., Bonds, A., Mansfield, B., & Lloyd, J. (2015). For slow scholarship: A feminist politics of resistance through collective action in the Neoliberal University. *ACME: An International E-Journal For Critical Geographies*, *X*(X), 1–24.

Nadia, C. (1997). Your politics are boring as fuck [Blog]. Retrieved 25 July 2021, from https://crimethinc.com/1997/04/11/your-politics-are-boring-as-fuck.

Newfield, C. (2011). *Unmaking the public university*. Harvard University Press.

Nocella II, A., Best, S., & McLaren, P. (2010). *Academic repression: Reflections from the academic industrial complex*. AK Press.

Oswald, A. (2018). *Middle-aged academics are at greater suicide risk than students*. Times Higher Education (THE). Retrieved 19 July 2021, from https://www.timeshighereducation.com/opinion/middle-aged-academics-are-greater-suicide-risk-students.

Powell, L. (1971). *Memorandum: Attack on American Free Enterprise System | Lewis F. Powell Jr. Papers | Washington and Lee University School of Law* Scholarly Commons Retrieved 15 July 2021, from https://scholarlycommons.law.wlu.edu/powellmemo/.

Rottenberg, C. (2018). *The rise of neoliberal feminism.* Oxford University Press.

Robinson, H. (1898). *Loom and spindle; or, life among the early mill girls.* TY. Crowell & Co.

Seis, M. (2020). Pondering the Neoliberal Public University with the Ghost of Foucault. In E. Juergensmeyer, A. Nocella II, & M. Seis (Eds.), *Neoliberalism and academic repression.* Brill.

Simmel, G. (1900). A chapter in the philosophy of value. *American Journal of Sociology,* 5(5), 577–603.

Tokumitsu, M. (2014). In the name of love. *Jacobin* (13). Retrieved 18 July 2021, from https://www.jacobinmag.com/2014/01/in-the-name-of-love/.

Williams, J. (2012). Deconstructing Academe. The Chronicle of Higher Education. Retrieved 26 July 2021, from https://www.chronicle.com/article/deconstructing-academe/.

Zerzan, J. (2008). *Running on emptiness.* Feral House.

13 Take Down the Wall: Higher Education at SLCC as Liberation for Incarcerated Students

DAVID BOKOVOY

Background

I was a professor of Bible and Jewish Studies at Utah State University when I first learned about the prison education program at Salt Lake Community College (SLCC). Although interested in the program, I had never seriously entertained the thought of teaching courses in a prison setting. I had pursued a doctorate in Hebrew Bible and the Ancient Near East from Brandeis University, and although I had always held a passion for social justice education and activism, I assumed I would spend my academic career teaching upper division courses in historical analysis of the Bible. That was my passion. True, I was drawn towards historical analysis of ancient texts such as Isaiah 61, which predict a day of liberty for captives and the opening of prison doors to those who are bound, but my interests in these ideas were more academic than practical. All that would change, however, in July of 2018 when I assumed the position of Director of Prison Education for SLCC.

Before moving forward, I want to make it clear that I am not a former incarcerated person and never committed civil disobedience for social justice, but I did know the penal system and punitive justice is flawed and destroys communities and people. This paper grounded in social justice, liberation, and a challenge to neoliberalism does not have the answer and is not striving to argue that I am saving anyone or I am doing this because of a religious calling or evangelical cause. Moreover, I am not arguing that prison education is the answer to create "good prisons." I am not in-favor of prisons. Neoliberalism is grounded in helping others for a financial reason by industries, corporations, organization, or individuals. Capitalism is the foundation of neoliberalism, which based all actions, goods, individuals, and elements with a value. Capitalism and prisons have a long and violent history. As the hard on crime perspective is being forgotten with the Clinton era, prisons are striving to market themselves as progressive and supportive of prisoners. Prison education, while used and abused on annual reports by the Department of Corrections is not striving to argue for "good prisons." Prison education can be liberatory and supportive of try reintergration, while understanding that we need to move away from prisons. Of course not all prison educators believe this, some prison educators, believe we should let people rote in prison and if possible torture them. There are prison educators that are in it for the money and others in it for the exotic excitement of meeting a prisoner. These two motivations need to be challenged and dismantled. THe only good thing that happened as a result of Clinton taking out college education from the prison, was the movement for prisoner support found out who was truly in it for the prisoners and not. It must not be forgotten the riots in the 1970s such as at Attica were caused because of demands by the prisoners, besides, healthy food and living, prison education was part of those demands.

Entering Prison Education

At first, I thought that it would be an interesting life experience—that I would enjoy the challenge of helping to bring higher education into the lives of incarcerated students. I had little idea that that opportunity would prove life changing, not only for the students, but for me as well. I woke up to a mass injustice of the penal system grounded in punishment, racism, classism, and oppression. Working in prison education has been both the most challenging and rewarding experience of my entire 18-year career in academia. When I first entered the Prison Education Program (PEP), it had experienced some significant changes, and several students expressed concern that SLCC might be disengaging from prison education. I assured those who had expressed the concern that this was not the case. On one such occasion, one of the students in an Economics course raised her hand and said, "Please help others understand. *This* is our sanctuary." As a teacher in Religious Studies, I felt deeply touched by that word and her description of the Community College courses she was taking—Economics, Math, English, Biology, as a sanctuary. A sanctuary is a place of refuge and protection from violence, harm, and oppression. It can describe the most sacred part of a religious shrine. If nothing else, it was a fascinating word to describe a course in Economics. I am not sure if we are a sanctuary, as much as a brake from her oppressive reality as a person incarcerated.

A few weeks later, while registering students for the upcoming Fall semester, I understood why this student described her college experience this way. As part of the registration meeting, our team handed to each student a copy of his or her Student Data report. This shows the students their GPA and the courses still required to earn their General Education certificates. When I handed one of the women her transcript, I pointed out her accumulated 3.7 GPA. "I'm so proud of you," I said. "That's outstanding work." The woman had been in prison for six years and was being released in a couple of months. Her reaction was deeply touching. The woman became quite teary-eyed and just stared at the score. "I can't believe I did this," she said. "I never thought I was very smart." "Well, you are," I replied, "and this now proves it. You've done really impressive work. And you're too smart not to finish this degree." Then Chuck Williams, my education assistant at the time added, "so come see us when you're out, and I'll walk you right down to the financial aid office and help you through the process of getting a Pell Grant that will pay for your classes and your books."

"I will," she responded. "I can do this. I can't wait to show this to my parents. They always said I was smart, but I never believed it." "Now you know that they were right," I replied. "Your parents were right!" She just sat there staring at her GPA with tears streaming down her cheeks, wearing a huge smile. Her parents were right. She is smart. I was hooked. I realized that this was not simply an exciting professional opportunity. It was much more. It was a chance to help bring education into the lives of extremely marginalized students and do activism.

At SLCC, we enjoy profound, critical liberatory experiences with our students on a regular basis. While registering the men for their Spring 2019 courses, I witnessed one hardened tattooed offender get quite emotional. He thanked us over and over again for what we're doing. The student told us that before SLCC entered the prison system, he wanted to take his own life. The man was beaming when he said, "I can't thank you enough. Because of this program, I got rid of all my drugs and contraband. I want to live. I have new direction." The students we work with are using education to become better humans. On one occasion, the Warden told me that 90 percent of the incarcerated population in Utah would eventually return to mainstream society. And as the Warden himself explained, "We have to educate them. They will be our next-door neighbors."

This effort to provide higher education to incarcerated students is essential, but especially so for the state of Utah. According to the National Institute of Justice, nearly 44% of inmates return to prison within the first year of their release. However, the state of Utah is currently higher than the national average with a recidivism rate of 50% (*World Population Review*). This is where higher education in the prison system can make a tremendous difference. An important study published in 2018 in the *Journal of Experimental Criminology* showed that inmates participating in correctional education programs were 28% less likely to recidivate (Bozick, Steele, Davis, Turner, 2018). Over a three-year period, every dollar invested in correctional education saves nearly five in incarceration costs. The United States Sentencing Commission has shown that inmates with less than a high school diploma had a 60% recidivism rate, whereas those with a college degree had only a 19 percent recidivism rate (McWilliams, 2019). These numbers prove meaningful. In Utah, they have led to a bi-partisan support of higher education in the prison since lowering the recidivism rate is not only good in terms of social justice, it quite literally saves taxpayers money. As a college committed to serving the community, SLCC has taken the lead in providing accredited college courses in the Utah prison system.

Founded in 2017, SLCC's Prison Education Program (PEP) provides a model for inclusive and transformative education in the lives of incarcerated students. We define inclusive education as not being discrimi based on individual identity such as sexuality, faith, politics, crime, age, race, class, ethnicity, gender, or citizenship. We define transformative education from the work of Paulo Freire in that the educate we provide must be liberatory, for the student and not for the school, promote social justice, radical action, and be critical of systems of oppression. The program operates upon the principle of open enrollment, accepting all students above the age of eighteen who have earned either a High School diploma or a GED. For those unable to successfully perform college level work, the PEP offers non-accredited courses in Mathematics designed to prepare students to successfully complete their General Education credits. Through higher education, the PEP changes the way incarcerated students see themselves as individuals and as members of a larger community. The PEP offers courses that alter the trajectory of students' lives, strengthens families that have been hurt or compromised, and enhances students' re-entry into mainstream society. The PEP operates according to the principle that every human being deserves education and that the community carries an ethical responsibility to ensure access to higher education within the Utah prison system. This education we provide is not about us or how we feel, it is about supporting others. It is not about exoticizing prisoners either, which many prison education programs do. This is not about making money from the state at the expensive of those incarcerated.

Many institutions of Higher Education involved in prison programs offer correspondence courses. However, incarcerated men and women often suffer from anti-social behaviors. Hence, bringing men and women together in a social context working directly with a professional instructor should always serve as an educational priority. SLCC's PEP offers onsite instruction to incarcerated students. Courses take place in classrooms where students engage face to face with both college professors and their fellow classmates. The courses are designed to succeed in a prison environment where lockdowns threaten to interrupt instruction on a regular basis. To address this challenge, each course is designed as a hybrid experience. The course is first and foremost a face-to-face encounter that assumes students will directly engage in a dynamic learning environment. Yet each class session is also designed with a corresponding set of readings and assignments that supplant seat-time in cases where either the instructor is unable enter the facility or students are not allowed to leave their cells. This hybrid design ensures that instruction moves forward in spite of prison safety regulations, control, and domination.

In addition to a full range of freshman and sophomore courses that transfer credit to the four-year colleges and universities throughout the state, the PEP offers a General Education Certificate comprising 34 credit hours that fulfills the General Education requirements at all the Utah System of Higher Education institutions. Since students in the prison system do not have internet access, they are unable to actually build SLCC's General Education e-Portfolio. Nonetheless, incarcerated students are required to complete the same requisite (a Gen Education Signature Assignment and Reflection) through print medium.

Students may also pursue an Associate's degree through the program. The Associate's Degree in General Studies is made up of 61 hours—34 in General Education and 27 electives. The degree is accepted at all USHE institutions. While a General Studies Major does not articulate to any specific focus at the baccalaureate level, the courses within the AS degree have been selected to provide a solid foundation for many Majors in the Social Sciences and Humanities.

In the PEP, courses are designed to meet the needs of incarcerated students in two ways. First, all instructors are taught to employ practices that research suggests lead to greater gains in learning and personal development. While many "high impact" practices such a Learning Communities, Service-Learning, and Study Abroad are not possible in the prison, there are others exercises such as Writing-intensive, Diversity/Global Learning, Undergraduate Research (albeit limited); Assignment and Reflection Portfolios; and Collaborative Learning that PEP students perform. These practices help students develop the ability to both analyze and synthesize ideas, and appreciate diverse perspectives and lifeways The PEP pedagogy is designed to assist students develop an ability to successfully discuss these issues outside of the classroom, transfer and/or apply the learning in one course to the material in another (or to nonacademic arenas), judge the value and credibility of information, and critically examine their own ideas. Moreover, while high impact practices increase the depth of learning for all students, research strongly suggests that they are particularly effective in helping underserved students (underrepresented minority, low-income, and first-generation students) become successful learners. Since prisons hold a disproportionate number of marginalized and underserved students, and the range of college preparedness among incarcerated populations varies significantly, it is imperative that prison education programs develop and utilize teaching and learning strategies that research shows to be most effective for underserved groups.

Second, all PEP instructors participate in workshops that help them build into their classes a humanistic and laboratory pedagogical approach. Incarceration involves structures, processes, and procedures that punish, limit agency, and deny individualism. In an effort to address these challenges, SLCC's PEP provides opportunities for students to gain knowledge and understanding of disciplinary ways of thinking. It also seeks to inspire and empower individuals, many of whom bring with them ideas and experiences shaped by oppressive environments and systems that predate their incarceration. SLCC instructors teach with compassion, respect, and sensitivity as they rely on a dialogical approach that recognizes the central role students themselves assume as active learners.

Prior to the beginning of each new semester, the PEP staff sits down for a one-on-one interview with all SLCC students. Interviews are scheduled for a ten-minute time period. During the interview, students are provided with a copy of their Student Data report. This allows students to discuss their academic progress with the staff, including GPA, course/teacher evaluation, and student progress towards the completion of the program. During the course of interviews, the PEP staff provides academic advising while counseling with students concerning their academic plan. The staff encourages students to register for the courses that will lead directly towards either a General Education certificate or an Associate's Degree in General Studies. During the course of interviews, students have the opportunity to select and register for the upcoming semester. This selection process transpires with the assistance of the PEP staff and in accordance with their academic advising. Since incarcerated students do not have access to the internet, the PEP provides a paper form for the student to sign. The signature indicates the students' desire to officially register for the SLCC course. The form is then taken by the Program Coordinator in order to create class rosters.

New students are typically admitted the week prior to interviews. The PEP staff holds a general orientation meeting for interested students explaining the responsibilities and expectations of the PEP. Students then fill-out by hand an admission form that is taken by the PEP staff in order to admit new students. Upon admission, students are allowed to register for a single course. This allows them to show to both the program and themselves that they can successfully complete college-level work in a prison environment. At the time of their admission into the program, students sign a promissory note concerning future payment for courses taken in the PEP. The note indicates that upon release, students will do their best to pay off the debt acquired by taking classes in the program. Incarcerated students in the PEP do receive a reduced tuition fee for SLCC courses. This reduction is due to the fact that incarcerated students do not have access to the same resources available to on-campus students.

Enrollment as a student in SLCC PEP is a right for all insiders. Some people this it is a privilege, it is not. It is a right and our goal is that prison education is offered in very incarcerated location in the U.S., until we move into a more transformative justice society without a penal system. Students are expected to comply with the rules and regulations required by both the PEC and the Utah Department of Corrections. In order to attend class, students must maintain a high level of privilege. This allows students to stay out until 8:30 PM. This is an absolute requirement since most PEP courses conclude at 7:45 PM. Students who lose their that level of privilege are immediately dropped from classes and placed upon on the waiting list until their appropriate level has been earned. No one, however, is dropped from the program, as long as they wish to continue working towards their degree.

In 2020, the Federal Government designated SLCC a Second Chance Pell institution, This means that incarcerated students can use federal Pell Grants to attend the institution. SLCC was among a cohort of 67 colleges and universities invited by the U.S. Department of Education to participate in the Second Chance Pell experiment, intended to pilot higher education opportunities for incarcerated students. This was the first time a Utah college or university was selected. The restitution of Pell Grant will allow the PEP to significantly expand its efforts to provide transformative education in the lives of its students.

To conclude this summary of the program, I would like to provide a few narratives from some of our students. Although the names have been changed to protect identity, these unsolicited statements illustrate the feelings SLCC students have towards the program and the pursuit of higher education. They illustrate the power of higher education to alter the way students who are incarcerated see themselves as individuals and as members of a larger community. Further, it is important as a white economically privileged able-bodied cis-male to step-aside to allow those that are marginalized to share their stories. We can learn a lot about prisons by those incarcerated.

J. (SLCC Incarcerated Student, 2019)

When living at home with my wife and kids, I was not able to help my kids with Math or English because I had forgotten most of what I learned over many years (I am 49 now). I only went to one semester of college when I was a teenager. Thank you for providing me the opportunity in prison to learn so I can be a better father to my children. I have been calling my kids and teaching them what I am learning and helping them with their schoolwork over the phone, because I am now smart enough to do that. Thanks to great instructors and classes. You are helping me build relationships with my kids who I miss so much. This education will also help me in my work when I get out and help me to be a better citizen so I do not recidivate and go back to prison, which will also save taxpayers lots of money. God bless you for helping a criminal to be better. I hope to pay it forward!

K. (SLCC Incarcerated Student, 2019):

Having been incarcerated now for 20 years, I've witnessed firsthand the difference higher education programs make in prison and what happens when they disappear. A fully functioning higher education program of Liberal Arts especially, creates an atmosphere of striving for knowledge and improvement. It has ripple effects that permeate the rest of the prison population.

The presence of higher education in prison gives us a chance to radically change our lives for the betterment of everyone. Other inmates see there is another way, one of dignity and true respect, rather than just fear. This creates a subcultural pathway back into society, undermining the predominant criminal prison culture. It gives us a chance to replace our criminal cultural values of strength and cunning for values like cooperation, empathy, reason, and discipline. We begin to see in ourselves and each other the character traits that are the very foundation of community and civilization and come to understand their value. It is through higher education that we grew to understand the value of society and thereafter our anti-social opposition.

My years of experience have taught me that strenuous, rigorous education in critical thinking is the only effective deterrent to crime. We don't all recognize this immediately. Many of us need convincing that education itself is an investment with enormous returns. Higher education itself is the best convincer toward its own value. The convincing grows easier when it is clear to everyone that the community, that society, understands this and anticipates our return to society with wise foresight.

J (SLCC Incarcerated Student, 2019):

My names is J. and I have been with SLCC since the program started in 2017. Prior to getting involved with this program, I was 120% invested in doing "Prison Time." What Prison Time consisted of was sitting around on the block gang bangin', doing and selling drugs, which eventually led to me getting stabbed 26 times. I was beginning to become restless after being incarcerated at that time for 11 years. I knew I wanted to be more than what I was being, but just didn't know how or where to even begin. I've been down now for 12 years, and still have 13 years left to the board. That can be discouraging at times. Then the opportunity came around to get involved with this SLCC Program. I've been involved with this program now for over a year and in that year, I've managed to get moved off of what is considered to be a "troubled block," and moved onto an honor block. I now am employed with the Prison maintenance.

My conversations with my parents are the best I've ever had. All the relationships I'm involved in are all healthy ones. I've stopped going bangin' and am actively trying to get a ministry started to help others out that are still struggling to find out how they can become that better man they've always wanted to be, but just don't know where to start. This program has undoubtedly changed my life. If it has had such a positive impact on my life it can many more. This program will make everyone that participates in it a better man. Thank you so much for all your guys' help and support, and most importantly believing in all of us. Thank you from the bottom and the most sincere part of my heart.

G (SLCC Incarcerated Student, 2019):

My name is G,, and I'm a student in the SLCC Prison Education Program. I enrolled in the Summer of 2018. Since I had the opportunity to educate myself through SLCC, it has changed my life in ways that I never knew were possible here in prison. I have been in prison for currently 14 years. And throughout that time, unfortunately, I lived as a gang member and utilized my time in a non-productive manner. You see, I wanted to change, and in most ways I did, but what I needed was a real opportunity to succeed. Then came the signup sheet for the SLCC Prison Education Program. I seized that moment to grab what I had been looking for all along. At registration, Chuck and Dave made me feel real comfortable to be joining SLCC. I was a bit nervous to attend college. Where I grew up, you were lucky if you graduated from High School. But this staff made me feel like I belonged to something great. I could see how passionate they are with this program. I wasn't looked at like just another man in prison. They encouraged me to continue my path for success. Since enrolling in SLCC, I now live in an "Honor Unit," and have a job at the Green House. If it wasn't for this education opportunity, I would have most likely given up hope and continued being negative. The professors who come here to teach choose to be here. So that means a lot knowing that this program is invested in us. I hope SLCC continues to change people's lives as it did mine. So as long as there is the opportunity then people have hope. Thank you!

Trevon (SLCC Incarcerated Student, 2019):

Hello, my name is Trevon. I have been a student of SLCC since 2017. I had no idea SLCC would accept me at the time due to my low academic scores. Upon interview of starting my first semester, I realized how the Director David Bokovoy's sincerely in getting my on the right track. Despite my doubts and my special education background, Bokovoy reassured me that... You can do this, and it was in the best interest of SLCC to see me succeed and that they will work with me.

I'm proud to report that since that day I have improved in all areas of academics with Math being my most challenged subject making the Honor Roll. I'm also the first person to go to college in my family. I'm about two more semesters away from that big day and I have not told my Mother because I would love to give her my degree as a Mother's Day surprise. I want her to be proud of me.

I am more confident and now believe I can do it. SLCC has changed my life because they chose to work with me, accepting my learning challenges and doubts. The professors are amazing in how they are teaching. I have learned so much; it has started to bleed into my daily conversations and letters I write. When I talk with family on the phone that have no idea I'm in school, they compliment my input and "level of insight." SLCC has also increased the potential in my future employment moving forward. I hope to continue my education with SLCC and that others can benefit from the opportunity the college has laid out for us. So to all those associated with the development of the prison ed. Program, Thank you so very much!

Take Down the Wall: Higher Education

In 2019, Trevon completed a Creative Writing course through the PEP. I conclude this essay citing one of the assignments he completed in the course. He has granted me permission to use his words. Together with his testimonial cited above, it provides a powerful witness to the fact that Higher Education liberates the captives:

To Whom It May Concern:

Hi, my name is Nobody. That's who I became when I took the life of Somebody. I didn't know what Domestic Violence was. I didn't think I had that problem. I received a Life Without Parole sentence for my reckless actions. I have myself to blame because I'm the one that did it. The whole thing happened in about 3 minutes. Now I have the rest of my life regretting what I did. I wish I could of got help, but I didn't think I had a problem. I was a controlin' person. I was a jealous person. I was insecure.

I'm hopin' that you listen to the words of Nobody, to help you become Somebody. If you are at a point in life to where you "Don't Care" about nothing or no one, you are in danger of an "Explosive Outburst" caused by layers of unconscious behavior. If you find yourself "Acting Different" when "Your Girl or Your Man" is talking to the opposite sex, you are in danger. If you drink or use drugs just so you could become "the person" you like when you're drunk or high, then you are in danger. If you want to start a fight because it makes you feel strong, then you are in danger. In danger of what? Well...

Becoming a Nobody like me. You see, once you get sent to prison, everyone forgets about you. They don't like a Woman Beater, a Child molester, an Animal Killer, a Thief, a Murderer, you name it. So the best way to avoid a dead end road is to stay in school, graduate, learn a trade. It's not too late to become Somebody. It's not too late to own up to some problems you see in yourself.

It's not too late to change. In fact, Step One is knowing and admitting you have a problem with whatever. So if you're aware of any situation of what "your issue" is, then it's not too late to switch lanes and go a different direction. Life is beautiful looking at it from behind bars....

That tells you how much I took society for granted. This is your LAST CALL!.... If you don't listen to Nobody then the only time you will become Somebody is when you get your prison number. Yeah, the number you get when you become a Nobody. LOOK! Life is really what you make of it. You can do what you want and that's the great thing about America but, once you break the laws, you put yourself at a disadvantage because a felony could stop or prevent you from getting a job. When you could and should be taking advantage of every open door opportunity that could lead you to success. So don't give up! You still have a chance. Learn form this situation and make new plans. Think about it. P.S. hashtag "Nobody Cares"

Conclusion

The goal of the prison education program is to promote the incarcerated voices and to provide education. We want to provide transformative education, which challenges colonial-settler dominate teaching and schooling. We are wanting to promote transformative justice and an end to the penal system, but in the meantime, we want to promote educate, build relationships, healing, taking accountability and responsibility, providing space and place for incarcerated voices, and developing an alternative to punitive justice.

Epilogue
Suggestions to University/College Trustees: An Interview with Anthony Joseph Nocella

Anthony J. Nocella II

You have been a member of several boards of directors for nonprofits and board of trustees for colleges. What do you believe is the mission of a board?

The mission of a college or university board depends on the nature of the university's current structure and stability. Depending on the governing structure, a board may have four missions: first, a government funded college; second, a privately funded college; third, a university primarily funded by endowments that create financial stability; and fourth, a university with declining enrollment and its related financial situation. In case number one, if the school is funded by the government, the purpose may be skewed or politically driven, with a decreased emphasis on educational quality and fundraising by board members. In cases two and three, the mission should ensure that students attain theoretical and practical knowledge with ethical sensibilities to provide dedicated service to those who are marginalized. In this mission, fund raising is often the key responsibility of the board. Donations are reviewed to ensure that they are consistent with the board's purpose and values. In case four, the mission of the board is primarily strategic planning, achieving financial stability, and fund raising. A trustee is primarily responsible for the financial wellbeing of an institution and fulfilling its mission. All of these cases are different from a board of managers or directors who direct the activity of the officers of the organization and govern all the activities relative to financial planning and oversee the success of the organization for the benefit of the owners of the institution. A nonprofit or college's mission and values should align with cases two and three.

What are the foundational values that college board of trustees should embrace?

The college board of trustees should embrace the foundational values of a holistic, integrative problem-solving education to utilize a foundation to improve stability through financial goals. These values should be continuously checked against the trustees' and students' prevailing beliefs. To do this, the trustees should nurture a mentoring relationship and a lifetime learning experience. There should be an open pursuit of truth and human potential. The concept of the liberal arts (from Latin liberalis "free" and ars "method"), which can be found in many cultures and societies under different titles, is the foundation of all professional success.

The scholar, trustee, and the recent graduate should be examples of these values, as shown by many elite institutions, but fall short at other schools that have entirely specialized courses of studies and exclude the ability to think freely. Examples include the Wall Street attitude that led to the Enron scandal, which resulted in one of the largest bankruptcies in US. It was generated by business leaders who assumed they were just wiser than everyone else. From Michael Milliken's leveraged buyouts and junk bond catastrophe to Madoff's Ponzi scams, there have been other Ponzi schemes that have brought the entire global economic structure crashing down.

Trustees have the responsibility and the authority to approve the annual budget and methods for fundraising. The structure of the board is used as a networking fundraising group and are often unwieldy with as many as 40 members with management attending the meetings.

Work is divided by expertise; each board member is on a committee, and the committee chair presents a summary of its work to the board of trustees. Any diversion from its mission or values should be reported to the entire board but, in many cases, is not. The budget reports new projects and donor programs to the entire board for approval. Any expectations by the donors or the creation of new values by the projects should, at this point, be presented for approval.

The board is usually collegial and utilizes Roberts Rules of Order so any business outside the agenda of the chairperson of the board and the committee chairs is extremely rare. The foundation and structure of the board of trustees can become suboptimal.

Epilogue

What type of education should be required to be a college board of trustee member?

A robust, practical education that enables the student to follow a career is essential but often is not a strong preparation for career in business and the sciences. Professional skills require that liberal arts should be taught within the context of values.

Let me give an example of a few practitioners. Roger Smith was a long-time chairman and CEO of General Motors who suggested that companies need employees and executives who have a liberal arts education. Smith also suggested that companies import them by hiring liberal arts graduates and pair them with technical people.

Years ago, in a speech that I gave regarding the Wall Street economic markets, I stated that education should include the principle of ethics and the process of moral engagement. It helps to understand what is appropriate against an internal set of standards, thus avoiding the Ivan Boesky problem, where insider trading cost investors billions of dollars.

Todd Cooke, CEO of the largest bank in Pennsylvania once upon a time, said it is very discouraging that we frequently experience bright ambitious and alert individuals who have performed well at the technical or supervisory level, but when promoted to the management level, fail. Their failure is a lack of grounding in liberal arts disciplines and the resulting inability to conceptualize, and articulate priorities both orally and in writing. Liberal arts is the key and foundation of good quality education.

As you observe the college board of trustees nationally, what are a few trends that concern you?

Trustees are navigating many challenges—lower enrollments, skepticism about the value of a college education, and reduced donations.

Communication between the board and the president needs to improve by establishing rigorous goals and objectives. The reliance on the finance team to create financial scenarios and the board simply following the scenarios rather than the values and the mission of the organization. The examination of its academic quality should be ongoing. Stakeholders should not strictly measure the practical nature and foundation of its education on how many jobs can be created by the university/college.

Instead, education should be a building block of a holistic approach to the graduate, which is the foundation of a society, ideally a healthy, inclusive, equitable, just, diverse, democratic society. In the United States, higher education was deemed necessary for the advancement of society, whether in the arts and humanities or the sciences. The argument for higher education being the foundation of society was how universities/colleges began to make groundbreaking social change.

A liberal arts education creates the basis and foundation for socially conscious critical thinkers who can challenge the status quo and challenge the ethical standards of our society.

For the last few years, an argument has been made that state schools should just create job seekers, but with the high amount of student loans, the effect is the students' inability to make a sizeable enough income to pay back their debt.

This condition creates the idea that liberal arts is just a waste of four years in school. Today's world is constantly changing because of technology, too often graduates wrongly believe that the essence of their education is what they do on the first day that they walk out the door as a graduate. But it's clear from my experience that these graduates need to be prepared to deal with the necessary communication skills and the ability to use them to create an innovative environment. A key technical skill is gathering intelligence and information to develop ideas that can be communicated and formed grounded on fact-based information.

One of the most important byproducts of a liberal arts education is the specific social justice innovations from the very beginning of the Ivy League schools, which helped accept economically disadvantaged students and foster the rights of women. Pat Sloan, a colleague who was one of the first female managing directors of an investment bank on Wall Street, graduated in the first female class at Harvard. Her process through the school was difficult but was surrounded by a nurturing environment that considered human dignity to be extremely important.

There is a significant difference between the job mill schools and the liberal arts-oriented colleges, the result being that the graduates believe that they can change the world and make it a little better. The job mill schools, grounded in a factory model, only look to how much they will earn. Volunteerism is a critical job that graduates must practice to become visionaries in a changing world.

As we live in a global COVID-19 pandemic, with global warming and food insecurity at an all-time high, what do you think is the role and responsibility of colleges toward the world, their community, and their students?

The requirements of living with global COVID-19, climate and starvation create a situation where virtual learning has become necessary. But hybrid education needs to be followed up by a strong mentoring process.

This process should not force the reduction of college/university revenues and the reduced quality of education. The financial capacity to carry out the college's mission and values and to educate the truth about just wars and global warming without political bias is critical to continuing a quality higher educational process.

Afterword
Don't Look Anywhere! Learning Without Stock Markets

PAUL R. CARR

Neoliberalism and the USA

Resisting Neoliberal Schooling: Dismantling the Rubricization and Corporatization of Higher Education is an important and compelling volume on a subject that needs to be further addressed and discussed. It is a pleasure to offer some thoughts on the subject, knowing that these few words at the end of the book will not adequately capture the full richness and expansive examination of the myriad dimensions of the question. My intention is not to summarize or synthesize the many wonderful and excellent ideas, proposals and problematizations of the effect, influence and meaning of neoliberalism on (higher) education; the editor and the authors have already presented a critical framework from which we can continue to explore how to develop and construct a more engaging, meaningful and responsive educational system. I, therefore, humbly hope that my analysis and comments will help continue the reflection and the debate.

Although the book is clearly and viscerally located within a United Statesian context, it is clear that this is equally a global problem. At the same time, although the USA leadership, importance, actions and resources is clearly waning on the global stage as it is being increasingly contested and delegitimized at many levels—owing to the debilitating and senseless quest for warfare and military expansionism, the void in international organizations, protocols and missions, and a fragilized normative democratic structure—, the country still plays a significant role in articulating and shaping a vision of the world.

Of course, the USA has taken some extreme and polarizing stances that fly in the face of global solidarity. These include stances in relation to healthcare, military interventionism and peculiar constitutional interpretations, especially pertaining to gun ownership and women's rights. The freneticism related to elections also sets the USA apart, not only in terms of the duration, the spending, the polling, the strategizing and the like, but also in the simple administration and counting of votes.

To be clear, as a Canadian, I am not seeking to malign one country here. Canada has its share of problems and issues, including the longstanding obfuscation to reconciliation with the First Nations, among a host of other concerns. All countries are facing issues related to the environment, migration, racism/sexism/poverty, xenophobia and social justice. Thus, it is important to understand collectively that the USA is not a separate island floating away from the world, even if the particular contextual issues make it all the more relevant in many cases. If the USA can't fund healthcare, diminish poverty levels, temper the war industry…, how difficult will it be for others to do so? Or is it a question of values, philosophy and cultural cohesion? Neoliberalism has tethered all of us together, even if we wish to opt out of a system of exploitation that specifically marginalizes so many. Ultimately, we are all affected by the policies, programs, processes, and decisions of a neoliberal justice, law enforcement, military, healthcare and education regime within the façade and trappings of normative democracy that trickle down and through much of what we do or wish to do.

The Political Economy of (Higher) Education

The political economy is fundamental to ascertaining what we know, what we do and how we can change. The production of armaments, for example, is still underpinned by national governments and political decisionmakers. The arms are subsidized, creating employment, then developed, marketed, sold and used. Killing takes place, the rinse cycle repeats. During the pandemic, arms sales have gone through the roof! Space exploration is underwritten with military objectives and backing. We become blinded and complicit, and billionaires happily float around in outer space seeking publicity, sympathy and more hits/sales/contracts. We're not always sure how these arms are used, who is killing whom, why those drones intended to procure GPS

Afterword

driving assistance and delivery prowess have become torture toys for the Pentagon and others....

Funding for everything is premised on potential return, and crypto currency represents a better option of social services and human development for many investors. Hedge-fund speculators, start-up managers and dot.com creators are on a fishing-expedition to determine how to maximize profits, even if there is an incubation-phase to see where the snapchat, the tic toc or a million other apps and gimmicks might monetize themselves. I'm not against creativity but am also in favor of considering the human conditions and social inequalities that underpin all of this idle gaming and investment focus.

What does any of this have to do with neoliberalism in (higher) education? The many contributors to this book have provided a broad range of the dimensions and details related to how (higher) education has been clogged with corporate and hegemonic interests. Inequality and disadvantage are endemic and flawlessly embedded within the processes and structures that frame (higher) education. I continuously place (higher) in brackets because it is understood to be a logical and inextricably connected extension to pre-school, primary/elementary and secondary education. By the time we make it to university/college education, if we do make it there, we will have been uplifted, integrated and "educated" or, conversely, perhaps down-trodden, marginalized and propagandized, or some other combination of potential outcomes. Of course, what happens within the formal educational context is significantly influenced by home-life, informal and nonformal education, community, culture and the political-economic context.

Higher education is increasingly being privatized or chipped away for private funding/benefit. The State, generally, no longer views it as a fundamental extension to the educational, citizen and societal development project (many countries still do offer free access to tertiary education but there are still may issues of financial support, access and conditions). The emphasis is increasingly more on job creation and economic indicators that shun low-paying professions and once knowledge-worthy fields that are not considered to have impactful employment potential. This philosophy further devalues building socially-just communities and societies, and emphasizes private (individual) return. Thus, placing a name on a building (which comes with a healthy donation and nebulous strings attached) and providing sports scholarships, within some contexts, are as important as developing learning programs and supporting students. The USA context is somewhat different with regard to the sporting industry as it does not really exist elsewhere, at least not with the burgeoning scholarships, stadiums, coaching salaries, specialized services and the like that supposedly bring in funding to support the academic enterprise (if college sports is so beneficial to universities, why does student tuition continually increase and professor salaries are deflated?). Should sports and (higher) education be linked, to what end, and for whose benefit?

Favoring MBAs over MSWs undoubtedly affects the societies we are developing. Cooperative learning is often supplemented and overtaken by specialized training for industry interests. Tenured faculty are increasingly replaced by contractually-limited instructors. Class sizes are increased, teaching loads are augmented, pressure to secure outside funding is constant, programs are opened and closed based on the basis of profit-based economics, and there is a constant feeling that engaging in dialogue, social change, solidarity and transformative learning, while not impossible or fully outside of the mission of the university, is greatly threatened within the contemporary framework.

Neoliberal friction is accentuated by bellicose political discourse that aims to discredit, undermine and diminish the value of (higher) education. Populist movements jump on the bandwagon, barking out the need to mock "intellectuals" and thoughtful debate. Talk radio replaces, to a certain degree, public engagement on climate change and the environmental destruction of the planet, war and conflict, and why poverty is so entrenched in a society of such enormous wealth. Does (higher) education help us to deliberate and contribute to the public good, and, if it does, why is there so much public antipathy toward it?

The question of who should pay is central to this debate, and tuition-rates that submerge people into permanent debt that literally mortgage the future after (higher) education means that we are, ultimately, ensuring that society will become even more neoliberal. Largely indebted bankers, lawyers and doctors will need to, or are enticed to, charge exorbitant, usury-like fees for their services that will ensure that the public purse is on the hook to subsidize the wealthy, while further hiving off finite resources to assist, support and develop those who do not make it through the educational labyrinth or who choose to study in areas that uplift society in other ways. What type of culture is neoliberalism constructing through (higher) education?

Similarly, the disproportionate emphasis placed on securing international/foreign students as money-generators for universities can further suffocate the mission of "higher learning". The obsession with having students from China come to just about every university in North America over the past few decades was never really intended to enrich intercultural engagement. To be clear, I am not against "studying abroad," and gladly acknowledge that my two-year séjour in France as a student a number of years ago was an extremely significant and transformative experience for me. My concern is the neoliberal, mercantile exchange involved, which can often overshadow the critical engagement and socio-cultural experiences that mark and define who we are. Universities have a unique and fundamental role in cultivating these spaces for diverse students/people, one that is increasingly being shrunk through economic prioritization.

Many of the examples provided in the previous paragraphs are more specific to the USA context but, as I mentioned at the beginning, the USA still carries some favor with how the world sees itself, and, thus, (higher) education is affected and influenced by USA trends. The language of conferences, journals, knowledge and debates has been disproportionately in English, and through the eyes of the USA, which, in my view, is increasingly deleterious and dangerous to considering the world's richness, cultures, ways of being and knowledge-systems. Clearly, the USA experiences, in the plural, and the vigorous tradition of debate and dialogue within universities in the USA is a necessary component to seeking peace and breaking down hegemony. The rising tide of neoliberal interests is quickly limiting these spaces, and the pandemic has further accentuated the move toward distance learning (which is not negative in and of itself but it has serious implications for the central mission of higher learning).

So What's the Upside?

Don't look up!, the Hollywood film on Netflix, distributed in late 2021 has became a metaphor for anti-science and trivialized power politics that rides a crest of populist decision-making. Fully marinaded within USA culture, the film is both entertaining and insightful. I'm not a movie critic so there is no need to explore the cinematographic merits of this creation but the fact that the film has taken hold internationally—not unlike *Squid Games*—is a symbol and signifier that people may not want more, and that they do read between the lines. The "system" is not working for most people, and the formal power dynamics, media representations and educational frameworks—from the curriculum to the evaluations to the diplomas through the knowledge validation—is being contested, constrained and reimagined by many thinkers, groups and movements around the world. This book is but one example, and there are also myriad social media applications, creations, discussions, organizations and developments that go under, through and around the official radar to assist in this process. The upside is that formal hegemonic power configurations are not the only way to conceptualize our lived realities, although no one would suggest that they are unimportant.

Don't look anywhere! This could be a rallying-cry for some of what is happening in the USA (and around the world, for that matter). If we don't look, we won't see, and without human compassion and solidarity, what/where are we? The educational experience should be about emancipation, social justice, conscientization (all inspired by Paulo Freire and the many wonderful colleagues who have continued his work) and feeling more human/humane, I believe. Neoliberalism has made us believe that we need to be share-holders busting unions in the 1980s Reagan/Thatcher mold, or independent contractors responsible for our own healthcare and well-being, or entrepreneurs (even at the academic level), with each of us generating (individual) wealth. We need to measure everything in terms of profit, margin, growth, impact, efficiency, comparative advantage.... Indeed, this is a sickness, and when education embraces this dance, willingly or unwillingly, we become locked into a COVIDesque merry-go-round. We can't get off, we can't breathe (which, sadly, reminds us of what happened to George Floyd), and we are, often, encouraged to *Don't look anywhere!*

I spent five years (2005-2010) teaching at a university in Ohio as well as another fifteen at home in Canada in English- and French-language institutions. It has been a wonderful and transformative experience. I have learned much, have collaborated widely, have participated in a range of projects, and have been extremely fortunate to travel widely (especially before the pandemic, and I do realize the environmental paradox) around the world. The USA is not an island, and there are many incredibly important and significant activities, actions and people engaged in the process of striving to create a better world there. There is a great deal of transformative work/research/engagement undertaken by colleagues in (higher) education, individuals motivated and supported, to varying degrees, to cultivate social change. At least, that is my perspective and experience.

So why write about the strangulating effect of neoliberalism on the academy? Because of the real, far-reaching and immobilizing effect that it has on how we wish to live together would be my gut-reaction. This book carries the torch a bit further, and there is much inspiration to be found within it. The process of critically engaging makes us more connected and, I believe, meaningful, even if the tide we're facing is more of a tsunami than a few waves washing ashore. Regardless of where we look (up, down, sideways, nowhere...), we will need to be engaged and open to thoughtful dialogue, a part of which emanates from (higher) education.

An end-run around the pandemic without the critical engagement and dialogue within the boiling cauldron stirring the neoliberal stew is as unlikely as end-run around poverty, sexism, racism and warfare. There is no quick, proverbially "magic bullet" to bring forth the required change, only a lot of mobilization, resistance and solidarity that would likely be almost unthinkable without critically engaged education. There is lots of work to be done but there is also a tremendous amount of engagement and action for change, not only in the USA but around the world. More solidarity between peoples, cultures and (ironically) nations will strengthen the resolve for a more just world and planet. The educational piece allows us to continue this work, despite the financial/economic window-dressing, and I hope that the necessary changes will happen in an inclusive, dynamic and transformative way, considering an end to warfare, addressing global climate issue, and spreading the net for human dignity to all corners of the Globe. Ironically, as with COVID, which is/was not simply a health issue, neoliberalism is not simply an economic issue. They are political issues, and the education component links us all to citizen participation. We need to *Look (and be) everywhere!*, in peace and solidarity....

Contributors' Biographies

Adalberto Aguirre, Jr., is Chair and Professor of Sociology at the University of California-Riverside. His publications and research interests are in the following areas: neoliberalism and higher education, critical race theory, public policy and immigration, and race/class inequality. He is co-author of *American Ethnicity, Women and Minority Faculty in Higher Education, and Racial & Ethnic Diversity in America*. He has authored publications in journals such as: *Social Problems, Journal of Comparative Sociology, Qualitative Studies in Education, Research in Higher Education*. He is collaborating with Ruben Martinez on a project regarding the inefficiency of higher education organizations that target diversity as a neoliberal practice.

Will Boisseau, is a trade unionist and independent scholar from London. His research focuses on the place of animal rights within the British left, particularly on the relationship between the anarchist/direct action and legislative wings of the movement. His work explores the class and gender issues influencing this relationship, the marginalization of animal rights in mainstream labor politics and a range of concepts including speciesism, total liberation, critical animal studies and intersectionality. Will is currently involved in trade union politics in the UK.

David Bokovoy holds a Ph.D in Hebrew Bible and the Ancient Near East and a Master's degree in Jewish studies from Brandies University. He has taught at Brigham Young University, the University of Utah, and Utah State University. He is a former chaplain at Harvard University and the current Director of Prison Education for Salt Lake Community College.

Paul R. Carr, Ph.D. is a Full Professor in the Department of Education at the Université du Québec en Outaouais, Canada, and is also the Chair-holder of the *UNESCO Chair in Democracy, Global Citizenship and Transformative Education (DCMÉT)*. His research focuses on political sociology, with specific threads related to democracy, global citizenship, media literacy, peace studies, the environment, intercultural relations, and transformative change in education. He has eighteen co-edited books and an award-winning, single-author book (*Does your vote count? Democracy and critical pedagogy*) as well as a recent book with Gina Thésée (*"It's not education that scares me, it's the educators...": Is there still hope for democracy in education, and education for democracy?*).

Ashley "AC" Cox is an Associate Professor of Marketing at Salt Lake Community College. He is distinguished as the first African-American graduate of the PGA Golf Management Program at Mississippi State University. Cox is a recognized 21-year veteran in the golf industry and a past member of the Colorado PGA Section Board of Directors. He is a current member of the Utah PGA Section Board of Directors and a marketing doctoral candidate. His research interests include behavioral economics, consumerism, and conspicuous consumption.

Lauralea Edwards is an educator activist who integrates business and technology to make higher education affordable, accessible, and sustainable. Her research humanizes data to dismantle systems of oppression and inequity. Dr. Edwards has twelve years of experience building data-informed processes to effectiveness of strategic goals in higher education. She has been publicly recognized for innovation in leveraging technology to improve business processes. She holds a BS in Behavioral Science from Andrews University, a Master of International Affairs from Columbia University, and a Ph.D. in Cultural Studies and Social Thought in Education from Washington State University.

Frank A. Fear is professor emeritus, Michigan State University, where he served as a faculty member and administrator for nearly forty years. A sociologist by education he is interested in how public and nonprofit institutions—higher education in particular—support and enable support democratic action. Fear is the lead author of *Coming to Critical Engagement* (2006) and has published in various journals, including *The Journal of Higher Education Outreach and Engagement*, *About Campus*, and *The Higher Education Exchange*. He has also authored book chapters recently on topics associated with community-engaged scholarship. Fear is MSU Senior Fellow in Outreach and Engagement and received MSU's Gliozzo Award for International Public Diplomacy. Academic units under his direction won the MSU Phi Kappa Phi Award for Interdisciplinary Scholarship, the MSU Excellence in Diversity Award, and the Templeton Foundation's "College and Character" designation for promoting students' ethical and citizen-minded development. Involved also in community affairs, Fear served as a two-term president of the Greater Lansing (MI) Food Bank, and he currently serves as vice president of Women's March Fort Myers. Since retiring from university service, Fear has authored social/political commentaries for public audiences, most notably in *LA Progressive* and through his podcast, *Under the Radar hosted by Frank Fear*. Fear is also managing editor of *FutureU*, a blog that highlights the pernicious impacts of Neoliberalism on higher education and society at large.

Steve Gennaro, Ph.D., explores intersections of media, technology, psychology, and youth identity. He is one of the founding members of the Children, Childhood, and Youth Studies Program at York University and is the author of Selling Youth (2010), co-editor of *Youth & Social Media* (forthcoming 2021), and co-author of *The Googleburg Galaxy* (forthcoming 2022). Dr. Gennaro regularly publishes in areas related to the philosophy of technology and education, and critical theories of youth, media, identity, and politics.

Rich Van Heertum, Ph.D., is a faculty member of the New York Film Academy LA and has also taught at UCLA, CUNY, the Art Institute and Drexel. Richard has a doctorate in cultural studies and education from UCLA and an MA in Economics. He has published four books - *The Fate of Democracy in a Cynical Age, Educating the Global Citizen, Hollywood Exploited* and *The Selling of Bohemia* - over 35 academic essays and chapters and hundreds of articles in the popular press on movies, music, politics and sports. He is currently completing a book length manuscript for Routledge on contemporary politics.

Caroline K. Kaltefleiter, Ph.D. is Professor of Communication and Media Studies and Coordinator of the Anarchist Studies Initiative at the State University of New York at Cortland. She is the author of "Self-Care and Black Girls Saving Themselves" In Black *Girlhood Studies*. A founding member of Riot Grrrl D.C., she's written numerous papers on anarcha-feminism, girls' media production, and activism. Her activist work includes Occupy Wall Street, Black Lives Matter, and multiple Mutual Aid Projects throughout New York. She co-edited *Smash the System: Punk Anarchism as a Culture of Resistance*, published in 2022 by Active Distribution.

Douglas Kellner, Ph.D., is Distinguished Research Professor of Education at UCLA and is author of many books on social theory, politics, history, philosophy, and culture, including *Herbert Marcuse and the Crisis of Marxism* and six edited volumes of the collected papers of Herbert Marcuse. His work in social theory and cultural studies includes *Media Culture, Guys and Guns Amok: Domestic Terrorism and School Shootings from the Oklahoma City Bombings to the Virginia Tech Massacre,* and *Media Spectacle*. Most recently, he has published two books on *American Nightmare: Donald Trump, Media Spectacle, and Authoritarian Populism* and *The American Horror Show: Election 2016 and the Ascent of Donald J. Trump.*

Lea Lani Kinikini, Ph.D., received her doctorate from University of Auckland, New Zealand, masters from University of Hawai'i, and bachelors from University of Utah. She is a researcher and educational practitioner who has worked internationally in Hawai'i, New Zealand, Oceania and now Salt Lake County. Her research has examined the school to prison to deportation pipeline with a focus on case law and Pacific Islander youth gangs. She has conceptualized how legal fictions are extrapolated both in the public sphere and in the legal realm to produce ranked or 'marked' populations underlined by racial classes. She currently is the Chief Diversity Officer at Salt Lake Community College working on building solutions to over-incarceration and is committed to creating equity through educational justice innovations.

Roderic Land, Ph.D., is the Dean for Humanities and Social Sciences at Salt Lake Community College. Having received his doctorate in Educational Policy Studies, Land committed his life and work to higher education. As a scholar-activist, he has insisted on bridging the gap between theory and practice. As a professor, his academic range includes sociology of education, educational policy, hip-hop and social justice education, Critical Race Theory and Ethnic Studies. His research is committed to liberatory educational practices with a sound pedagogical approach. Land insists that race and racism, coupled with other historical, oppressive realities are continued battles in the 21st century and are important to the millennium scholar.

Rubén O. Martinez, Ph.D. is professor emeritus of sociology and former director of the Julian Samora Research Institute at Michigan State University. His scholarly interests include Latino community issues, diversity leadership, education and ethno-racial minorities, youth development, Latino labor and entrepreneurship, environmental justice, neoliberalism, academic freedom, and institutional and societal change. He is the author of numerous

Contributors' Biographies

articles and books, and is the editor of *Latinos in the U.S.* book series through Michigan State University Press.

Victor Mendoza earned an Associate's - Law Enforcement Forensics (Odessa College, 2015); Bachelors – Homeland Security (Sul Ross State University, 2017); Masters – Criminal Justice (Sul Ross State University, 2019) and currently a PhD candidate - Administration of Justice (Texas Southern University). McNair Scholar (2017 – 18) who presented at McNair, American Society of Criminology and American Criminal Justice Society conferences on crimmigration, prisons and criminological theory. Former member of African Criminology Society, Convict Criminology Society, currently employed at Texas Department of Transportation and over 25 years' experience with Texas Department of Corrections/Criminal Justice – Institutional/Pardons & Parole Divisions.

Anthony J. Nocella II, Ph.D., (they/he) long-time intersectional total liberation scholar-activist, is an Associate Professor in the Department of Criminal Justice and Criminology in the Institute of Public Safety at Salt Lake Community College. He is the editor of the *Peace Studies Journal*, and managing editor of the *Transformative Justice Journal* and *Green Theory and Praxis Journal*, and co-editor of five book series including *Critical Animal Studies and Theory* with Lexington Books and *Hip Hop Studies and Activism* with Peter Lang Publishing. He is the National Director of Save the Kids, Director of Academy for Peace Education, and Executive Director of the Institute for Critical Animal Studies. His work has been translated in Spanish, Russian, Portuguese, German, Korean, and Japanese. He has co-founded numerous concepts and the fields of critical animal studies, Hip Hop criminology, lowrider studies, disability pedagogy, terrorization, academic repression, and ecoability. He has published over one-hundred book chapters and articles combined and forty books. He has been interviewed by New York Times, Washington Post, Houston Chronicles, Fresno Bee, Fox, CBS, CNN, C-SPAN, and Los Angeles Times.

Anthony Joseph Nocella is one of the founders of the mortgage-backed securities market including the sale of the first commercial and residential mortgage-backed security. Throughout his life, Nocella has continues to be and influential American banker and philanthropist. Born on October 13, 1941, in South Philadelphia in a blue-collar Italian neighborhood, Nocella voluntarily joined the U.S. Air Force during the Vietnam War. After returning from the service, Nocella graduated from La Salle University, Temple University, and University of Pennsylvania's Wharton School, all while working full-time. Nocella helped shape one of the first publicly owned hospital systems in the U.S. – American Medicorp. Under his guidance and leadership, Nocella brought four companies public. One of those companies, PSFS, was the largest IPO in the world at the time. Nocella also served as the Vice-Chairman and co-founder of Bank United, the largest bank headquartered in Texas from 1989 to 2001.

David Robles is an Assistant Professor in the Department of Criminal Justice at Salt Lake Community College. His disciplines include criminology, social justice, juvenile justice, public policy, emergency management, the criminal justice system and history, and victimology. He is a Squad Leader with the Salt Lake County Search & Rescue team where he provides mountain search and rescue. In this role he works closely with the Unified Police Department Canyon Patrol Unit as well as the Salt Lake County Sheriff's Office. David is the Editor in Chief of the Transformative Justice Journal, a project of Save The Kids. In addition, he has over 10 years of professional experience working in nonprofit organizations where much of his focus centered around juvenile justice, criminology, victimology, rehabilitation, and reintegration. David received his Master's in Community Leadership from Westminster College and a Bachelor's in Criminal Justice with an emphasis in Law Enforcement from Weber State University.

Clifton Sanders, Ph.D., received his doctorate from University of Utah and his bachelors from Hamline University. Sanders is the Provost Emeritus at Salt Lake Community College. He has more than 25 years teaching, administrative and leadership experience in higher education. He led the development of several STEM programs and is a collaborator on several local, regional and national initiatives on education, diversity and inclusivity, and workforce development. His scientific work resulted in six patents in biomaterials technology. He is a 2023 University of Utah Distinguished Alumnus and a 2017 University of Utah Chemistry Department Distinguished Alumnus, and he coauthored a 2009 paper on music and democracy published in *Radical Philosophy Review*.

Laura Schleifer created the word 'artivist' to describe her vocation. An NYU Tisch graduate (BFA, Drama), she's toured the Middle East with a theater/circus troupe, taught in China, Nicaragua, and at Wesleyan University's Green Street Arts Center, performed off-Broadway, and arts-mentored homeless/targeted youth. Her screenplay, *The Feral Child*, was a Sundance Lab finalist. Her essays appear in *The Leftist Review, Project Intersect, The New Engagement,* and an upcoming Black Rose Books Kropotkin anthology.

Currently, she's writing a book, *Liberating Veganism*, for Vegan Publishers. Laura is also the Institute for Critical Animal Studies Total Liberation Director and co-founder of Plant the Land, a vegan food justice/community projects team in Gaza.

Elisa Stone, English Professor, helped create Salt Lake Community College's Gender & Sexuality Student Resource Center and helps plan the Utah Pride Center's genderevolution conference. Via SLCC's Beloved Community Project, Elisa co-educates students about Martin Luther King, Jr. She received SLCC's Unsung Sheroes Award, President's Inclusivity & Equity Award, and Utah Campus Compact's Engaged Faculty Award. Elisa's SLCC Community Writing Center Teens Write Mentoring Program won Innovation of the Year and National Bellwether Finalist. Joining an anti-stigma campaign for the Desmond Tutu HIV Foundation, Elisa connected with Nobel Peace Prize winner Tutu following his Peace with Justice Award in Cape Town, South Africa.

Emily Thompson is the Competency Based Education (CBE) Program Manager and supports CBE across the Salt Lake Community College (SLCC) system. She has master's degrees in psychology from Purdue University Global and English with an emphasis on trauma and postcolonial African literature from the University of Oregon. She holds a Bachelor's degree from The Evergreen State College. She has also completed the Comprehensive Training in Hakomi Mindful Somatic Psychotherapy. In her former job at Purdue University Global, she created and led an Innovative Learning Technology Team and served as the CBE Faculty Lead coaching and supporting 200 faculty teaching CBE courses while working as a Full-time Adjunct. Outside of academia, she worked as the executive assistant to the Cabinet Secretary for Cultural Affairs in New Mexico. Emily is skilled at supporting collaboration across a wide range of stakeholders, developing faculty resources, writing faculty training, adapting academic policies to enhance student agency, and supporting students to effectively advocate for community change. She is committed to prioritizing critical pedagogy, student agency, and fostering a liberatory, decolonized learning environment that grounds pedagogy in the lived, felt-sense experiences of students.

Riley Clare Valentine, M.A. is a doctorate candidate in Political Science at Louisiana State University. They research the neoliberalization of presidential rhetoric in American politics and its resulting moral framework. Alongside this, they do extensive work on care ethics as an alternative political model to neoliberalism. Valentine has been published in books such as *Vegan*

Entanglements and *Unlocking Social Theory*, as well as academic journals, and popular academic websites as well. Outside of their scholarly endeavors, they are a dedicated educator activist.

Elizabeth Vasileva finished her doctorate degree on anarchism and immanent ethics in 2018 in Loughborough University. She has been a co-convenor of the Anarchist Studies Network for the past two years. She is currently organizing and teaching at Free University Brighton and is an organizing member of Free University London.

Index

A

Ableism 25
Ageist 29, 53
Anarchism 65, 66, 69, 75, 196, 197, 230, 234
Animal Liberation 63, 66, 74, 77
Assimilation 2, 3, 5, 6, 8, 19
Attica 202

B

Bigot(try) 35
Blackboard 20
Black Liberation 50
Black Lives Matter 17, 39, 70, 90, 158, 230
Boyz n the Hood 24, 26

C

Cancel Culture 29
Cisgender 41, 146
Citizenship 6, 22, 158, 159, 204, 228
Civilization 74, 201
Classism 24, 25, 41, 57, 202
College Culture xii, 36, 45
Collectivism xvi, 129, 130
Communism xvi, 3, 88, 89, 129, 136, 176

Cooke, Todd 215
Corporatization xi, 188, 190, 220
Corrupt 34, 74, 105, 137
Critical Animal Studies 9, 63, 227, 231
Critical race theory xi, xvi, 2, 8, 70, 90, 101, 117, 168, 173, 174, 190, 230
Cultural Expansionism 177
Cultural imperialism 176

D

D2L 20
Diederich, Paul 5
Diploma Mill 20
Domination 8, 23, 26, 29, 59, 68, 157, 178, 205
Donations 198, 213, 215

E

Elitism 16, 23, 133
England 17, 64, 96
Ethno-Nationalism 135, 137

F

Faith(ful) 36, 97, 188, 204
Fanon, Frantz 6, 7, 86
Fascism 128, 133, 136, 137

Financialization 188, 189, 191, 197, 198
Freedom School 90
Freire, Paulo 7, 19, 97, 104, 105, 157, 162, 204, 224

G

G-7 178
Game Theory 134, 136
G.I. Bill 84
Globalization 82, 95, 155, 156, 157, 158, 160, 161
Gramsci, Antonio 53, 193

H

Hate 26, 39
Hawaii 56
Hegemony 4, 5, 67, 103, 157, 223
Hip Hop 7, 58, 231
Holistic xvi, 3, 9, 22, 137, 214, 215
Hoover, Edgar 88, 173
Humane 130, 224

I

Imperialism 2, 3, 6, 8, 17, 22, 59, 62, 176
Institute for Critical Animal Studies 63, 231

L

Left-wing 137
Lowrider 2, 9, 58, 59, 60, 231

M

Manufactured Consent 190
Market-based 57, 87, 149, 178
McCarthyism 10, 89, 90, 92
Milliken, Michael 214
Modernism 98
Multi-culturalism 2

N

Nazism 21, 176
Neoconservatism 3, 28
Non-binary 40, 70, 71
Nonprofit(s) 5, 16, 104, 176, 177, 213
North American Free Trade Agreement 17

P

Pink Floyd 5, 20
Police Brutality 75
Political Prisoners 75, 77
Police State 81
Praxis ix, xi, 53, 69, 156, 188, 231
Prison Education 11, 201, 202, 204, 206, 207, 209, 210, 212, 227
Privatization 17, 82, 84, 86, 131, 135, 136, 167, 173, 175, 176

Q

Queer 7, 34, 36, 37, 41, 42, 43, 44, 56, 71, 72, 74

R

Racial Justice 39, 91
Racism 24, 25, 39, 41, 43, 45, 53, 57, 58, 59, 61, 70, 72, 76, 90, 112, 126, 135, 173, 224
Rand Corporation 134
Rape 26, 101
Redlining 53
Red Scare xvi
Retaliation 46
Research 2, 3, 4, 8, 16, 21, 22, 23, 27, 33, 45, 50, 56, 58, 59, 63, 64, 65, 73, 75, 84, 85, 86, 87, 91, 98, 99

S

School to Prison Pipeline 25, 50

Index

Schooling xi, xiii, 1, 7, 21, 29, 59, 104, 116, 120, 121, 159, 170, 171, 212, 219
Sexism xvi, 25, 64, 71, 72, 76, 146, 220, 224
Sexuality 35, 36, 42, 204, 233
Slavery `xv, 23, 26, 38, 121, 131, 173
Social Justice xvi, 6, 7, 8, 9, 10, 18, 25, 28, 29, 35, 37, 46, 63, 74, 87, 92, 97, 104, 106, 107, 135, 156, 161, 189, 196, 201, 204, 216, 220, 224, 230, 232
Social Stratification 45
Sociology Liberation Movement 89
Solidarity 26, 34, 50, 58, 70, 72, 74, 75, 76, 77, 107, 188, 197, 198, 220, 222, 224, 225
South Africa(an(s)) 36, 37, 233
Speciesism 71, 227
Standardization 1, 6, 7, 8, 9, 19, 98, 120, 136, 152
Stigmatization 43, 44
Student-consumers 45, 98
Student Nonviolent Coordinating Committee 87
Supreme Court 112, 131, 171, 176, 187

T

Tenure 56, 60, 61, 85, 99, 101, 102, 103, 105, 106, 165, 174, 175, 195, 222
Terrorism 158, 230
The Heritage Fund 174

Tokenize 27
Total Liberation 29, 70, 71, 227, 231, 233
Toxic Masculinity 41
Transformative Justice 29, 50, 58, 207, 212, 231, 232
Transgender 25, 40, 41, 149
Transphobic 29
Trump, Donald 21, 57, 95, 97, 100, 101, 102, 170, 173, 184, 230
Tutu, Desmond 36, 37, 233

U

Ugandan 43
Un-American Activities Committee 89
Utah ix, xxi, 3, 9, 34, 40, 49, 51, 52, 54, 58, 59, 61, 62, 201, 203, 204, 205, 207, 227, 228, 230, 232, 233

V

Veganism 74, 223

W

White Power 59
White Supremacy 5, 8, 25, 53, 56, 58, 90, 116, 117, 149
World Trade Organization 17

Anthony J. Nocella II, and Lea Lani Kinikini

Series Editors

Liberatory Stories and Voices from Community Colleges, an international peer-reviewed book series published by Peter Lang Publishing and co-edited by Dr. Anthony J. Nocella II and Dr. Lea Lani Kinikini, is a grass-roots community-focused radical transformative critical decolonizing anti-authoritarian book series on the political delineations of transforming education for liberation in communities occupying Indigenous territories and stolen land on Turtle Island (North America). This book series, supported by JEDI4ST, the interdisciplinary researcher center at Salt Lake Community College, will provide space and place for marginalized communities, students, staff, public intellectuals, activist-scholars, and frustrated administrators laboring in community colleges to critically resist and amplify their counter-stories which demand that in the rollout of the neoliberal corporate factory academic-industrial complex agenda, that public education must be affordable, inclusive, equitable, inclusive, just, transformative, and open to all. This book series foregrounds writer's agency with authentic story-telling, autoethnography, collective biography and life writing narratives and is a place for disseminating participatory action and social justice activist research. It seeks critical teaching and critical writing that resists Eurocentric pedagogies and methodologies such as denotative reports, standardized metrics and rubrics, corporate, neoliberal, capitalist, standardized, colonial, factory education that colonizes the mind. Instead, the series privileges radical liberatory praxis and makes space for outstanding embodied action research tied to teaching, transformative participatory projects created with not 'on' marginalized communities that centers the margin. Many of the students and faculty are at community colleges not merely because it is affordable, but moreover because community colleges defend political spaces for and with the oppressed: whether first generation (code for "working class"), the racially, territorially and marginalized 'others' that are pandemically silenced by repression and oppression. This series holds space and place that the community college is the last hope of democracy from which knowledge from and for the margins emerge as powerful countercurrents and disruptive discourses that liberate. This book series holds space and place for these voices who brave the world with knowledge in one hand and resistance in the other to liberate all.

For additional information about this series or for the submission of manuscripts, please contact:

    Anthony J. Nocella II, Series Editor; nocellat@yahoo.com
    Lea Lani Kinikini, Series Editor; lealani.kinikini@slcc.edu

To order other books in this series, please contact our Customer Service Department:

    peterlang@presswarehouse.com (within the U.S.)
    orders@peterlang.com (outside the U.S.)

Or browse online by series:
www.peterlang.com

www.ingramcontent.com/pod-product-compliance
Lightning Source LLC
Chambersburg PA
CBHW061710300426
44115CB00014B/2625